THE KINDNESS
OF
STRANGERS

WISING UP ANTHOLOGIES

ILLNESS & GRACE, TERROR & TRANSFORMATION
2007

FAMILIES: *The Frontline of Pluralism*
2008

LOVE AFTER 70
2008

DOUBLE LIVES, REINVENTION & THOSE WE LEAVE BEHIND
2009

VIEW FROM THE BED: VIEW FROM THE BEDSIDE
2010

SHIFTING BALANCE SHEETS:
Women's Stories Of Naturalized Citizenship & Cultural Attachment
2011

COMPLEX ALLEGIANCES:
Constellations of Immigration, Citizenship, & Belonging
2012

DARING TO REPAIR:
What Is It, Who Does It & Why?
2012

CONNECTED:
What Remains As We All Change
2013

CREATIVITY & CONSTRAINT
2014

SIBLINGS: *Our First Macrocosm*
2015

THE KINDNESS OF STRANGERS

Heather Tosteson & Charles D. Brockett
Editors

Wising Up Press

Catalogue-in-Publication data is on file with the Library of Congress.
LCCN: 2016959711

Wising Up ISBN: 978-0-9826933-6-0

Wising Up Press
P.O. Box 2122
Decatur, GA 30031-2122
www.universaltable.org

DEDICATION

To all the strangers, aka friends-in-the making, who have helped create this book—and to all those who find something in it that speaks to them. May our worlds continue to expand in such gracious ways where and when we least expect—and most need—them to.

TABLE OF CONTENTS

HEATHER TOSTESON
THE KINDNESS OF STRANGERS   *1*

I. RE-EVALUATION/REVELATION

MARGARET HASSE
BLOOD ORANGES   *24*

WILLIAM CASS
NEW YEAR'S EVE   *25*

NORITA DITTBERNER-JAX
JAZZ TRUMPETER   *32*

LOWELL JAEGER
GETTING WHERE WE NEED TO GO   *34*

GEORGE J. SEARLES
RESOLUTIONS   *37*

LAURA CHAIGNON
KNOWING GRINS AND SUSPICIOUS LOOKS   *38*

KATIE GLAUBER BUSH
SOLE MAN   *41*

SUSAN AUSTIN
THE SWEET AND DARK   *44*

SUSAN CLAYTON-GOLDNER
THIS WEIGHT I CARRY   *46*

GINA VALDÉS
BORDER DUENDE   *48*

REBECCA TAKSEL
OMEGA   *51*

KAREN SKOLFIELD
WAIT FIVE MINUTES   *57*

MEIA GEDDES
GIFTS FOR THE CRANE LADY   *58*

MK PUNKY
TAKE CARE OF EACH OTHER   *59*

II. CROSS-IDENTIFICATION

PAUL HOSTOVSKY
STARING AT THE BLIND — 64

FR. ROBERT J. KUS
MARCELINO — 67

DARCY SMITH
TATTERS — 71

RACHEL SQUIRES BLOOM
WHO'S THIS GIRL IN THE PICTURE? — 72

KAREN SKOLFIELD
WELL-BEHAVED — 74

JESSICA NAAB
SINNERS ON SIXTY-SIX — 77

LAURIE KLEIN
BEHIND HER EYES — 91

MURALI KAMMA
BRAHMS IN THE LAND OF BRAHMA — 97

III. HELP WHEN WE NEED IT MOST:

SHIREEN DAY
UNEXPECTED STRANGERS — 108

PEGI DEITZ SHEA
WHO EVER YOU ARE — 113

NORMAN KLEIN
VETS — 116

STEPHANIE HART
AN UNEXPECTED KINDNESS — 124

NORITA DITTBERNER-JAX
UNIVERSAL DONOR — 128

PATTI SEE
TO GIVE AWAY: ONE USED KIDNEY — 131

DOROTHY OLIVER PIROVANO
THERE WHEN HIS BODY FAILS HIM — 134

JOEL WACHMAN
THIS IS GETTING OLD   139

KEN STALEY
MISSING   148

IV. WEAVING A NEW FABRIC

MARGARET HASSE
AND ALL POINTS WEST   158

LINDA MAXWELL
THE BUSINESSMAN'S TRUTH TABLES   160

JENNIFER L. THORNBURG
ALL SOULS   164

RUPERT FIKE
TUTORING MOHAMMAD MOHAMMAD   173

OUR LIBERIAN STREET PREACHER, MISS EDNA,   176

RICK KRIZMAN
CANTALOUPE ISLAND   179

FRANK HABERLE
ROAD TO HAINES   188

ALETHEA EASON
HOLIDAY COVE   199

STEVE KOPPMAN
THE RUSSIANS ARE HERE   208

PAULINE KALDAS
AMONG NEIGHBORS   221

PATRICK CABELLO HANSEL
WASHING AWAY   227

LOWELL JAEGER
AFTER SECOND SHIFT   228

NATURAL HISTORY   230

NEIGHBORS   231

WHAT SORT OF MAN   232

THE LIBRARIANS   234

JOHN KING
COMMENCING AGAIN   236

V. HOW MUCH IS ENOUGH?

ANUSHA VR
CORN ON THE COB   244

JENNIFER SCHOMBURG KANKE
CRANK CALLS FROM GOD   247

FORGIVE ME KENJANEA   250

BRING YOUR OWN REDEMPTION   251

MARIANNE PEEL
HAPPY HOUR AT PF CHANG'S   252

TEETLE CLAWSON
FOLLOW-UP APPOINTMENT   254

WILDERNESS SARCHILD
CHARITY   256

JOHNNY TOWNSEND
THE GIRL FROM TREPONEMA   259

JOHN TIMM
A GOOD DAY AT THE OFFICE   267

JASON A. NEY
UNTIL IT HURTS   277

JANA ZVIBLEMAN
BUCKET OF WATER   292

ACKNOWLEDGEMENTS   313

CONTRIBUTORS   316

EDITORS/PUBLISHERS   325

HEATHER TOSTESON

THE KINDNESS OF STRANGERS IN AN ESTRANGED SOCIETY, AN ESTRANGING TIME

> *The point, though, is that we all go forward with the presumption of good faith in our fellow citizens because that presumption of good faith is essential to a vibrant and functioning democracy.*
> *Barack Obama*

Why Now?

Pondering this introduction as we developed this anthology, I was often mentally connecting images and scenarios that demonstrate our keen current need for kindness as a society. There is no dearth of them. Once invited in, they kept coming faster and faster, indeed in no time at all it felt like I was treading roiling, treacherous water. But suddenly, for no reason I can point to, my spirits lifted and I began to feel almost giddy as words rose up from the depths: *We're all in the same boat.*

Paradoxically, another set of images began to flow, ones that genuinely lifted my spirit: Falling into an unexpectedly intimate conversation with a stranger on an airplane flight, both of us free to share in a way that we couldn't with our closest friends, feeling, as I said good-bye and walked away, like a treasure chest, their confidences and revelations stored deep inside. Going into a grocery store, the library or post-office and sharing that small comment that would let the person I saw, a recent refugee from Nepal or Ethiopia, the new pharmacy tech, the cashier, know that I saw them as a vivid and welcome addition to my real and my imagined community. The face of the young man in a wheelchair who spun around immediately when I asked to take his picture for our *Remembering Kindness* series, agreeing as soon as he knew I wouldn't show the cigarette he was smoking, the way his face opened into a beautiful smile as he said, "Oh yes, I have the memory right here in my mind." *Right here. Kindness.*

We're all in the same boat. I can see it. The deep blue paint of the hull is blistered, peeling; the gunwales scuffed; some water swishes in the bilge; it holds more passengers than it was intended for. But it fills me with optimism. So many skin colors, so many personal histories, hidden talents, so much drive not only to survive but to thrive. The boat lands, we tumble out, gain our land legs, scramble off. Now I can see an elevator where, having come to an unexpected pause between floors, we're suddenly alive to each other in ways we haven't been before. Looking for each other's strengths. That tall quiet woman's mechanical ability. That burly man's calm. Wondering what I myself can add to the mix. But sure we'll find a way out, together.

As I write, I step back bemused by the profound, almost nonsensical sense of social trust these images imply. Where on earth did it come from? I've seen photos of those boats heading off from Egypt and Libya, I've watched the twin towers fall over and over again in videos.

But in my current mood, the images and memories keep coming. I remember a man I heard speak a year after 9/11, the husband of someone in my spiritual direction program. He was one of two survivors from the floors above where the first plane hit. He described his horrifying descent. But he laughed when he described how, as he made his way down the floors, he discovered a second man, also miraculously alive, only his legs visible under a desk, whose first question when approached was, "Do you accept Jesus Christ as your personal savior?" "Perhaps we can discuss that later," the husband of my classmate said. "Let me help you out from under there."

I remember the day we voted in the 2008 presidential election, what it felt like standing in line in my predominantly African-American neighborhood on the outskirts of Atlanta, looking into all those faces which bore expressions so similar to mine, as if some huge weight had been lifted from all of us: we knew we at last really could be what we claimed to be, a country of equal opportunity, *essential* equality, a beloved community.

I don't really know the origins of this generalized social trust, but I do know it is deeply rooted, probably ineradicable. I know as a single mother I always told my son, wherever we were living—Greensboro, NC, Athens, OH, San Francisco, Narberth, PA, Mexico City, or Watertown, MA—"If you're in trouble, knock on a neighbor's door. Any door." I had friends, also single mothers, who warned their children never to answer the door, never to speak to strangers. I didn't teach that to my son because I didn't, and I still don't, believe it. I feel that if you are in need and hammer at a door, any door, long enough, they will not *all* leave you comfortless. They *will* come to you.

Perhaps this attitude developed when, at two, still unable to speak, I was shooed out into the world alone and unchaperoned by my mother, who was in the grip of a violent postpartum depression following the birth of my younger brother. Even years later, she felt it was the wiser course. "I knew you were safer out there than you were inside with me," she told me. I was irrepressible, a climber, and would find my way to a nearby playground and climb to the top of the jungle gym. I did not know how to reverse my steps, so I would wait until an unsuspecting adult passed by, at which point I would throw myself without a sound into their arms—and they would, white-faced and judgmental, return me to my mother. So we could start the whole drama of expulsion and rescue again. It wasn't a tragic one. They may have shamed my mother, but no stranger ever dropped me.

I regularly played a variant of this primal drama a few years later, running away from yet another home in yet another state, this time on my own initiative. I would run as fast as I could toward our neighbors' house, my older sister yelling after me from the front steps, "I'll tell, I'll tell." I didn't care. I knew the old couple would let me climb into their warm bed, feed me breakfast, then take me by the hand to gather eggs from the hen coop. I knew what to call that experience: homecoming.

Perhaps the word to describe my general stance toward strangers is xenophilia: I experience a preferential option for the compatible stranger, who I am more likely to trust than someone bound to me merely by genes. As a child, my son often remarked, somewhat resentfully, on this obvious tendency of mine, for when he brought friends home he felt I favored them. My friends called it my kibbutzim attitude toward child rearing. I thought of it, deep down I probably still do, as normal. *We are all in the same boat.* My child, yours, they both need care.

But what does this stance toward strangers, whatever its origin, have to do with kindness, in particular with depending on it? This anthology, like all our anthologies, like our press in general, has depended on the kindness of strangers, twice over, actually, because not only did we put a call out to writers but we also conducted a companion photo project, *Remembering Kindness*, that also depended on the participation of total strangers. To be so generously met around a subject of such immediate and intensely personal concern to us, and also to those who responded, has been a source of solace and encouragement at a time when some of those basic assumptions of mine about kindness and strangers are being challenged. *What does kindness to strangers mean at such an estranging moment in an increasingly estranged society?*

"I never realized so many people harbored so much hate in their hearts," I blurted out to my husband after watching only a five minute clip of people leaving a political rally. Reading about it was a completely different experience from seeing it, hearing it. I never imagined the slogans on the T-shirts, never imagined the aggression, the righteousness, the exultation, the vision of us as a people and a country that energized it. Lock *them* up. Kick *them* out. It is as if all the hidden transcripts of betrayal, domination, loss, retribution, revenge, corrosive rancor have become holy writ, declarations of independence, bills of rights.

Watching, however briefly, I felt my belief in our essential kindness as a country greatly challenged because, more than perhaps I realized before, one foundation for my own generosity is my sense of identity as an American who believes that part of our national identity is our core commitment to the *intrinsic* value of *all* people, but especially the outsider, the outlier, the poor, the hungry, the huddled masses, all those who yearn to be accepted and free. For me, to be an American means to stand for that value in the wider world, to embody it in practice as much as possible. To see national identity used to evoke fear, to disparage and reject the stranger inside and outside the country challenges me at many levels. It makes me feel more estranged inside my own country than I have ever felt before. I know I am not alone in this. People everywhere along the political spectrum, even the apolitical, feel this.

Estrange: Verb transitive. To remove from customary environment or associations. To arouse especially enmity or indifference where there had formerly been love, affection, or friendliness.

I did not know, truly, the depth of hatred we harbor in our hearts. I don't know if my naiveté also extends to the belief that at the heart of that hatred is a terror of estrangement, of social exile, invalidation, that, too, is deserving of empathy, *kindness.*

I know I am not alone in any of these responses, but that doesn't mean I know what to do with them. I resist opening my heart to that unmodulated anger, raw hatred—to the image of the society it evokes. I resist closing my heart as well.

Even more troubling to me than the vitriol of this election year are two recent local events. The first is the accidental death of a woman in her early sixties at the hands of her supposedly doting husband, a wealthy lawyer in his early seventies. She was shot in the back while sitting in the front passenger seat when the loaded gun her dozing husband in the backseat casually rested on his lap accidentally discharged. He had asked her to give it to him when they passed a major homeless shelter in Atlanta late on a Sunday evening on their way back from their country house to their home in Buckhead, the most expensive area in town. A prominent lawyer, a member of the state election board, why was his first response—riding on a public street in a large, locked car, *just passing by* a group of men without homes, without means—to pull out a gun, remove the safety? Who was in greater danger from the stranger?

The other image is of middle-aged militia members, armed with automatic weapons, massing in front of the courthouse in Newton County to protest the building of a mosque and graveyard in the county. They are protecting the country from Islam by fully exercising their right to open carry, free assembly, and free speech. "Where are we going to bury our children?" the imam asked. "They were born here." The imam was clear what the members of the mosque needed to do. They needed to meet their neighbors. He was sure that once people met them face to face, talked with them, their fears would diminish. My own course of action is less clear. I'd rather go to jummah at the mosque than cozy up to a man holding a semiautomatic rifle. But I know who feels like the greater stranger.

But these images, these sentiments, mine and the militiamen's and the wealthy lawyer's, all make me grieve. They all get to me, get *in* me. They make the world we share feel as strange to me as it must feel strange to them. I don't *see* what they do when I speak with a homeless man, visit a mosque. I want no part of their guns, their fear, their violence, and yet their faces and their actions work in my imagination in ways that have nothing to do with words like *xenophobe, misogynist, demagogue, predator, supremacist, racist, dispossessed, unemployed, the 1%*—or *xenophilia.*

These responses of mine have nothing to do either—or do they—with the word *kindness?*

Kindness and Kin:

When we talk about kindness we aren't talking about beneficence, benevolence, altruism, generosity, or sympathy, all of which in one way or another hold us apart from—and a little above—the recipient of our good will. With kindness, we're talking about something more visceral and egalitarian. Something that has at its core the physical origin of the golden rule. Recent neurobiology teaches us that we are hard-wired to know the inner states of others, our own muscles fire with their muscular intentions. We attend remarkably early to kindness, as young as nine months, particularly kindness to the less powerful. Toddlers voluntarily offer help to someone they perceive to be in distress (although they don't necessarily offer to share). Our brains' pleasure centers light up when we are generous or kind, a powerful intrinsic reward that is actually diminished by external ones.

When psychologists and social psychologists discuss core prosocial behavior, along with empathy they include perspective taking, theory of mind, and moral commitment. But if those capacities don't have a basis in our bodies, a felt sense of "that could be me, that can be me," they don't really partake of *kindness*.

The word *kind* comes from Old English, gecynde, meaning "natural, native or innate, with 'the feeling of relatives for each other'" and shares a root with kin. Kind as an adjective refers to the behaviors we have when we empathize and identify with someone and wish to help them in some way. Close synonyms might be warmhearted, friendly, tender, compassionate. Kind the noun refers to the capacity of our abstract mind to see a similarity, a type, a category. So, it makes sense that we are kind to kin. We see them as the same kind as us.

I do have an image of what kindness is—and it is how my father-in-law responded when he found his niece, in the throws of addiction, passed out on the floor, alone and helpless, and didn't hesitate, immediately leaned down, picked her up and said, "Don't be afraid, sweetheart. You are going to be okay. Don't be afraid, it will be all right." His action was immediate, instinctual, unplanned, genuine. It was exactly the response she needed if she was to recover in spirit as well as body because it let her know that, once through rehab, she would be welcomed back into community, that her essential nature was still visible to her uncle even when it was lost to her. Many decades later, describing that moment still brings her to tears. He doesn't see it as unusual, rather what was natural to the occasion, the person, the relationship. He is fundamentally kind, and she is kin.

Strangers and Kindness:

As an adjective *kind*, or as a noun *kindness*, the actions we are referring to are based on a *physical* understanding of our shared human condition (what it means for *anyone* to bleed, to fear, to feel joyful, encouraged, enthusiastic, happy, loving, doubtful, anxious, helpless, lost, alienated, enraged, *estranged*), an understanding that can easily expand beyond kin. When people describe who they commonly act generously toward, they usually say someone who they are related to (but don't necessarily feel similar to) or a stranger they feel 'at one' with.

For some of us, responding positively to strangers is less problematic. We may just find it easier to feel 'at one' with others, familiar or unfamiliar. Kindness toward strangers may often be a matter of instinct, not principle. For example, years ago, I was struck once when visiting my sister at how similarly both of us responded when we heard screams coming from a merry-go-round in the park. Immediately and without reference to each other, we both set off running toward the sound. Once we had made sure there was no danger, we returned to find my brother-in-law and nephew placidly finishing their sandwiches. They weren't convinced of the danger, didn't see how their presence would contribute. Our response, in the opposite direction, had been just as instinctual. None of the responses were moral, but for my sister and me, our body's sense of who our 'kind' was might have been broader.

Those who respond to strangers positively and easily are probably those who score high on several of the basic character traits psychologists call the Big Five, particularly openness, agreeability, and extraversion. Studies have shown our openness to, or anxiety toward, new stimuli even at two is predictive of our value orientations as adults, anxiety about new stimuli being associated with an emphasis on stability, familiarity, and hierarchy.

We're also more likely to respond positively to strangers if we ourselves have been in the position of being the stranger at different times and in different settings, for then we have a range of physical, emotional and intellectual experiences that can enrich our understanding of what the other person may be feeling. It is also easier if we have a vision of community as something we actively create together, rather than something we inherit. If we feel others are basically trustworthy, the distinctions between the familiar and the unfamiliar become more fluid. None of these seem to me to be conscious choices, matters of will, but they may predispose us to act kindly towards those we don't know.

But kindness to the stranger is not as innate to many people. They don't feel that sense of basic identification for various reasons—indeed they may feel fear or antipathy. If we feel fear, we don't approach. If we feel our actions will bring us condemnation from the groups we most want acceptance from, we don't intervene. If we feel it is someone else's responsibility to act, we stand aside.

I point to an American ethos to support my own affinity for strangers—but there are many American values that actively impede kindness: our emphasis on self-sufficiency (taking care of ourselves and our own), our competitiveness, our feeling of social insecurity and threat in a pluralistic society where we feel we have less and less political power, economic stability, and normative value. If we feel we are barely making it ourselves, that no one would come to our own aid, that there is danger in coming to someone else's aid, that by helping we are encouraging others to be helpless or manipulative or exploitative, we stand back.

Estrangement: The Stories We Tell About "Them"

"Stranger danger" is an American term developed in the U.S. in the 1960s. Our sense of stranger danger has only increased since then—the danger of strangers within our borders and strangers without. The Danish social scientist Christian Larsen has an interesting study on why social cohesion in Denmark and Sweden increased in the last fifty years even when these countries were facing the destabilizing factors that are used to explain the loss of social trust in the U.S. and the United Kingdom: loss of industrial jobs, the diversifying work force, immigration, the weakening of the nuclear family, and increasing income inequality. The greatest differences he found were in levels of income inequality, in the number of people who felt securely part of a meritocratic middle class, the number of people they believed were on the 'bottom,' and, most significantly, in the stories the middle class believed about those who were less fortunate. When the middle class comes to believe those who are less fortunate are *essentially* different, not sharing the same motivations, aspirations, core values, sense of responsibility, or the *kindness* of the middle class, the less social trust there is throughout the whole society.

Larsen emphasizes that these beliefs are stories, acts of imagination. They are not based on direct experience, face-to-face interactions, *real* life, rather on what people see and read in the media, people who are *not* like our kin, our kindly if rigid grandfather, our frightened but well-meaning grandmother, our hard-working brother, our sensitive niece, our belligerent and blustering cousin or son-in-law. But if we standardly overestimate the size of our poor and its racial make-up, if we standardly deny *them* the same values, aspirations, commitments, complexity, *and a good will equal to our own*, if we begin to understand anyone unlike us (the very rich, the very poor, the older and whiter and less educated, the multicultural young, the immigrant) as living by rules and values that bear no relation to ours, the less we feel kindly toward *them*, the more we feel estranged and distrustful.

The quality of our imaginings when we are estranged, threatened, devalued and feeling helpless is essentially different from when we are feeling accepted, appreciated, and competent. Adrenalin-driven imagination, which is a product of our left brain, is cartoonish. It is a world of flat characters driven by primal urges—anger, hunger, lust, greed, aggression, revenge, domination. Characters tend to be elaborated from and explained by a single attribute. Someone is a liar, a cheat, a miser, a bully and they predictably and inevitably act the way they do because they are a liar, bully, cheat. The range of feeling, complexity of motives, assumptions of essential goodness and vulnerability we give ourselves we don't extend to these strangers. Strangers by race, gender, religion, class, education, wealth, party affiliation. *They* do not bleed as *we* do, painfully, vividly, unjustly. *They* do not yearn or grieve or have second thoughts, and we respond to them with the broadest of emotions, anger, fear, hate. Our behavioral responses are flight, fight, freeze. All our affiliative emotions are suppressed. *They* do not elicit kindness for they are not like us. We do not imagine being related to them, sharing a Thanksgiving dinner table, a close friend, a picket fence, much less a gene pool, a physiology, a country. We do not "go forward with the presumption of good faith in our fellow citizens."

Remembering Kindness
This anthology, thank goodness, invites us to a very different place. A place where we have the time and safety and sense of community needed to explore what at times has allowed us to reach out to help others who do not seem to be like us and what we have learned from doing so—about ourselves, about the people who inspired these actions, and about the world these acts of kindness help create.

The images in the book come from our companion *Remembering Kindness* photography project. People were asked if they were willing to share a photo of themselves remembering a moment of kindness given or received. If I took the pictures, I asked participants to let me know when they had the memory clearly in mind, and when they indicated they did, I took several photos.

Several participants shared their memories: A woman remembered when work colleagues collected money to send her home for the holidays the first year that, newly divorced, she lived out of state, a gift she has quietly tried to pay forward ever since. A young boy remembered a man taking the time to read a book aloud to him. An Ethiopian visa lottery winner, who had arrived only two weeks earlier, was eager to share his happiness to be here "because I love freedom." A young woman remembered how many times, moving to a new city, she has been embraced by organizations that have felt "like family," a reception so reliable she has now begun to assume it. A restaurant manager remembered the pleasure of serving people in the right spirit. A waiter remembered conversations with customers that were far more valuable than tips.

One woman remembered how her shyness as a child was resolved so that she now knows no stranger. She contracted polio in 1954, a year before the vaccine. She became the poster child for the county March of Dimes and her photo was posted in all the stores to encourage donations. Everywhere she went people recognized her and wished her well. So this illness, which could have been traumatic and isolating, led to an experience of inclusion at several levels. She knew she stood for others, including the ten other children she personally knew who also had contracted the virus. She knew she was seen as worthy of a sympathy and support that included her but expanded beyond her. She contrasted her own assumptions of social trust and support with the attitudes of her father, a policeman, who focused on potential dangers. "But it hasn't been my experience," she says now, at seventy. "There's nobody I won't talk to. I always assume they mean well. I can't help myself."

Election day, we were visiting Savannah and we wandered the city inviting people to remember kindness with us. We made an intentional effort to engage people who appeared as if they might be on different ends of the political spectrum. The stories we heard included an account by a couple from Florida of how they came to give extravagant tips to waiters and waitresses at the holidays. The wife explained, "We were at Cracker Barrel and we had this very nice waitress and we looked at each other and I said, 'I think we should give a really big tip. What does $100 sound like to you?' And my husband said, 'I was thinking the same thing. That's perfect.' It didn't mean that much to us, and it meant so much to the waitress. She came out to us in tears, she was so grateful, and we decided that from then on, we were going to do it on a regular basis." With equal pleasure, a shy young art student, much tattooed, spoke of her own recent moment of illumination standing in line at the local

Starbucks, seeing the young girl ahead of her was short ten cents for her coffee and thinking, "I can do that! I have ten cents. I can help her."

A man who had been staring up at the weathervane on the steeple of one of the many churches in the city refused to have his photo taken but eagerly shared this memory from thirty or more years earlier in New Jersey where he grew up. "You know New Jersey is not like here. It is a snatch-and-grab place. It was in the winter, snow and slush on the ground. I was going into the supermarket and this old white man was leaving the store and his wallet fell out of his coat. When I called out to him, he wouldn't turn his head or acknowledge me. But I walked up to him, he was just beginning to realize that he had lost it, and I said to him, 'This may be what you're looking for,' as I put the wallet in his hand. He still wouldn't look at me. But when I was about ten feet away he called out, 'Boy, God will bless you.' Now, I didn't mind that 'Boy' since I was from the Caribbean. I called out to him, 'God has already blessed me. I did what I needed to do.'"

A handsome man taking a lunch break from a construction project told us about his older brother giving him a kidney when he was twenty and his brother was twenty-six. "He was married with kids, so it meant he couldn't give one to either of them in the future if they might have needed it. But I don't remember him saying anything about that. I'm sixty-five now. I've had his kidney more than twice as long as I've had my own and it's still working fine, even without medicine. When I moved here sixteen years ago, I stopped the medicine because it was so expensive, but my brother and I were such a close match, it doesn't matter. My doctor tells me I'll probably die of something else before this kidney gives out on me. My brother died at forty-eight of cancer."

As I went to sleep after the election, I said to my husband, "I am so glad we spent the day the way we did." Those stories, those faces, were an invitation into a far more embodied, and *kinder*, imagination, one that had room for attentive and empathic conversations, finding genuine common ground with people whose skin color was similar to mine but whose political convictions probably weren't. It was an invitation I needed to accept.

Just as I drifted off to sleep, I remembered one last conversation, with a couple a few years older than we are, who were in town through the generosity of their daughter and son-in-law to celebrate their fortieth wedding anniversary. They were happy to meditate on that, be photographed for our project, and proudly introduced us to their children, who also participated.

They were also curious about the photos I had been taking of a shop window, indeed the husband had taken a picture of me doing so. "It's the T-shirts," I said.

Stomp my flag, I'll stomp your ass. POLICE OFFICER: My job is to save your ass, not kiss it. E.M.S.: My job is to save your ass, not kiss it. Family, Faith, Friends, Flags, Firearms: Five things you don't mess with. There's plenty of room for all God's creatures: right next to the mashed potatoes. She was short and fat and had a big mouth, so I let her go. NURSE: My job is to save your ass, not kiss it.

"I keep trying to imagine what it would feel like to *wear* them," I said. I remembered the look on the their faces. They *understood.* I could see it, feel it, in real time.

Reciprocity

One of the great challenges of kindness whether to kin or to strangers— —a challenge we see as core to our own commitment to a universal table with a place for everyone—is the reality that our good intentions and actions may be well received but not reciprocated. *What does it mean to make a place at the table for someone who would not make a place for you? To be kind to someone who would not be kind toward you or anyone like you?*

In the aftermath of a remarkably corrosive election, in an increasingly estranged and estranging society, these questions are alive to many of us. They are frightening in their implications, especially because they are directed at those who might be our neighbors, certainly are our fellow citizens. At what point does that fear cause us to shift from the kind of imagination that builds on our direct, complex, face to face, mirror neuron to mirror neuron, heart to heart, flesh and blood interactions with one another to the abstracting imagination that strips the other of the full range of complexity (compassion as well as ire) we grant ourselves, a bloodless but violent, fear-mongering and conspiratorial, kindness-sapping imagination that gets picked up so rapidly and is amplified so loudly by social media that it transforms *us* so tragically and dangerously into *them*?

More importantly, how do we hear that shift and reverse it? I think it begins with taking a deep breath, recognizing our own vulnerability and having compassion for it, and taking the time to listen in with that same kindness to others, listen in with that most necessary of all presumptions, good faith.

What You Will Find Here

The sections in the book developed naturally from the selections themselves and present various stages in the experience of being kind to strangers or receiving kindness from them. Kindness isn't always spontaneous, it isn't always reciprocated, its effects are as various as its origins.

I. Re-Evaluation/Revelation

In the first section, individuals reconsider the nature of kindness, what it is, when, and where we find it. We are often surprised into an awareness of its presence and of its effects, sometimes at the moment, sometimes years later.

Margaret Hasse, responding to a vividly dressed and expressive woman on the bus, says, "I envy her, wrapped in a woven shawl like a choir of crayons./For months, I've tried to pull my heart up/ like a heavy stone from a well of disappointment." Hasse envies the exuberant and flamboyant woman, but also finds her energy contagious, an invitation to look at the world they share with more receptive eyes. In William Cass's story, "New Year's Eve," he describes the flow of kindness between neighbors, that in the ominous flow of world events we often don't notice: "But these other things happened, too, and would keep happening, no matter what."

Lowell Jaeger in his essay, "Getting Where We Need to Go," meditates on the nature of kindness, what exactly it was about the way an old man gave her money for gas that truly got through to a car-jacking young girl: "Is kindness, true kindness, more an attitude than a thoughtful gesture? In my own life, the people who have moved me and shaped me most are people who have truly wished me well." This answer seems too simple, too obvious—or is it, this simple stance of truly wishing someone well, in its unvarnished, unconditional directness a necessary precondition for anything else we may wish to convey?

Revelations come to us at different ages, sometimes years after an event. Katie Glauber Bush, at eighteen, watching her father, a podiatrist, tend to the feet of a schizophrenic women several times each week for free, discovers a completely different side of him from the rule bound and rather impatient man she knows at home. Rebecca Taksel does not fully recognize the unusual generosity of the chicano family who took her into their simple home, opened up their lives to her as a young, footloose woman until many decades later.

The narrator in MK Punky's "Take Care of Each Other" brings us face to face with the many ways we all blind ourselves to our general need for the simple sign she carries, one that is equally admonition and invitation:

> *My story is just as boring and horrifying as everyone else's:*
> *bad choices, etcetera you don't want to hear it believe me because it*
> *will heartbreak you and then it will send you off on a there-but-for-*
> *the-grace jag that will make you feel better about your life of Netflix*
> *and artisanal cupcakes and treadmills but somehow it won't make*
> *you feel deeply enough to consider why you take better care of your*
> *dog*
> *or your gerbil*
> *than you do the woman sleeping in a tent beside the freeway.*

II. Cross-Identification

We are more likely to be kind to those strangers we feel 'at one' with, although the source of that cross-identification may not always be apparent to bystanders, the stranger, or even ourselves to begin with. Becoming aware of its source can often send us off in very new directions, as we see in Paul Hostovsky's "Staring at the Blind." Hostovsky describes what attracted him to Paul, a blind man he met on a subway and then followed out onto the street: "He looked exposed, yet determined; vulnerable yet independent, fragile and at the same time, I don't know, girded." He goes on to say, "I stared at him like that for a long time. I stared at him for years. Literally. I helped him cross that street that day, and the next day and the next. And soon we became friends." Indeed, he opened up another career for Hostovsky, as a Braille transcriber as well as sign interpreter for the deaf. But he also opened him to a new sensibility that could include vulnerability and strength as fused rather than antithetical qualities.

The impact of Marcelino, a Honduran immigrant, on Robert Kus, a Catholic priest in Wilmington, North Carolina, was even more profound. Father Bob invited Marcelino to move out of the local homeless shelter and come and share his rectory. This instinctive act and the friendship across nationality, culture, and class that develops from it lights something in Father Bob himself, something that continues even after Marcelino returns to Honduras, providing a much larger and more inclusive frame of reference and meaning for Father Bob's own pastoral activities and also for those of his parish, which becomes a sister parish for Marcelino's parish in Honduras.

More challenging forms of cross-identification are found in Jessica Naab's "Sinners on Sixty-Six." Her often amusing and refreshingly honest narrator explores how her ideas about herself and her society change when she, a socially awkward young woman, begins taking the bus to work and makes the acquaintance of men from the local halfway house: "Oddly enough, I wasn't the least bit afraid to be standing at the bus stop in near darkness with a murderer. Maybe because he wasn't *just* a murderer. He was a murderer named Rich who had befriended me when no one else had."

Both Laurie Klein's essay "Behind Her Eyes" and Murali Kamma's story focus on insights triggered by cross-cultural relationships. Laurie Klein describes the complex, and ultimately tender, relationship she develops with an older Thai widow whose behavior towards her originally appears, and feels, assaultive, triggering memories of early molestation. It is only when she can see that there may be some shared experience here that she is able to respond differently: "One day, our gazes locked. And I wondered: had Yai been shamed? As the days passed, the stories I made up about her in my head began to reflect my own." The Indian host in Kamma's "Brahms in the Land of Brahma," finds that the sympathy that allows him to move through his sexual prejudice with his homosexual American houseguest also gives him the courage to make changes for himself, allowing him the inner permission he needs to move beyond caste taboos in his own culture.

III. Help When We Need It Most—Illness and Accident

We clearly are most in need of help when we are most vulnerable, but to have kindness go with that help is something that often causes us to reconsider some of our assumptions about the values we place as a society and as individuals on self-sufficiency and autonomy. Shireen Day, as she describes all the ways people came to her daughter's aid after a terrible car accident, while she waited, helplessly, 2,000 miles away, must also rethink the teachings she has received through her life about family as the only reliable source of protection and safety: "As I thought about my daughter, the highway, the stranger, I would have given anything to be with her. She needed her mother, not some unknown person. *How could someone that didn't know her actually help?*"

In Norman Klein's "Vets," we see how that most American of values, self-sufficiency, can impede the resolution of post-traumatic stress, but how the coexisting value of interdependence, having each other's back, can counter-balance that—both summed up in that single word *Vet*. The story clearly conveys the healing power of kindness based on physical empathy and simple presence, a theme that is echoed in Stephanie Hart's "An Unexpected Kindness." Hart describes the impact the encouraging words of a young man who had also survived cancer had as she was beginning to recover from her own treatment: "I was aware of a warm glow in my chest as if a light had just been turned on inside of me. For the first time, I had the certainty that I would be well and thrive."

Other selections in this section emphasize a strong sense of interconnectedness in sickness as well as health that is both appreciative and matter of fact. Patti See describes why she donated a kidney anonymously: "I've always been blessed; my donation was a way of sharing that good luck, good life, and good health with another. What I've received in return may not be as tangible as a new organ, but it is just as life-changing." Dorothy Pirovano describes with humor and appreciation the number of times, the number of settings, when her husband, who has Parkinson's, has fallen and the wide range of people—young women, policemen, businessmen and joggers—who have helped him find his footing again: "as long as we are able, we will maintain a united front. It will be made easier knowing we are surrounded by people who take time to show you they care. They emerge from out of nowhere in a moment."

Joel Wachman's honest but uncomfortable memoir, "This Is Getting Old," explores his feelings as his mother loses her independence and comes to depend heavily not only on him and his brother but also on strangers, the staff in the emergency rooms she often frequents, the staff at the nursing home. Although obviously responsive and attentive, he resents the demands his mother's age and loss of self-sufficiency place on him even as he meets them, resents himself for resenting them and her, a feeling that is heightened by the relative ease, grace, and simple kindness with which others seem to be able to meet his mother's needs:

> *Caring for an old person suffering irreversible decline is not my idea of fun. Yet the stranger on the sofa, taking a break from being my mother's crutch, was able to find satisfaction and humor in it. If I am too squeamish to help my mother with her pressure stockings, does that mean there is a hole where my heart should be?*

Ken Staley's story, "Missing," describes how a small community is able to absorb the changing health status of its older residents as they go missing through dementia, embracing the unexpected dimensions of their personalities, holding a place for them in illness and death through their own affectionate memories.

> *Mabel slipped away quietly, slowly, but much further. Ruth seemed to have some deep seated understanding of where home and hearth was and stayed right close to Uncle Ed's store. Mabel always wanted to be somewhere else, somewhere pressing and urgent called her; places to visit demanded her attention and she'd make up stories about living in places she'd heard about but never seen.*

IV. Weaving a New Fabric

The stories in this section are longer and more expansive in time, revealing the role time itself plays in transforming conventional relationships between strangers into a sense of community. The first several selections focus on the lasting impact of caring unfamiliar adults in giving young people a sense of what they can expect in the larger world, providing a much needed promise of belonging. In Linda Maxwell's poem, "The Businessman's Truth Tables," two young girls traveling with an impatient mother and older sister are entertained by a businessman sharing their row in coach, who teaches them how to solve puzzles, including the very important one of how they too might find a place in the world when they grow up, a small lesson that as adults they still cherish and pass on. Jennifer Thornburg's story, "All Souls," evocatively describes the experience of three young children from the wrong side of the tracks on Halloween, the tension between family loyalty and the desire to belong, which is modulated by the kindness and redefining power of their neighbor Steve from the Ukraine: "We were *good* children, he had said. Maybe you didn't have to live on the right side of town to be good. His blessing rang in my ears, and though I carried a pillowcase heavy with that evening's plunder, I have carried Steve Sieveshenko's words all my life."

Rupert Fike's freely associative and funny poem, "Tutoring Mohammad Mohammad," shows how much goes into becoming acculturated, a process as baffling to the native-born as to the immigrant, as the strangeness of our own culture becomes more and more evident when seen through new eyes. Rick Krizman's "Cantaloupe Island" captures the angst of a teenage musician struggling with obsessive-compulsive disorder and the surprising way his peers come to his aid, allowing him to see his own struggles in a new light.

In Frank Haberle's "Road to Haines" two older women from Illinois befriend a young man also heading for Alaska. The story is a fascinating combination of the direct and indirect, the women's kind clear-sightedness evident in their prayers for their young hitchhiker: "And dear Lord, we hope you help him find his friend, and himself, and a purpose for this journey he's on." Whether he finds his purpose or not, they know their own—to provide a helping but unintrusive hand.

In Alethea Eason's "Holiday Cove" the narrator, after calling child protective services, to her own surprise finds herself inviting the young mother she has reported over for dinner. By the end of the story, she is able to consider what they have in common and claim the kindness that now binds them: "I want to believe she's taking stock of her life, coming to terms with being a mother, growing up as she sits beside me. I don't trust my thoughts. Who really grows up? But, I know I'll keep rooting for her."

The ambivalence present in Eason's story (for she is a little suspicious of her own kind gestures) is heightened in Steve Koppman's story, "The Russians Are Here," where a middle-aged American, a civil servant, finds himself volunteering with Russian refugees, whose possibilities in the United States he feels are perhaps greater than his own: "He hated more than anything to explain himself. When he thought too hard about it, his life seemed a terrible series of misunderstandings he wished he could straighten out but never actually could." The description of the tensions between the narrator's desire to do good to others and his need to feel his own life still has real value and possibility capture well the tensions in many Americans' relationships with immigration: "He wondered again why he was there with the Russians while thinking he should really come more often."

Pauline Kaldas' memoir, "Among Neighbors," traces the slow, organic growth of community among young couples on a street in Binghamton over several years, developing first through husbands, then children, then wives: "Had we met elsewhere, we probably would have never come to know each other. But sharing space can force an intimacy, stretching us beyond our seclusion. For me, that rainy evening was one of the rare moments when I felt located in one place, when cultural identity seemed superseded by being neighbors."

In John King's essay, the flight of associations that accompany Colin Powell's commencement address at King's third graduation from Rice, his first having taken place in 1967, allows him to ponder the incremental impact of various moments of "humanity in action"—from a policeman helping a sick child, the university's decision to integrate, to the city of Houston taking in 250,000 refugees from Katrina—that have shaped his view of human nature.

V. How Much Is Enough?

Our discomfort with what is reasonable to expect of ourselves and for others to expect of us, with how much is enough, is the central theme of this final section. We've heard echoes of it in earlier selections, for example, in Joel Wachman's "This is Getting Old" and in Steve Koppman's "The Russians Are Here," but here the uneasiness comes sometimes from the writers themselves and sometimes from us as readers. We wonder about an action that could be variously interpreted: Was that really kindness? We ask ourselves when we hear about sweeping or sustained acts of kindness: Is that within our range—and should it be? For scale is an important dimension here, used both playfully and seriously.

Anusha VR in her essay, "Corn on the Cob," describes being befriended during a rainstorm after a very frustrating day at work in Bangalore. The street vendor who comes to her aid both feeds her and also gives her a frame of reference for the travails she faces as a young accountant. The vendor, who has raised and educated two sons by her own efforts scolds this relatively wealthy young woman: "If I had stood under a shop crying like it is the end of the world, then it would have been the end of the world. You have to fight for yourself."

Jennifer Kanke's poems move back and forth across the line between compassion and something much less affirming, a keen sense of how often and how willfully we fall away from it.

. . . Instead, I pass out cards to those in need
saying, "Sorry, I gave in my childhood," because I am no

infinite dharma font. I am a squirrel on a tree limb, balanced
on one foot scratching my fleas,
holding tight to my own little acorn.

In Teetle Clawson's disturbing poem, "Follow-up Appointment," the poet interprets the doctor's transgressive action as a kind invitation back to life after deep loss and invites the reader to view it in the same way: "I know he's doing this for me./I know he's risking his career."

The narrator in Johnny Townsend's "The Girl from Treponema" practices kindness daily, nearly incessantly, as a matter of course. He works at a center that provides mailboxes and other services for the destitute. He knows his customers personally, their stories, their quirks, their aspirations, cuts out coupons for them. As he tends to their needs kindly, he also unsentimentally reviews the various love relationships he's been in that have also thrown him into a caretaker role, one that seems to nourish rather than deplete. We, as readers, feel a little abashed at the scale of his good deeds.

A laid-off manager finds employment at a Walmart in his home town in John Timm's "A Good Day at the Office," a job he manages to infuse with dignity and care, even when it may go against company policy: "I'm on camera. You're always on camera here. Most of the time I forget about it. Sometimes I resent it. Right now I don't give a damn. If they want to give me crap because I helped out a customer, too bad."

Jason A. Ney's "Until It Hurts" forces us to laugh, cringe, and ache for the narrator and his wife, who, through a circuitous path it quickly becomes difficult to reconstruct, end up taking into their home a very manipulative woman who is pregnant. They are torn between their belief in kindness and their reactions to the selfish actions of their exploitive houseguest, who they are having a hard time getting to leave: "There it was. It wasn't the first time I'd heard it, our friends and family constantly mentioning what a 'good thing' we were doing. *Then why doesn't it feel like it?* I would think. *Why has doing this 'good thing' made us so miserable?*" The author comes to an understanding of his inner imperative, and the nature of sacrifice, that we will honor, but probably will be reluctant to emulate.

The closing story by Jana Zvibleman, "Bucket of Water," takes a similar situation in a more comic direction when a wedding officiant asks herself what the Dalai Lama would do and decides to officiate at the wedding of a young woman whose honesty and spirit appeal to her—with unexpected benefits all around.

We hope that you will find people here to identify with, situations that echo with some you have experienced and also ones that seem completely new, responses that reinforce your own best instincts and ones that acknowledge the inner doubts that can accompany those best instincts or hold us from them, and many invitations to think more boldly about what we are able, stranger to stranger, to give each other and why it matters that we do so.

BIBLIOGRAPHY

Batson, C. Daniel. *Altruism in Humans.* New York: Oxford University Press, 2011.

Blau, Melinda and Karen L. Fingerman. *Consequential Strangers: The Power of People Who Don't Seem to Matter . . . But Really Do.* New York: W.W. Norton, 2009.

DeWall, C. Nathan, ed. *The Oxford University Press Handbook of Social Exclusion.* New York: Oxford University Press, 2013.

Larsen, Christian Albrekt. *The Rise and Fall of Social Cohesion: The Construction and Deconstruction of Social Trust in the US, UK, Sweden and Denmark.* Oxford: Oxford University Press, 2013.

Music, Graham. *The Good Life: The new science of altruism, selfishness and immorality.* New York: Routledge, 2014.

Padilla-Walker, Laura M. and Gustavo Carlo, eds. *Prosocial Development: A Multidimensional Approach.* New York: Oxford University Press, 2014.

Pfaff, Donald W. *The Altruistic Brain: How We Are Naturally Good.* New York: Oxford University Press, 2015.

Smith, Christian and Hilary Davidson. *The Paradox of Generosity: Giving We Receive, Grasping We Lose.* New York: Oxford University Press, 2014.

I. RE-EVALUATION/REVELATION

MARGARET HASSE

BLOOD ORANGES

A woman came on board the bus today
carrying blood oranges in a string bag,
her lips like red cuffs on the sleeve of her throat.

Others in winter coats sit like spools of black and blue,
the shock of a Monday workday freezing our morning faces.
I envy her, wrapped in a woven shawl like a choir of crayons.
For months, I've tried to pull my heart up
like a heavy stone from a well of disappointment.

Standing, she flirts with the driver in a foreign language
that clicks like knitting needles.
Her voice filling the aisle could melt the blue slush on the floor mats.
Laughter opens her mouth to a diva's O plucking a high C
like a cherry from a tree.

Down the aisle she floats by our plastic pews.
As if happiness has a hand on her breast, as if happiness
is taking her body apart in pieces of dazzled joy.

She is rickrack on a funeral dress,
a peacock's tail fanned against a gray wall,
a handful of bright corn to feed the birds.
She smiles with a candle's lick of flame that doesn't leave when it lights.

The sun shoots golden arrows through the dirt-pocked windows.
I stand to stop the bus with a tug on the white cord.
The accordion doors open to a sidewalk shoveled clear of snow.

WILLIAM CASS

NEW YEAR'S EVE

The year was grinding to a halt. It held the memories of bombings, mass shootings, a gridlocked Congress, civil wars, terrorism, an increase in global warming. These things happened, as did others.

)( )( )(

Early in the year, a late season hurricane destroyed much of a town in Alabama. The entire west side was flattened; no building left standing. One of those who lost his business was an auto repair shop owner named Carl. He was an army vet who'd served as a mechanic; his wife kept the books and knitted afghans and scarves for their church thrift shop. Carl employed three assistants who all lost their homes, too.

There was only one other auto repair shop in town. It was larger and operated by a big guy named Terry. He came by after the storm, pulled his car to curb nearby and watched Carl sort through the rubble where his shop had stood. The late afternoon was overcast and dim. Terry waited until the streetlamps blinked on to climb out of the car and lumber up the street. Carl heard him coming through the rubble and turned around. They recognized one another from separate photographs in the yellow pages where they'd studied their competitor's advertisements. They'd crossed paths a few times in the auto parts departments at local dealerships, and each had avoided the other.

Carl dropped the shingle he'd been holding. Terry stopped a few feet away, looked around, toed the debris. They were silent for several moments.

"Well," Terry finally said, "I'm awful sorry about your loss."

Carl nodded and looked around at what had been his shop. He sighed and shrugged.

"So," Terry said. "I've cleared out a couple of bays for you at my place.

You bring your guys over there and set up shop for as long as you need."

Carl frowned and regarded the big man.

Terry said, "Your tools all gone?"

"No, we were able to salvage most of those."

Terry nodded. "That's good. You can use whatever you need of ours, too."

Carl shook his head, folded his hands into steeples, and touched his fingertips to his lips.

"My daughter is my secretary," Terry said. "She set up a desk next to hers in the office for you, emptied out some file drawers."

"My wife," Carl said. "She does that for us."

Terry nodded again. "For your wife then. We keep a coffeemaker in there for customers and the workers. You can use that, too. And we hung a frame above those bays in case you want to put up a sign."

Carl kept shaking his head. "I don't know what to say. Thanks, I guess, to start."

"Sure. No problem."

Terry held out his hand. Carl took it in both of his.

✗ ✗ ✗

In the early spring, Ralph's wife, Judy, went into the hospital due to an auto-immune deficiency problem. The doctors weren't able to determine an exact diagnosis, but her symptoms were severe enough that Judy was kept there on a prolonged admittance. Ralph had been retired for only a few years. He couldn't sleep in their bed alone, so he stayed in her hospital room each night on a recliner that folded down into a kind of cot. He ate his meals in the hospital cafeteria. Judy slept most of the time, so he sat next to her holding her hand, thinking or watching the muted television.

During the time she was admitted, snow melted and the earth thawed in that part of the Northeast. Buds appeared on trees, and the tiny white curls of the first crocuses opened. Ralph sometimes visited briefly with neighbors when he came home every few days to shower or change clothes. He spoke most often with the Fred and Jenny Miller who had lived across the street for nearly three decades. Their children had grown up and gone to school together; they'd shared bar-b-ques, birthday parties, graduations, weddings.

The flower beds in Judy's front yard had long been her pride and joy.

After the admittance passed the one-month mark, Fred and Jenny went to the nursery and bought flats of pansies, petunias, and mums of different colors. They spent a Saturday planting them in the beds across the street, adding potting soil and vitamins to each hole. When they finished, they put down weed barrier and spread bark. Then they sat on their neighbors' front step while they turned the sprinklers on the beds that day, and Fred did the same each evening afterwards.

An afternoon finally came soon after when Ralph didn't arrive alone in the driveway of their home in their big maroon sedan. He trotted around to the passenger side, and helped Judy out of the car. He lifted her suitcase out of the backseat and held her elbow as she made her way to the front door. She stopped suddenly when she saw all the flowers in full bloom; Ralph did, too. When they turned to look across the street, their eyes were wide and their mouths were open. Fred and Jenny stood watching together from their living room window. Judy saw them, patted her hand to her heart, and pointed to them. Jenny repeated the same gesture.

)( )( )(

It was a rainy summer that year in Seattle. John's postal route largely involved a neighborhood of old homes in the northern portion of the city. Many had moss growing along their concrete foundations and roofs or gutters that sagged. John had been on that route for eleven years. Because of the climate, most of the deliveries were to slots in front doors or to boxes hung under front porch eaves. A lot of the people in that neighborhood were elderly and came to the door to meet him; they weren't busy and often engaged him in idle conversation.

One old man, Mr. Faulks, lived alone in a plain brick house that sat back from the road under a canopy of evergreen trees and was dark even at the height of day. Mr. Faulks was tall and stooped; his eyes behind rimless glasses drooped at the outside edges and his lips always curled into a quiet smile when he greeted John at the front door. He had worked as a librarian, and his wife had been dead for a number of years when John first made his acquaintance. Mr. Faulks kept coin and stamp collections, and John could often see one or the other spread out with a magnifying glass on the dining room table behind Mr. Faulks in the open doorway in the light of a gooseneck lamp. There were sometimes quiet strains of classical music coming from an old console in the living room.

Over the years, Mr. Faulks' trips to his front door grew less frequent. He began to use a walker that was difficult for him to maneuver. When he gradually came to need a wheelchair instead, John rarely saw him anymore; the dining room table through the front window remained empty and unlit, and the house was silent. However, the mail had always been collected each morning when he arrived.

One day in July, he stood on Mr. Faulks' front porch sorting through his bag to ferret out the correct items to slide through the old man's slot. As usual, these were mostly flyers and advertisements, but there was one item out of the ordinary that caught his attention: a postcard from a dentist's office that held a pre-stenciled birthday greeting. John stood looking at the card and blinking. He thought of his own father whose birthday would have been that same week if he was still living; John considered the years that had passed since his father's death and estimated that he would have been about the same age as Mr. Faulks.

John cut short his lunch break that afternoon and went to a florist nearby where he bought a bouquet of birthday balloons. He returned to Mr. Faulks' house and tied them to the handle of the front door with a tiny card before resuming his route. Through the window on the door, he could see the mail that he'd delivered earlier that morning still scattered below the slot on the hardwood floor.

The next day, the balloons were gone, but there was a post-it note waiting for him on the flap of Mr. Faulks' mail slot. It said simply: "Thanks. That's the nicest thing I can remember."

✕ ✕ ✕

Maggie and her husband had been married for seventeen years, and together for almost twenty, when he told her he was leaving her shortly before Thanksgiving. They both worked in the same small school district outside of Fresno, California. Almost all of the students there were children of migrant farmworkers and most could speak very little English. Maggie taught fourth grade in the elementary school, and her husband provided tech support to all the sites and the district office.

He was sitting at the end of their bed when she came home from work the day before Thanksgiving vacation. A small suitcase perched next to him on the bed.

She stopped in the doorway. He sat with his head bowed, his hands folded between his knees. After a moment, she asked, "What's going on here?"

He looked up at her with sad eyes. "I'm unhappy. I feel trapped."

Her knees buckled under her. "Is there someone else?"

"That's only part of it. I respect and admire you, but I don't love you anymore."

She shook her head, and kept shaking it. She heard herself say, "No."

"I've settled," he said. "We've settled."

"I haven't settled."

He took the handle of the suitcase. Maggie stepped toward him and held out her hand. "Don't go," she said. "Please."

He stood up and pushed past her with the suitcase. She heard the back door open and close, and then his car start up and drive away from the curb on the side of their house. She collapsed onto the bed. It felt as if she was falling, falling into a well and couldn't reach out to stop it.

He didn't come home that night, and didn't return any of her calls to his cell phone. The next morning, she went into school, but moved in a daze throughout the day, through the first Thanksgiving play in the school hall, through the spelling test, through the free choice time she allowed her students at the end of the afternoon. After dismissal, she sat perfectly still at her desk staring off over the desks. Vaguely, she heard other teachers' classroom doors lock closed and the sounds of voices and footsteps diminish until the school was silent.

Maggie sat there until she became aware of one of her students, Susana, and her mother standing in the classroom doorway. Susana came up to her desk carrying a dark carton of waxed cardboard. Her mother remained in the doorway. They were both smiling.

Susana set the box on the desk. She was one of the best students in the class and had picked up more English than most. "This is for you," she told Maggie.

Maggie looked at the box, which was filled with heads of lettuce, still unwashed from the fields. She heard Susana's mother say something in Spanish from the doorway.

"She says you're a good teacher," Susana told her. "That I'm the first person in my family to learn to divide."

Susana's mother nodded from the doorway. Although it was already dark and cold outside, neither of them wore a coat.

Susana said, "We're leaving to follow the crops to the Imperial Valley. We hope to be back next fall, and we hope you're still here."

Maggie looked from mother to daughter and began to cry. Susana stepped forward and hugged her for a long moment. Maggie held the embrace with her eyes shut tight.

)( )( )(

The last hours of New Year's Eve crept by. Across the nation, people took stock, reveled to forget, considered the somber events of the past year. But these other things happened, too, and would keep happening, no matter what.

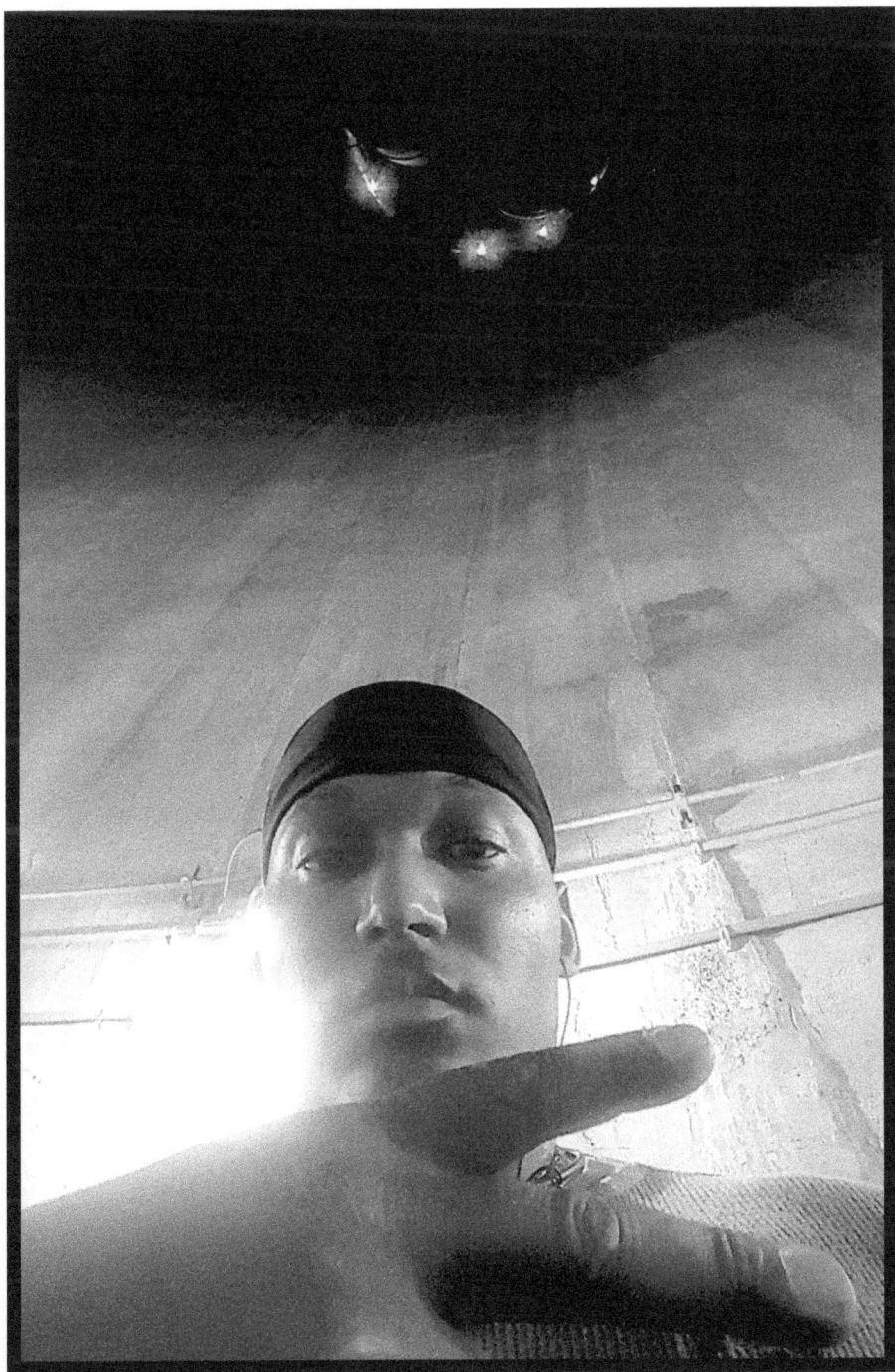

NORITA DITTBERNER-JAX

JAZZ TRUMPETER

> "You are not who this country says you are."
> Hannabal Lakumbe

His voice is soft
and he stops often.
The young black men
around the table,
fidget with their braids,
sprawl.

Doing the right thing
he says, is harder
than 100 Chinese push-ups.
A pause for push-ups.
The boys take turns
making the triangle
with their hands on the floor,
getting their chins down
into that triangle.

He wears them down
with his voice,
his silence. He waits
for them to find their way
and they do: one
tells of the grandmother
related to Ida B. Wells,
another to Leadbelly.
None of these boys
is nothing.

On their faces,
a sense of calm
as if some confusion
has been ordered,
bodies upright,
hands quiet in their laps.

He takes up the trumpet,
the slow wail,
shows them what to do
with sorrow.

LOWELL JAEGER

GETTING WHERE WE NEED TO GO

I've given them sixty seconds to ponder, and Taz is first to raise her hand. Think of an instance, I'd said, when a stranger delivered unto you an unexpected kindness. Eight "troubled teens" and I are sitting in a circle on metal folding chairs; we've just finished reading a poem about a woman in an airport who risks lending companionship to calm a panicked Palestinian grandmother. The grandmother is lost and alone, on the verge of causing a scene.

"I know how that old woman feels," Taz says. "Once I was stuck all by myself in a truck stop. I'd been driving for hours, the gas gauge said empty, and I discovered I'd left my purse at home." She tells us how she'd parked at the pumps and sat sobbing, her head braced against the steering wheel . . .

And she tells us how this old guy, a Good Samaritan pumping gas nearby, notices her distress, fills her tank, and hands her a twenty for good measure. Then he says, "Hope that gets you where you need to go, Sweetheart." Or something like that. Taz can't remember exactly what he'd said, but he was really, really nice, she says. She's "like amazed" at how nice the old guy was; it was "like awesome."

We all nod.

"He even stopped on the highway to offer help after the cops had pulled me over," Taz continues, rakes her hair back out of her eyes and looks around the circle.

Cops? I'm the only one in the circle who doesn't get it.

When finally I do comprehend, I want to laugh out loud, but the group's hushed, sympathetic faces cause me to rally restraint. Turns out Taz had stolen the car. Turns out the Good Samaritan was unwittingly aiding and abetting a runaway teenager crossing state lines. How ironic, I'm thinking, how absurd. How beside the point of the poem. But as I continue to listen to Taz and her compatriots, I begin to glimpse complexities I'd scarcely considered before.

I'm struck in Taz's story that kindness is more than a free tank of gas or a twenty dollar windfall. Action speaks louder than words, we say; I'm sure Taz appreciated the free tank of gas, but what does she mean when she says the old guy was "really, really nice?" A bright star lights in her eyes when she says it. Does it have to do with him not quizzing her, judging her, lecturing her? Does it have to do with him not expecting applause and Taz's thank you, thank you, thank you? Does it have to do with him simply and sincerely wishing her well?

Is kindness, true kindness, more an attitude than a thoughtful gesture? In my own life, the people who have moved me and shaped me most are people who have truly wished me well. I think of my junior high English teacher who could have written me off as hopelessly loud and unruly, but instead . . . in ways that to this day still seem a bit mysterious . . . when she looked at me, I felt she liked me, she wished me well. Why would she do that? Initially, of course, she scarcely knew me, and when over time she learned more about who I am, she surely uncovered a wagon load of mighty obvious flaws. But she went on wishing me well, and it was "like awesome."

Consider this: Why was I surprised my English teacher would like me? Why was Taz "like amazed" that the old guy was really, really nice? By junior high age, I had experienced precious little well-wishing, especially from adults. I suspect it was a bit of a mystery to Taz why the old guy should lend his kindness, should wish her well, should hope she would get where she needed to go. The tank of gas and the twenty dollars are long gone, but the old guy's open-hearted attitude remains. Similarly, for me, I'm sure whatever grades my English teacher friend gave me were over-generous, windfalls that moved me forward in the system when I could just as easily been held behind. The grades are faded ink now in some obscure file, but her kind, perhaps naïve, vote for me that I might someday amount to something more than an attention-seeking chatterbox is now rooted in my core. In my own teaching, I've bumped into students from years past, students I could scarcely recall, who've expressed how their interactions with me in the classroom were of lasting worth. I wonder, what did I offer them more than every opportunity I could find to let them shine, and compassion and acceptance when they fell short of their own potential?

As I write about this notion of kindness as an attitude of sincere well-wishing, I want to argue against my thesis. Is this all just soft-headed nonsense? Taz needs to learn it's not a good idea to steal a car. To keep our communities livable, we need cops, we need probation officers, we need finger-waggers and frowners. To coax students forward in the classroom, we need also to offer honest, rigorous, objective critique. Sometimes we wound with "tough-love" in an attempt to wake the ones we love, to guide them. Tough-love surely is also an attitude of kindness, intended to help people get where they need to go; so are classroom standards and the disciplinary codes of juvenile probation.

Why did the old guy who came to Taz's aid in the truck stop do what he did? Most of us would have kept our distance, wouldn't we? Maybe he should have dialed 911 and let the cops sort it out to begin with. I wonder if it had been his own daughter sitting there in a teary funk, would he have done the same he did for Taz? Sad but true, it seems easier for me to offer open-hearted aid to other people's kids than it is to be "really, really nice" to my own. I wonder if it had been his own daughter, would the old guy have wanted someone to call the cops? I think it's too easy to answer yes to that question.

We can't know for sure why the old guy filled Taz's tank and handed her a twenty. I'm thinking it's a sort of faith that moved him, faith in the outcome of tangles complicated beyond his ken, beyond his control. Maybe he hoped his open-hearted attitude would turn Taz around. Maybe it did, at least in some measure. Whatever the specifics of the crisis in which Taz had become embroiled, she seems most eager afterwards to tell about the Good Samaritan. Wonder what the old guy thought when he watched the cops cuffing Taz?

It's an intricate question of right and wrong. The world keeps spinning on its upright axis, but it's situations like this which cause a little wobble. Taz is learning, the hard way, the limits of the law. That's tough, we say, that's just the way it is. The old guy taught Taz something else: people can care about us, people can wish us well, and the world can be a better place than we've come to expect. This is where we need to go, and the old guy is hoping we all get there.

GEORGE J. SEARLES

RESOLUTIONS

It was New Year's Eve again, but I had no date
and my friend Johnny—long dead now—was also
on his own that night, so we went to The Top Hat,
a decent little place on the other side of town,

and paid our $20 apiece and drank and ate and shot
the breeze until finally the ball dropped in Times Square
as everyone watched the TV and cheered and kissed
and Johnny and I started to feel like royal losers

and got drunker and drunker, finally lurching outside
into a full-blown blizzard that had already nearly buried
my bald-tired little car, a troublesome two-seater
I'd bought from Butchie, my ex-girl's scary older brother.

We brushed off the windshield, got in, and mushed along
the Boulevard, deciding to take a shortcut through the park
where—no surprise—we right away lost all control
and slid into a meadow filled with deep, immobilizing snow.

It wasn't easy to push the doors open, but we got out
and stood there, resigned to our plight and a long walk home
in the frigid night. Soon, though, this began to look like
the least of our problems when an old black Cadillac

full of young black men pulled up and the brothers got out
and advanced on us: silent, focused, businesslike.
They had no trouble at all lifting my car up, three on each
bumper, returning it to the road, wishing us Happy New Year,

and sending us on our way, back into the blinding whiteness.

LAURA CHAIGNON

KNOWING GRINS AND SUSPICIOUS LOOKS

People have always been nice to me, for as long as I can remember, with of course the occasional frustrated prick. They have always been nice, even people I am meeting for the first time. Cashiers, secretaries, professors, waiters, bankers, and people I brush past in busy streets. They always have that smile for me, that same discrete, knowing grin. I can see that they don't think about it when they do it, it just passes graciously on their faces when they look up. Effortless, natural. The kind of smile that starts in the eyes with a fleeting sparkle.

It sounds beautiful when I write about it. It sounds as if I have been experiencing the natural bond uniting us all, beyond all the structural chaos brought upon us by modern society, its addictions and its tragedies, which hide the threads uniting me to you. Which hide the human tapestry. It sounds beautiful and it should feel beautiful. But it does not. It always leaves me with a guilty bitterness. It never feels as natural as it looks, and I always fail to experience any sense of connection. It should feel blissful and perfect. I should feel like I belong in this world and that everything is how it is meant to be. But it feels as if these smiling strangers grin from the knowledge of a narrative I am unaware of. And they act as if I know exactly what they mean. They smile knowingly at me; they smile from who I am, starting sparkles in their eyes, when I struggle to understand what they see in mine.

I never knew what to make of this feeling of utter loneliness arising at waves of identical polite smiles. Until I knew, until it just struck me. They smile at me because they see a nice girl. A nice pretty girl. A nice pretty white girl. A nice pretty young white girl. A nice thin pretty young white girl. A nice thin pretty young white girl with fancy clothes. They see privilege. They smile at me because they recognize it in me. Like an aura, only more obvious. Like a tattoo on my face. I always fail to smile back, because I refuse to wear my tattoo with pride. It does not make me happy because it feels too obvious and sticky, it is glued all over me, hiding my personality, my tears, my immigration background, my money issues, the hard work and the constant struggles, the eating disorders, the self-hatred. They just see a nice thin pretty young white girl with fancy clothes, and they smile at me knowingly. Forcing me to acknowledge that I am so, forcing me to behave like so. But I am not so. That is when I truly understand that the unprivileged are tattooed all the same, from a different ink. They don't get knowing smiles and polite grins. They get suspicious looks, they get ugly stares, they get spiteful glares. To make them think that it is but what they are, forcing them to acknowledge that they are society's scrap, forcing them to behave like so. But they are not so. They are not so.

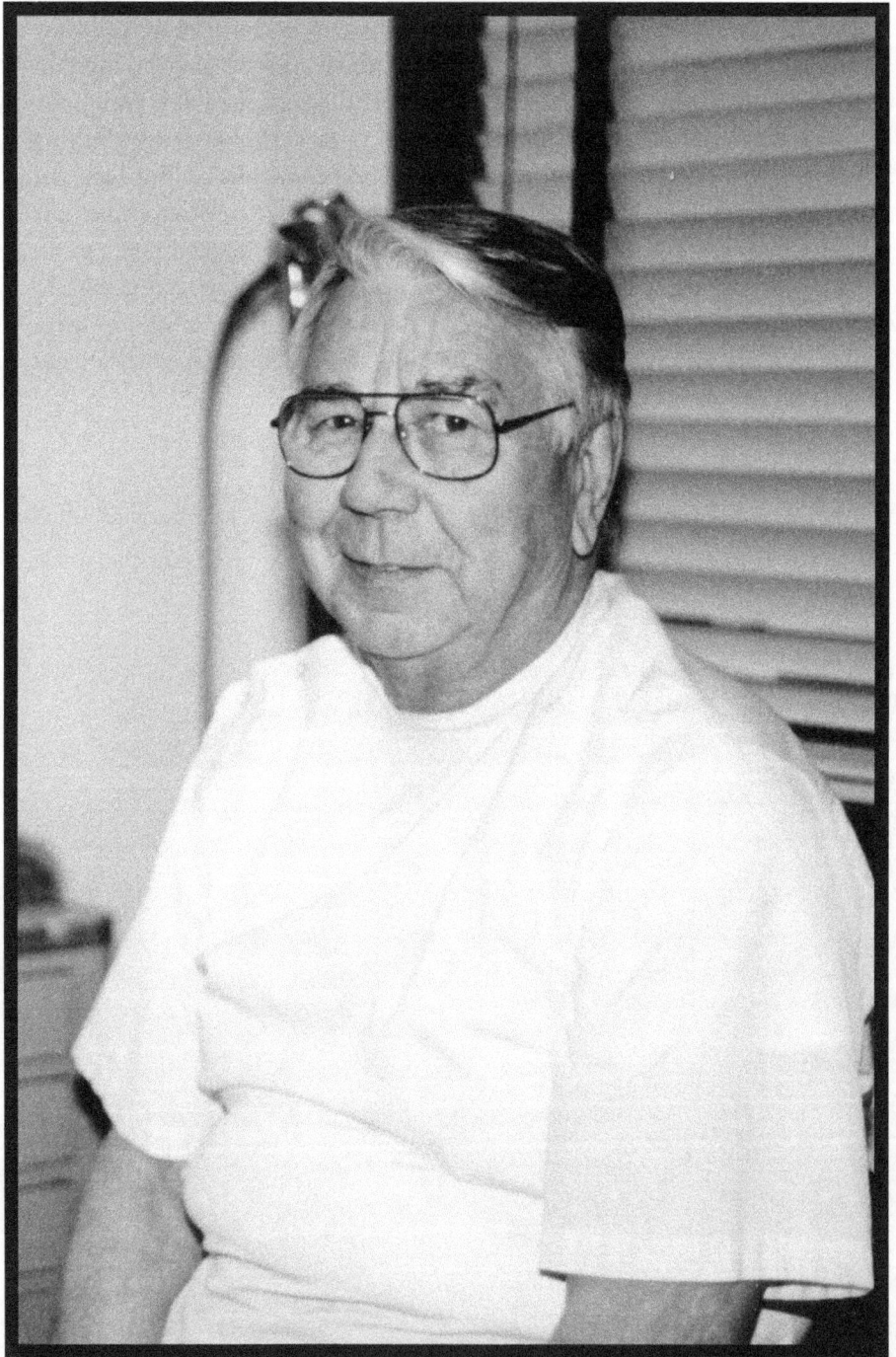

KATIE GLAUBER BUSH

SOLE MAN

Maybe it was those years in the U.S. Navy or his career working on people's feet, but to Dr. James H. Glauber D.P.M., you just weren't dressed until your shoes were shined. I was proud to walk down the street with him each morning as we traveled the two blocks from Skip's parking lot to his office on the seventh floor of the Starks Building. He wore a dark suit, white shirt and tie. His shoes smelled of Kiwi shoe paste and his fedora hat framed his ruddy face.

This doctor of podiatric medicine trimmed toe nails, made arch supports, tended to corns, calluses and bunions, and helped keep hundreds of store clerks, mailmen, teachers and working folks on their feet. My job was a little less grand. I answered Dad's phone, made patient appointments and swept up shaved calluses and toenail clippings from the floor after every patient.

That summer, as I approached my eighteenth birthday, my self-proclaimed job was to observe this man—so different from the uptight, beds-must-be-made, dishes-must-be-washed, chore-driven, no-nonsense, undemonstrative, time-obsessed guy who lived in our family home.

Once in the small office, he traded his coat, shirt and tie for his doctor's jacket. I took the instruments from their sterilizing bath and laid them in a straight row on his table. *Limp in. Leap out.* While my friends spent their high school summers waiting tables, selling magazines or lifeguarding, I spent my daytime hours assisting my dad, as he lived up to that motto hanging on the wall.

Sitting there eavesdropping on his conversations with patients, I realized he really did listen to us at the dinner table and knew of our recent escapades and successes. That summer, how proud he sounded as he told them of Pete's survival of basic training at Fort Knox, Ann's summer plans volunteering in Appalachia, my upcoming first year at the university, and the fact that Joe's height exceeded his skill at, but not his enthusiasm for, basketball.

That summer I also found out about Dad's other woman.

You could hear her coming long before you saw her. She would get off the elevator and start calling as she walked down the hall, "Doctor Glauber, Doctor Glauber, Doctor Glauber"—sounding like a priestess chanting a mantra. The first time it happened, Dad called to me from the examination room and asked me to go help Miss Sylvia.

The odor of kerosene and rotting onions preceded Miss Sylvia into the room filled with waiting patients. Some hid behind their *Life* magazines. I could feel the wide eyes of others on us, sheltered behind their *Ladies Home Journals*, as I moved forward to bring her in. I led her to one of the Danish modern chairs that lined the room and she visibly shrank as she lowered herself into it—now eye and elbow level with all the others in the room.

Dad walked out of the examination room with the patient he had finished treating. He stood there smiling and said, "Good morning, Miss Sylvia." He turned to the patient who was next in line and said, "Mrs. Metz, you wouldn't mind a small wait while I attend to Miss Sylvia, would you? Now, come right in here, Sylvia, and let's see what's bothering you today."

He led her into the exam room and pointed to the patient's chair. "Just be seated and my daughter will help you with your hosiery." I looked at Dad and his eyes told me this was important and I wasn't to argue. I held my breath to block her smell and got to work. Once my part was done, Dad washed her feet, massaged them with lotion, and then powdered them with wonderful smelling Amman's Powder. As he ministered to her, you could see the tension leave her frail body. Finally, he sent her on her way. No charge.

At the end of the workday, Dad explained that Sylvia's troubled, schizophrenic mind kept her anxious and roaming downtown for hours. He welcomed this street person each time she showed up that summer. She came to visit at least three times each week, and no matter how full his waiting room; he never denied her this kindness.

I spent my childhood clad in sensible Stride Rite oxfords and saddle shoes. With his choice of shoe, my father shaped my feet. It was his decision to be a foot washer that shaped my life.

SUSAN AUSTIN

THE SWEET AND DARK

These hot June mornings I walk in the shade of aspen, through
the willing grass.

I wonder if I might meet the grizzly sow talked about in town,
her three bright cubs sniffing the air like their mother.

It wouldn't be a pleasant end. Messy,

buried in a scratch of earth to ripen, the dead
and living forest for a blanket.

You have to know loneliness deep within your bones,
the willing marrow.

Once I saw a string of mucous stretch nose to foot
on a drunk man mumbling in the gutter. I did not want
            to dirty my new green dress.
He smelled like soured milk until he turned

to say, *I miss you.*

I helped two bikers haul him up a flight of narrow stairs
to the place he lived two blocks from the bar—

a stained mattress on bare coiled springs, a sink ringed with rust, a yellowed
toilet bowl, so everything he knew for certain about himself
          was right out in the open.

Tonight Venus, Jupiter and Regulus will line up straight as the crow flies
          in the western sky.

The sweet and dark.

One of the bikers, a woman dressed head to toe in silver studded leather,
she helped rinse the skirt of my dress in the sink.

SUSAN CLAYTON-GOLDNER

THIS WEIGHT I CARRY

On the March day my brother's big heart
stops beating, paramedics stand
at the foot of his bed and stare
at the huge mound hidden beneath cotton sheets
the color of a robin's egg.
Outside the room's only window, once again,
Forsythia burst into yellow blossoms.

While they struggle to hoist his swollen body,
sirens announce help is near. Even the firemen
can't maneuver him through the narrow, bedroom doorway.
Finally, a cousin saws a six-foot square
from the living room wall.
When they strap my brother to an oversized gurney,
his right hand, fingers thick as bratwursts,
dangles beneath the sheet's edge.
I look into the weedy garden
where one purple crocus opens.

Firemen erect scaffolding, drape tarps over pipes
to protect him from gawkers who gather,
like ravens, on the sidewalk.
Some clutch Bibles fat with God's mercy
for this housebound, church brother.
Each blade of grass seems numbered as it bends
beneath black boots that march him across his yard.
At street-side, a forklift loads him onto a flat-bed truck—
his transport to the morgue. When the show is over,
neighbors hang their heads and hurry home to bake
him casseroles. How easy it is to love what is gone.

As minutes tick back into memory, I disassemble
my big brother and me. Break us apart like
pieces of a gigantic puzzle, fragments of love
stronger than religion or his obsession with food.
When I connect them to the place fantasy and longing merge,
we stretch our arms, weightless as wings, and fly.
Together we'll wade barefoot in the shallow creek
behind our house in Collins Park, listen to our mother
sing hymns in the garden while our mud pies dry
on the flat rocks. We'll hold our funeral processions
for dead birds, oatmeal-box coffins lined with
fragrant orange peels that linger on our fingertips.
The ebony trill of my clarinet in the summer air.

GINA VALDÉS

BORDER DUENDE

This is a mystery I may never solve,
unless a border duende whispers the truth
and I wake to hear it.

Mamá (who worships the god of secrets)
will never tell what truly happened that night.

The air crackled with positive ions
that day in Ensenada: birds hopped
on electrical currents crisscrossing the sky,
uncombed cats slinked through streets,
curtains parted and closed.

Papá cornered me, the youngest, alone
in our yard. Was I staying or leaving?
Where was I going? When?

Papá was building a house of cedar
and sons, uninterested in daughters.
His moneyed sister fancied a family
with his three girls.

The evening sun sparked the sky red
and four plastic bags leaned near our door.
A woman in an old car cruised our unpaved street
scouting for our nonexistent house number.

All Mamá will tell: We fled at midnight
in a Ford steered by the aging American lover
of her young brother.

What a border duende reveals:
a hushed summer night
scented by sea breeze and laurel,
a lime slice of moon, a border guard falling
under the spell of Mamá's sad beauty;
on the eyelids of slumbering daughters,
the flutter and glimmer of dreams.
All three, nine, twelve, and fifteen,
asleep in the back seat of a beat-up Ford
in the defining event of our lives.

What potent powder did Mamá stir
into our evening's café con leche,
fearful that one or all
might choose Papá or wealth?

She will remain eerily silent, like the night
of our momentous crossing.

And we crossed with wings;
our U.S. birth certificates hiding
in the darkness of Mamá's purse.

Who needs papers in a charmed world?

When earth, moon, stars, wind, ocean, hills,
a one-eyed jalopy, a lovesick Americana,
and a moonstruck guard all conspire
to help: to answer a woman's silent cry.

REBECCA TAKSEL

OMEGA

California sits at the edge of an immense continent. It is the end, **omega**, Ω, the place where each evening the sun enacts the ritual of falling into the infinity of the sea. Many people, once they arrive overland in California, cannot think of making the return trip across the continent. Others do, but I believe they bring back something important with them. I was one of that second group of travelers.

I came to Los Angeles in 1965 to visit a musician I knew from my hometown. I had just graduated from college, and I had been writing to him. I thought I was in love. I wasn't sure what to expect when I got to Los Angeles. We'd made no plans and he'd made no promises, but I flung myself headlong into this adventure.

I crossed the country from Pennsylvania by train. It was a long, long ride, and I traveled coach class. I went to Chicago on the Capitol Limited and from Chicago to Los Angeles on the Super Chief, the express train of the Santa Fe line through the southern deserts.

I met Bill Halstead in the club car out of Chicago. He was a pleasant man with olive skin, very black hair, and a crisp moustache. He was probably under thirty, but to me he was an adult and I was not. I was on the cusp of the generation that would become the youth culture, and we would never feel grown up in the way we'd expected to. In a couple of years I'd call myself a revolutionary and get into blue jeans. Now I still wore babyish mod dresses, the ones you see in the black-and-white footage of early Beatles concerts.

Bill was quiet, easygoing and very polite. He befriended me, which was something more than being friendly. I wasn't aware that he wanted to protect me, but later I realized that this was his interest in me. Of sex there was none, not in his speech or manner towards me, and not in my thoughts towards him. (He was a grownup, a nice man, not dangerous, therefore not sexy. That was how my subconscious worked in those days.)

Bill taught me cribbage, and we played and played, all through the Southwest. We endured the long hours of no drinks through strictly dry Oklahoma, and we drank beer the rest of the time. I'm sure I talked a lot and drank and smoked too much. I'm sure I thought I was smart and sophisticated. Still, Bill seemed to be comfortable with me. He created an atmosphere of simple warmth around himself. Others joined us for cards and drinks, and for the space of a couple of days we lived happily in our glass-domed moving world with its great desert and mountain backdrop.

When we were pulling into Los Angeles, Bill gave me his phone number. I had told him where I was going, and he was quietly insistent that I keep his number and not hesitate to call him if I needed to. It was an offer of help, not an invitation.

The next few days were a nightmare, beginning with the musician's failure to meet me at the station. I went to the Hollywood address I'd been writing to, on a seedy-looking street. He was in his apartment, asleep in the middle of the day. A welcome note of sorts was taped to the door. It was actually a do-not-disturb sign. Had I had any sense or pride I'd have left right then, but my head was full of the fantasy of our romance, one I'd almost wholly invented, writing ten pages to his one.

Once he woke up and I'd spent a few hours with him, I realized I didn't like him or even know him; and he certainly didn't care about me. He was living in a world that was far too exotic for me, the new California folk-rock scene that was exploding into untold wealth for its stars and providing a collective identity for millions of white kids. This world, as everyone in the country would know in a few years, ran on seriously mind-bending and body-destroying drugs. My erstwhile boyfriend and everyone around him were living on eerie schedules dictated by the metabolizing of hallucinogens. I didn't belong. I liked beer and scotch, and I listened to hard-edged modern jazz and lyrical bossa nova. Still, I hung around for three days, an invisible chick, ignored and wounded and scared. Then I called Bill Halstead.

I didn't want to leave California. I was already in love with it. That had happened when the train came down through the Sierras into the soft summer-brown hills. I was in love with Baskin-Robbins ice cream, which was new then and reflected all the colors of the semi-tropical flowers that grew in Los Angeles gardens. I was in love with the suave, dry air that brushed over my skin as I walked along the bright streets, legs bare in my short dresses. I was in love with the vast, surreally clean and new Safeway store I'd visited with some friends of the man I'd come to see.

Bill came to Hollywood for me and drove me out to West Covina in an unbelievably beat-up, very old green car. I didn't know then that West Covina was an ordinary working-class suburb and that Bill and his family were probably struggling on the edge of poverty. To me the houses were pastel dream cottages, set on magical palm-lined streets in the cradle of the hushed brown hills.

Bill asked no questions about my brief stay in Hollywood. Nor did his mother, when he brought me into the house he shared with her. Mrs. Halstead (I never learned her given name) was a large, handsome, soft-spoken woman with brown skin and thick graying hair cut short and remarkably bright, almost-black eyes. She had taken Bill in after his disastrous marriage to a woman named Martha. Martha sounded like something out of Raymond Chandler, a movie woman, beautiful, darkly sexy, and entirely heartless. She had gone off with someone and left Bill with their three children. I had never heard of a woman doing this, and it added to her awful mystery. The little boys were good-looking, with those same dark, shining eyes. Two of the three were mentally disabled and moved slowly and tentatively. I could not help associating their fragility with the blow their mother had dealt them by deserting them.

Now Mrs. Halstead took me in, as she had taken in the unfortunate boys. She did not comment when her son talked about his wife, just looked at him and shook her head. Her voice was soft and low, the vowels round, the final consonants a little indistinct, in the Spanish manner. For his part, Bill spoke about Martha without bitterness, as if Martha were a cruel goddess who had simply fulfilled her nature and against whom there was no recourse. Like his mother, Bill spoke quietly, and the boys played around the house quietly, too. There was no anger in that house.

How many hours did I sit at the round white dinette table in Mrs. Halstead's bright, sunny tract house? How many days? I don't even remember. In my memory it is all one long afternoon, during which this woman with the beautiful, softly accented voice gave me California. Bill was there some of the time, and he took me on wonderful excursions to Santa Catalina, to Laguna and San Diego, even to a jai alai game in Mexico. But it was Mrs. Halstead who told me stories. She was what I only later learned later was chicana, a Spanish-speaking person of Indian and European ancestry born in California. Her family had been in California for a very long time, and the California she lived in was not the jumped-up mass-culture factory Los Angeles had by then become. Her California was old and deep, of no interest to the incomers like the ones I'd just left—young prospectors avid for gold in the form of million-selling records.

Mrs. Halstead's California was a country of vast farms and ranches owned by a vanishing aristocracy of families with lovely Spanish names like Verdugo. It was a country of expansive, arid beauty and hard work, yet open and entirely free of stuffiness. Sitting there listening to her, I grasped something of what I still think of as the essence of the West, a sort of ironic tolerance. California, I realized, allowed people to recreate themselves, to escape uncomfortable family ties, to leave behind the secrets and burning shames of unhappy childhoods. Listening to Mrs. Halstead's stories day after day, I felt something in me loosen and become as warm as the dry subtropical air. I saw my skin turning browner and warmer, too, more like the Halsteads' skin, as I spent more time under the sun, bare-armed and bare-legged.

Mrs. Halstead had worked as a nurse in one of the places we still called homes for unwed mothers. She was used to waifs. She and Bill seemed simply to assume my presence. Bill insisted that I learn to drive his pickup truck, which was even older and more dilapidated than the car that took him to his job—I don't remember what it was he did, something physical and routine. The truck, from the early 1950s, had gears so stiff I could hardly manage them, and under my direction the old thing bucked up and down the grid of quiet streets to the nearby market. I felt proud of myself for driving, proud that Bill trusted me to drive his mother. The truck was a farm truck, an appurtenance of the vanished landscape of Mrs. Halstead's memory.

I sensed something of the possibility of a different life there in West Covina, one in which I would live enfolded by the hills and by history and by the kind of love that makes no demands. But I didn't stay. I got on the train after a couple of weeks and went home to begin a restless life in the East. I hope I remembered to send a thank-you note to Mrs. Halstead.

I saw Bill once more when he came to Washington, D.C., where I was living in the late 1960s. By then my revolutionary persona was firmly in place, and Bill seemed conventional and uninteresting to me. I didn't bother to hide my impatience with him.

But in those years I would sometimes find myself picturing beautiful scenes of Southern California again. Through the prism of my memories I would see, reflected against the landscape of hills and palms and cactus and cascades of pink and white flowers on pastel houses, the faces of Bill and Mrs. Halstead. When the television showed images of Cesar Chavez and the striking farm workers, I saw the face of Mrs. Halstead over and over again in the crowd, strong, dark-eyed, gentle. At that time there were almost no faces like hers in the Eastern cities and suburbs where I lived and visited. But now my map of the United States changed, expanded to take in all of California and the rest of the Southwest. I could suddenly hear the Spanish language as part of my own inheritance as an American, learn the meanings of the names of cities and states and mountain ranges and rivers of the West. I could begin to put pieces of the puzzle of our country together, to acknowledge what I'd never been taught in school: that Santa Fe was the oldest city in the United States to become a state capital and that the Western settlement had followed an earlier and quite different path from that of the English colonies.

More years had to pass until I acknowledge properly the more personal gift I had been given by the Halsteads. I had been too wrapped up in youthful dreams and youthful egotism to do that when I met them. I never got in touch with them again, though I went back to California several times and fell in love with it all over again each time. But I began to tell the story of their kindness.

When I told my story of California, I spoke as if the place, and my experience there, had existed on some other plane, in some other dimension. That was how I felt, and how I have continued to feel for all of my life. Through a chance meeting on a train, I had been admitted into a sanctified place. One of the quietly kind, good people had found me and saw that I was wounded; he invited me into the care of a healer. When I remember Mrs. Halstead's little round white table, I see it as a circle of pure compassion. The Halsteads showed me, in their quiet, modest way, that there is a kindness that forgives everything and accepts anyone who is in need of that kindness and compassion. When I finally grew up, too many years after that first trip to California, I was able to reach back into my memory and let their lesson inform my life.

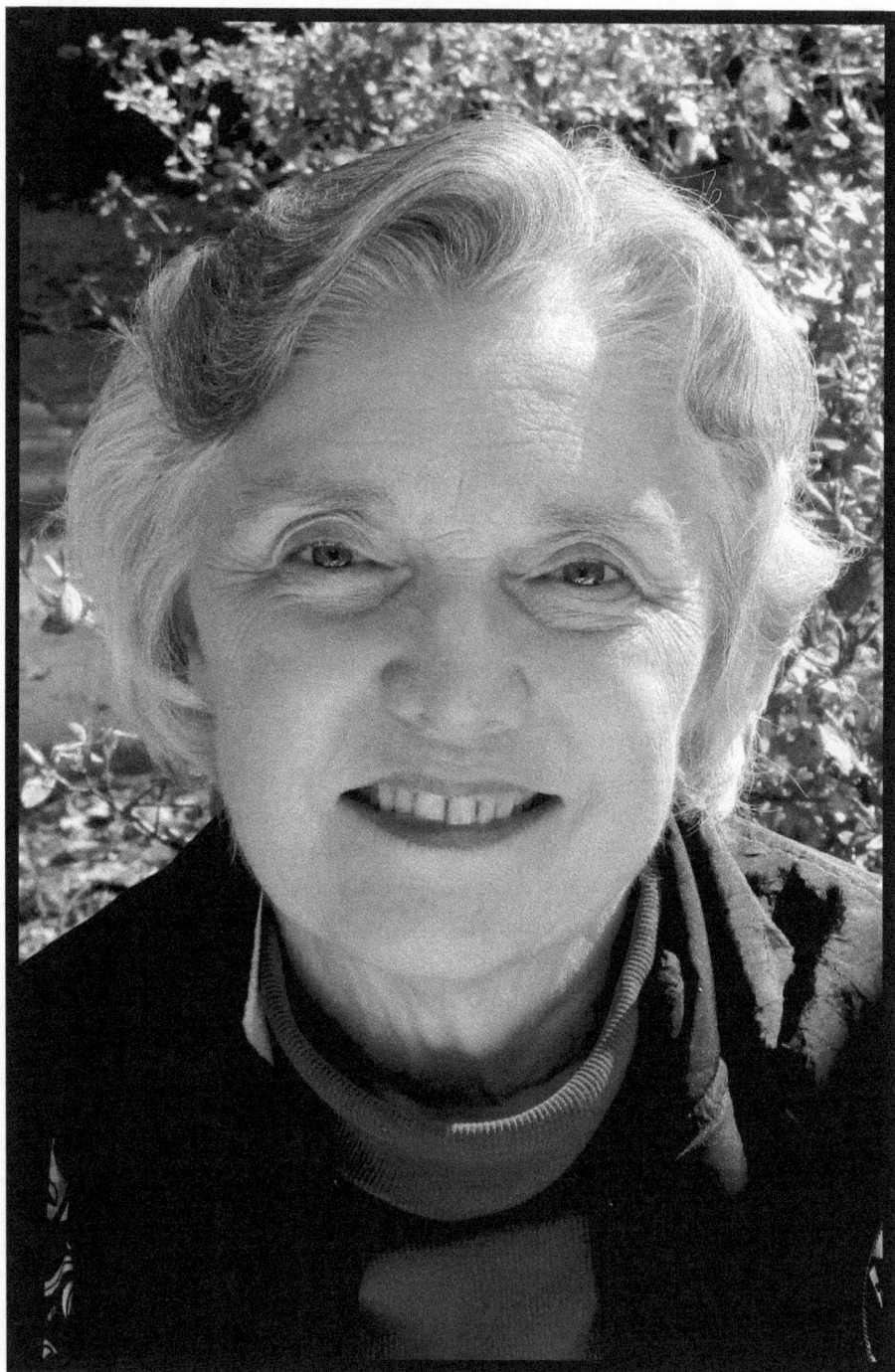

KAREN SKOLFIELD

WAIT FIVE MINUTES

I duck into the Visitor's Center and shake the water off my jacket. The woman behind the desk asks if the rain's stopped. When I say not yet, she says if you don't like the weather here, just wait five minutes. Well isn't that true, I reply. What I like about the five-minute statement is that it's always said with the air of a grand but knowable secret being given away. It takes both people speaking their lines, nodding and smiling at just the right times. I like the predictability of it, and when someone says it to me, which is often, I play right along as if it were new and wondrous, a thing to be turned over and over. Sometimes I'm even the one to start it, and the other person will look at me with an air of gratitude and say Well isn't that true. How much fonder could I get of humanity? In New England, it's as close as we get to hugging. Another batch of visitors comes in and I can feel my heart swell. Soon enough we'll greet each other. Outside the rain goes on and on.

MEIA GEDDES

GIFTS FOR THE CRANE LADY

Sitting at a booth and standing on the street,
Handing out little paper cranes to passersby,
Feeling like I was handing out little bits of myself,
I did not know I would receive so much in return.

I have been the lucky recipient of
A mooncake, banana, flower, coffee, and tea.
I have been gifted a selfish wish, a guidebook, newspapers, magazines.
I've met Doctor Tea and sung "Stand By Me" for the first time busking.

I don't know what I'll do with some of my gifts,
Like the yellow sunglasses (hashtag #WeWillWin on the side),
But I tucked away the custom superhero sketch, charcoal portrait,
Wikipedia articles, business cards, and advice.

I even memorized that belly stab wound,
And still recall the Harvard Kennedy professor
Who donated $20 with the request
That I give a string of cranes away to a deserving little girl.

I don't recall how to make clothing waterproof,
And those Fado renditions of "Matchmaker, Matchmaker"
Are fading in and out like the chess games we played,
But I will try to remember what I learned,
That a stranger friend will always come along.

MK PUNKY

TAKE CARE OF EACH OTHER

The sign I carry says "Take Care of Each Other"
because that seemed to be the distilled essence of my essential
message, the guiding mantra
        the reason why I was put here
so far as I can figure.
People find it funny in a darkly satirical ironic melancholy way
        that someone who looks like she can't take care of herself
        walks around downtown all day
or sits in silent meditation with her sign turned outward leaning
against a wall
        urging the world to accomplish the impossible
while her mission quest crusade is for vacant toilets and showers,
            impolite fluid receptacles
reminding us we're all human,
even the losers without a place to wipe away
        the stench of living.
I'm used to it by now, the invisibility.
They turn away.
But I watch their eyes, the corners, and sometimes I see them
        reading my sign.
Often they chuckle or snigger or swallow down a true and powerful
feeling
        suppressing
        a sense of connectedness
        when confronted with the end

of the line, where all your capitalist dreams go to die.

Those are the moments

I know I'm doing something good with my life.

I'm getting through and I'm getting by.

> That's marvelous. And I am dumbstruck with gratitude.

There are days, I confess, that the only thing I seem any good at is
being ignored.

Being disconnected from the grid and from someone to care for.

> I'm an expert at that. Have been for some time.

> I grew accustomed to irrelevance long before the street.

> Nobody listened then so you can understand why I don't
really expect anyone to listen now.

My story is just as boring and horrifying as everyone else's:

bad choices, etcetera you don't want to hear it believe me because it
will heartbreak you and then it will send you off on a there-but-for-
the-grace jag that will make you feel better about your life of Netflix
and artisanal cupcakes and treadmills but somehow it won't make
you feel deeply enough to consider why you take better care of your
dog

or your gerbil

than you do the woman sleeping in a tent beside the freeway.

Maybe I could walk your dog. Maybe that could be my career

> my Lifepath

my way of earning a rightful place in your highly celebrated society,
somewhere near the bottom, of course, yet

> officially part of the game,

> still an eligible receiver of illegible messages transcribed for future

broadcast.

I would be helpful, not an unpleasant manifestation of the system's
waste products.

May I walk your dog? I no longer have useful references and for that
I apologize but I believe you'll nonetheless find me eminently
qualified to walk your dog to the organic pet food store so that we
can both try sample biscuits

and she can move her joints and then her bowels while you're away doing more important things than spending time with your best friend.

She deserves it. You deserve it.

Someone to simply *be there*. Like a security guard.

Someone to look after your prizes, the stuffed animals you won at the carnival thanks to hard work and perhaps a little luck and more hard work.

You are a winner. You earned what you've got. And now you've earned my service.

May I, Madame?

May I, sir?

Or do you think, would it be better

to grind me up,

to reform me as appetizingly crunchy pellets and

feed me lovingly

by the handful

to the fluffy just-shampooed creature you care for most?

Although I smell unpalatable to you, I am high in protein and loaded with nutritious disappointments

that dogs and cats and some confined birds find delicious.

Please consume what is left of me. The body and the blood.

Let me be your Jesus. Let me walk your dog.

If I can take care of you in this way, like the sign says,

maybe you could take care of me?

Or someone else you don't know.

Or someone you do.

Let's call it even and everyone is happy.

That's all I've ever asked for.

Take care of each other and everyone is happy.

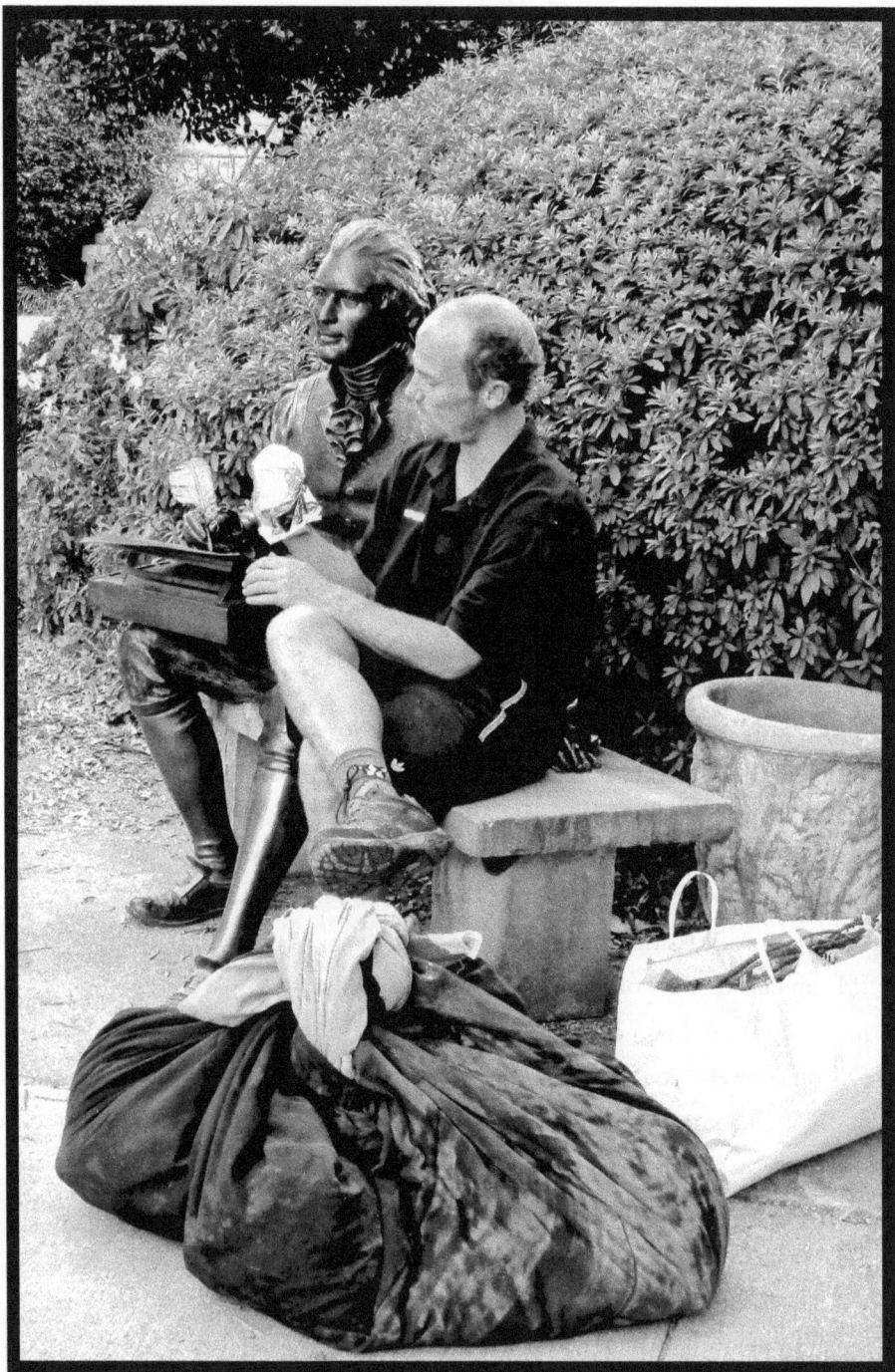

II. CROSS-IDENTIFICATION

PAUL HOSTOVSKY

STARING AT THE BLIND

I first noticed Delbert on the subway, sitting directly across from me, a Braille book closed in his lap, his hand inside it, gliding back and forth, reading. He was in the seat nearest the door. It had one of those signs above it, in print and in Braille, that said *Please offer this seat to an elderly or disabled person in need of it.* I had often noticed those signs, especially when the subway was crowded and I was forced to stand by the door and hang onto a handrail or a pole, with nothing to read but the advertisements and the collective glum face of the ridership. Then my eyes would sometimes light on one of those signs with its official-looking plea for kindness, and I'd try to figure out how the Braille dots lined up with the print letters, how those pithy round bumps, which didn't resemble letters in the least, added up to the words in that sentence. And I'd wonder whether any blind people ever read that sign, if their fingers ever found those Braille dots or even knew they were there. And now, here was this blind guy, sitting in the seat opposite me, Braille above his head, Braille in his lap, the spilled white milk of his eyes staring upward and slightly to the left as his hand moved furtively back and forth inside the closed Braille book.

I wanted to ask him something. Something about Braille maybe, or the signage, or the public transit system, or the kindness of strangers. But before I had the chance, a rangy young man with a Van Dyke and a Bible plopped himself down in the seat beside Delbert and said in a loud, conspicuous voice to no one in particular: "Let us pray." Then he yanked Delbert's hand out of the Braille book, and held it in his own hand, and raised it above Delbert's head in the manner of prizefighters and referees, and asked Delbert his name. When Delbert, visibly shaken, said "Delbert," the man continued in an incantatory voice: "Dear Jesus, we pray, together, that you please heal our brother Delbert of his blindness right NOW." Then he closed his eyes tightly, presumably the harder to pray, while Delbert opened his eyes wide, presumably to say he saw nothing remotely amusing or efficacious in what this man was doing. It did, in fact, look more like an assault than a prayer, and before I knew what I was doing I was up on my feet defending Delbert, whom I hadn't even met yet, but who impressed me as being someone worth defending, someone who didn't seem to need our prayers or Jesus's healing foisted upon him right at that particular moment by this fellow with his Bible and goatee and chutzpah. I stood above them, hanging on to the handrail, and I grabbed the man's Bible right out of his hand, held it menacingly over his head and yelled at him to give Delbert back his hand. The praying man blinked up at me, cowered a little, then let go of Delbert's hand, which immediately burrowed back inside the closed Braille book. I didn't say another word, but gestured with my thumb for the man to vacate his seat tout de suite. Then I gave him back his Bible and shooed him away. And I sat down next to Delbert.

"Are you alright?" I asked him, feeling a faint urge to slip my hand inside his Braille book and feel the dots for myself.

"I think so, yes," he said. "Thank you. But this is my stop." And standing up, he produced a folded white cane that suddenly rattled and clicked open with a sound vaguely like switchblades. It startled me a little.

"Mine, too," I said, wanting to offer him a hand, or an elbow, but not wanting to insinuate myself, especially after having liberated him from that pious insinuator who was staring at both of us now a little sheepishly from a safe distance at the other end of the subway car. So when the train stopped, I followed Delbert, walking behind him as he skillfully found the door with his cane, then, switching hands, followed the railing with his right hand down the three steps, holding the cane in his left hand and tapping the riser beneath each tread as he descended.

Once outside, he turned confidently to the left and started walking toward the intersection, his cane sweeping back and forth in front of him, alternating with whichever foot he put forward. Click, sweep, click, sweep, was the sound of his going as he made a beeline toward the crosswalk with me following a few paces behind him. I felt self-conscious, following him like that, like some guy stalking a blind guy, so when he reached the curb, I pulled up beside him to ask if he wanted assistance crossing the street. But before I asked, I couldn't help staring at him silently for a few moments as he stood there listening to the traffic. He held himself very erect and rigid, almost as rigid as the cane he was holding in his hands, completely vertical

now, the handle against his chest, his head swaying to the left and right as
the other pedestrians crossed without stopping to offer assistance. He looked
exposed, yet determined; vulnerable yet independent, fragile and at the same
time, I don't know, girded.

I stared at him like that for a long time. I stared at him for years. Literally.
I helped him cross that street that day, and the next day and the next. And
soon we became friends. And later, roommates. He worked at the National
Braille Press as a proofreader, and he taught me a thing or two about Braille.
Like how many dots it takes to say anything in the whole alphabet: six. And
he taught me a thing or two about sighted guide technique. Like how to walk
with a blind person through doors, or through a turnstile, or up and down
stairs, or with more than one blind person in tow. And he taught me a thing
or two about miracles, and Christianity, and the treatment of blind people in
literature, and in history, and on the subway.

And before long, I decided to learn Braille myself. And Delbert was
able to get me a job at the National Braille Press as a transcriber. And now
we take the train to work together. We sit next to each other on our morning
commute, reading, his hands on his Braille, my eyes on my book. But more
often than not, my eyes wander from my book over to his Braille, and then I
watch his hands reading, which is a beautiful sight to behold. I love to watch
his fingers flying over the dots, breezing over them with such a light touch,
a touch like the pursed lips of the wind, like a breeze kissing all the leaves
on the trees, lingering over them ever so lightly, almost imperceptibly, then
moving on.

FR. ROBERT J. KUS

MARCELINO

It was two days after Christmas 2006, and I was looking at the brick wall that two Hispanic men had just finished repairing on the St. Mary campus in Wilmington, North Carolina where I am the pastor. As they were finishing their work, I saw a young man walking down Ann Street and greeted him. His name was Marcelino, and he told me that he was from Honduras and was living at Mercy House, a local mission for men on Red Cross Street.

Marcelino did not speak any English, and I was very glad that all Catholic priests of the Diocese of Raleigh must speak both Spanish and English. Marcelino told me he had come to St. Mary Church—later to be named the Basilica Shrine of St. Mary—a couple of times. With that short interaction, he continued his walk.

For the next month, I saw Marcelino on and off at our Sunday Mass in Spanish, and he always stopped to say hello.

The relatively warm winter weather that we were enjoying began turning markedly colder. And as the nights became frigid, I began having nightmares. I began feeling incredible guilt at having a large, warm rectory to myself, when one of my parishioners was living in a mission.

When I got to the point that I could no longer live with myself, I drove to Mercy House just as it was getting dark. Marcelino was standing by himself outside, the only Hispanic among the group of men milling around. The men always stood around at that hour because the mission did not let them in the house until 6 p.m. sharp.

He was very happy to see me, and he readily agreed to go out to dinner at the Golden Corral. As the dinner progressed, I told Marcelino that I had a huge rectory with four bedrooms, and I asked him if he would like to live there for a while. Not only would it be good for him to have a decent place to live, it would also benefit me immensely because I would have an opportunity to improve my conversational Spanish. Naturally, he was thrilled with the offer.

After dinner, we went to Mercy House so he could say "good-bye" and "thank you" to the mission staff and some of the men. The place was incredible—nothing but rows of bunk beds with one man sitting on each mattress. I was so glad to get Marcelino out of that place.

With only a little grocery bag containing a couple of pieces of clothing, he came to my house where we talked for an hour before going to bed. In the morning, when I asked him how he had slept, he said that he had been so excited and happy that he could not fall asleep until 1:00 a.m.

In the morning, I drove him to where he had a landscaping job. I was astonished at how far he had to walk and how dangerous the journey was. There were superhighways across which he had to walk, and there were virtually no sidewalks to protect him.

When I got home from taking him to work, I could not help but reflect on "The Starfish Story" by Loren Eisley. In this story, a young man is seen walking along the beach and throwing a starfish back into the ocean. He knows that if the starfish remained on the sand, it would die from the sun. An old man came up to the young man and pointed out that there were miles and miles of beach, and there were thousands of starfish. The old man said, "You can't possibly make a difference!" At this, the young man picked up a starfish and threw it into the sea. Just as the starfish hit the water, he said, "It made a difference for that one!" Though I can't help every person, I certainly can make a big difference in the life of Marcelino and his quest to help his family back in Honduras.

I absolutely could not refuse to help Marcelino, for my conscience would not permit that. I have so much, and he has so little. He has only a second-grade education and can barely read and write in Spanish, while I have a PhD and two post-doctoral master's degrees. He is poor and is trying to support his wife and five children in Honduras, while I only have to care for myself. He was a stranger in a strange land, while I was surrounded by every support a person could want.

For the next ten months, Marcelino lived at my house, and eventually he worked full-time at St. Mary parish. He began to have new hope and dreams, believing that perhaps his life could become much better for his family and himself.

Then, in December 2007, it was time for him to leave and return to his family once again. After all, he had been gone for three years, and the whole burden of raising five children had fallen on his wife. She was extremely eager to see him, and so was his three-year old daughter Arleni who had never seen him.

On the morning of December 17th, Marcelino and I said our good-byes by the Christmas tree in my living room. It was the first Christmas tree that Marcelino had ever enjoyed. He turned to me and gave me a blessing.

I told him that I would go with him on the planes, for he had never flown before, and he would certainly never be able to navigate changing planes in Charlotte and Phoenix. He was fascinated by flying and filled with bittersweet feelings. On the one hand, he was very sad to say good-bye to me, and on the other hand he was so excited to be united with his family once again.

When it was his turn to board the plane in Phoenix to take him to El Paso where a Maryknoll Missionary priest was waiting to take him to Mexico, he asked me for a blessing. I blessed him with tears in my eyes. Right before he entered the boarding plank, he turned and looked at me, wondering if he would ever see me again. Despite my assurances, he could not believe that I would be part of his life forever. Then, after the glance, he boarded the plane and off he went to a new life.

On Christmas, Marcelino called to let me now he had arrived back home in Reitoca to his family at 11 p.m. on Christmas Eve.

Eight Christmases have come and gone, and Marcelino is still very much part of my life. I have adopted his parish—San Francisco de Asís, in Reitoca, F.M., Honduras—as St. Mary's sister parish. I visit it at least twice a year, and I'm even planning on retiring in Honduras someday and spending the rest of my life as a missionary.

Because of Marcelino, my parish helped build a clinic in Reitoca for the people, bought pickup trucks for the priests to make their rounds in this far-flung rugged mountain parish, gave scholarships to needy young people, helped them repair chapels that had washed away in floods, and a host of other things. We have even established two foundations to be sure help for the poor of this area are continued long into the future.

I am giving Marcelino and his family financial support every month and help pay for his children to have a good education. As for Marcelino, he has gained new confidence and hope, and he has been able to put many of his dreams into action.

As for me, I have learned so much from Marcelino. He showed me a simple but deep faith, a faith free from highfalutin' theological arguments and conflicts. Because Marcelino only has a second-grade education, he can read only very slowly. Because of this, he always listened intently to the Scriptures as proclaimed each Sunday in church, and he was familiar with all the Bible stories of the New Testament.

Each week, when I had written my homily for the coming Sunday and had it translated into Spanish, he would be enchanted while I read him the homily. He loved the stories I told, and he loved to reflect on them and show how the principles applied in daily life.

Marcelino also taught me how to see the world through the eyes of someone who has never had access to the wonders that I and other Americans take for granted every day. For example, he thought a string of multi-colored Christmas lights must cost a fortune because they had so many colors. He was shocked to learn that one could by them for less than $3.

Helping a person break the chains of poverty for himself and his family has been one of the most fulfilling experiences I have ever had. I just wish I had billions of dollars to help more. And when I think that all of this stems from God planting a spark in my heart, and me responding to this spark, I am amazed and grateful!

DARCY SMITH

TATTERS

A cloudless morning rounds my shoulders
light slips pearls from the sky. All I want
is to curl under her faded granny squares

gray blue pink, thread my fingers
through the holes left knowing that today
or tomorrow or next week or in an hour

while I'm at work, Nana will leave us.
My shared office in the psych center, a cramped
shoe box. The heat rattles, bakes my insides out.

I'm certain that my colleagues can see the holes
in my work. All the little bits that don't fit quite
right without Nana to coax me back to confidence.

I'm lost in her afghan, her lavender lotion.
Don't even notice the new guy pacing
too close, staring at my shoes.

He circles me, worries a scrap of paper
to tatters. Muttering secrets, he drops bits of
disjointed stories all around me. Stops and asks,

"Excuse me Miss, would you do a me a favor?
It'll only take a minute.
Could you please just step on my feet?"

RACHEL SQUIRES BLOOM

WHO'S THIS GIRL IN THE PICTURE?

Held inside the photo's rectangle
she's beside me, our arms around one another.
We must've been close.
The photo is a quarter century old—
can't be, I feel nineteen. I can
locate the Dardanelles on a map, quote old
baseball statistics—why won't her name pop
up among these useless facts?
She's a blonde, like I never was
and wears pastel, which I never did.
I'm not sentimental, don't
see photos as time frozen.
Her hair has most likely darkened;
maybe she dyes it,
maybe she's dead.

Once we sat together in the cold tiled hall
outside Kindergarten. Big and pale,
she cried and cried. Our hips touched.
I didn't know why she cried
or what magic word I might know to make her stop.
I only knew that finally, at five,
I was in the presence of something Important.

I recall exactly how the dim
pre-winter sky tried to shine
into the hall, empty but for two girls:
one big and pale, one slim and dark,
one sobbing, one silent.
That lone beam of sun almost springs
the trap holding her name;
the hip-to-hip connection is borne across years.

KAREN SKOLFIELD

WELL-BEHAVED

The sunshine makes me wave at everyone.
Hi, stranger. Hi, stranger. The strangers
grin and wave. They walk their little dogs,
and their little dogs grin and wave.
Sometimes I'm walking, but mostly
I'm on the bus and always seem to ride
with a woman carrying six bags of groceries,
a baby in a sling, and a toddler who wants
to hurl himself out the bus window or crack
his head on the seat bars and she won't let him,
she has him by the wrist, and then it's her stop.
Someone always assists her. Sometimes it's me,
but usually it's a stranger grabbing up her bags
and helping her off, a college kid, a guy in his 50s,
and that makes us smile again for small kindnesses.
Let me tell you. I've been this woman.
My kids are two years apart. O'Hare airport,
me wrestling a carseat, a baby, a toddler.
A whole family of strangers swooped up,
lifted the carseat, offered to carry my screaming son
who, by then, I was holding football style.
We were in an airport, I figured,
how far could they run? and I handed them
the screamer. He was so startled he began
hiccupping, which the strangers thought charming,
and they laughed, and my son gave a damp smile,
and I burst into tears. I tried to cry into my arm
but I couldn't stop and we were in an elevator
and I turned my face from them.

It was the slowest elevator in the world.
I'd stopped crying by the time the doors opened.
I felt angry that my own children
and a few people I would never see again
could do this, and I was supposed to feel grateful.
And I was grateful, or I would be,
after I'd washed my face and made the connection
and a flight attendant rocked the baby
even though she was supposed to get
the first-class drinks and warm towels
and yet another stranger remarked
"your kids are so well-behaved"
which means they're not crying or yelling
or other things that bother his world.
I said "we've got a little reprieve"
and I said "I probably cry more than they do"
which I'd meant to say lightheartedly but choked
at the end and I turned away and he turned away
and we were glad not to know each other again.

JESSICA NAAB

SINNERS ON SIXTY-SIX

The wind whistled through the shoddy window insulation, waking me. *Another crap-tastic day.* But in the thick of an el Niño winter in Denver, Colorado, the weather was always bad.

I rolled out of bed, and my lower back creaked. At twenty-four, I wasn't old enough for those kinds of problems. But my body, it seemed, hadn't gotten the memo.

I heard my roommate and best friend, Alanna, tooling around in the kitchen. She wasn't normally a morning person, but she always seemed more awake than me, more alive.

I stayed in the shower longer than necessary and then picked whatever outfit wasn't dirty. When I pulled a long-sleeved shirt over my head, my back cracked again. Mondays were bad enough, but having my car repossessed on Friday made everything worse. Now I was already looking forward to this weekend. A weekend where I would do absolutely nothing, because that's all I ever did.

Here I was, a young woman who should be taking on the world. Instead, I was weary from everything I hadn't done. But, the thing about the rat race of life is that it is, indeed, a rat race. One that, even if you managed to win, you're still a rat in a cage.

I headed to the fridge and pulled out the sack lunch I'd made last night. Alanna sent me a chipper greeting, for which I internally begrudged her. How dare she be in such a good mood so early?

What was there to be in a good mood about? I had a snowy trek ahead of me now going to work. Life just kept getting better and better.

I began my trek to the nearest bus stop. Driving, it normally took ten minutes to get to the insurance company I worked for. By bus, it'd take over an hour. I'd spent the weekend testing my new route, and the subsequent hours crying about it.

I stepped onto the dirt trail that ran behind my apartment complex. Unease chilled me worse than the wind. The trail was a lot darker and quieter than it had been this weekend. It would be so easy for someone to sneak up and attack me. Too easy.

It wasn't like I lived in a particularly bad neighborhood. But I'd seen plenty of stories on the news. Violent offenses could happen anywhere, without rhyme or reason.

A harsh burst of wind urged my feet forward. My gaze darted around, ready for anything to leap from the shadows. Maybe all the offenders were still asleep? It *was* pretty early.

My boots crunched on the snow blanketing the dirt trail until they hit cement. A small congregation stood across the street. The bus stop wasn't one of those fancy ones that shielded you from the elements. It didn't even have a bench with a real estate agent's ad. It was simply a pole stuck into the ground beside the road.

I crept closer, my anxiety ratcheting up another notch. There were more people out at five in the morning than I'd anticipated. Or maybe more people took the bus than I'd thought.

When I crossed the street, a few watched me, but I avoided eye contact. It was a method I'd picked up at work. If you didn't look at people, they were less likely to engage you in conversation.

I stood off to the side, and was suddenly reminded of grade school. I'd always been the quiet type. The only friend I'd had was Alanna. We'd bonded over the polar bear Beanie Baby I'd brought to school one day, and the rest was history. Over the years, Alanna had attempted to exorcise my introverted behavior, to no avail. I was socially awkward as hell. Always would be.

So instead, I chose to watch them all from the corner of my eye. Some wore fluorescent-orange vests a construction worker might. They also all seemed to know each other.

I kept my distance the entire time, but bus number sixty-six arrived without incident. With a sigh of relief, I shuffled aboard.

One of the men sat next to me, so I popped in my earbuds. The thing about public transportation was that pesky obligation to make small talk, like in the elevator at work. So I stared out the window, as if snowy streets and traffic were the most interesting things I'd ever seen.

The train ran south and, even though a small shuttle would take me directly to my office from there, I chose instead to walk. The first bus had already been stressful enough and left me frazzled.

It went like that for several days. And each day when I returned home safely, I felt like an idiot for having been so afraid.

X X X

By the time Thursday hit, so had a big snowstorm. The sky had graciously dumped five inches, and I grumbled all the way to the bus stop. On the plus side, no attacker would be on the prowl in this crap.

I crossed the street and saw the usual suspects, but hardly noticed. All I focused on was my normal spot. The storm made it a mess of water and mud. I cringed and looked to where one of the groups stood on the sidewalk, entrenched in a heavy cloud of cigarette smoke. I moseyed over, taking hesitant steps.

One of the men noticed and waved. "Mornin'."

I smiled and returned the greeting, fighting the rising tide of panic. *Oh, Jesus, he's talking to me.*

"Cold as hell out here," he said beneath a flimsy plaid jacket with the hood pulled up. He wore a construction vest and work boots, so I had a pretty good idea of his profession.

He was a big man. Not fat, but strong, and appeared to be fifteen or twenty years older than me. I could see Hispanic traits clearly, yet they were watered down with enough Caucasian features to where I'd suspect him to be second or third generation American.

Just below his left eye he had a tattoo of three teardrops. Wasn't that some sort of gang insignia meant to brag about how many people you'd killed?

That's ridiculous. If he'd killed someone he'd be in prison.

"Sure is," I replied, not knowing what else to say. Then it occurred to me I could find out more about these guys. "I see you here all the time. Do you live in the complex?" I pointed to the apartments, even though I knew he didn't. His group always seemed to be coming from the opposite direction.

"No, we're from the halfway house." He pointed at himself, "Recently released."

One of the things I'd always been a champ at is schooling my expression, and, boy, did I tamp that shit down right quick. It all made sense now. Their attire, the tattoo, the fact that they all seemed to know each other.

"Oh, really? I didn't know there was one around here," I kept my tone neutral, like I didn't care one way or the other.

Great, I've spent every morning here with a bunch of criminals. I peered up at the man. Given his size, he could easily take me down, but surely he would've tried by now.

Plus, there was something in his eyes that told me he wouldn't—a weariness that tugged at the corners, right above the teardrop tattoo.

Oh, God, he had *been in prison!*

"Yeah, it's just behind that building there." He half-turned and pointed over his shoulder.

"Huh. And how long have you been . . . living there?" I asked, unsure of the verbiage. I mean, did one really live in a halfway house? Wasn't it supposed to be prison's ugly cousin or something?

"I've been there for about four years."

God, I thought, *having to take the bus everywhere for four years?* Then I remembered his previous street address had "Correctional Facility" on the first line. He probably thought taking the bus was a luxury.

"I get out in July. There's a buddy of mine who's hooking me up with a place downtown close to my work." He extended his hand, "I'm Rich, by the way."

I put my gloved hand in his. "I'm Renee." The other two men who'd been silently listening to our conversation made no moves to introduce themselves, so I ignored them. "What kind of work do you do, Rich?"

A grin split his face. "I install granite countertops for a home remodeling company."

Given his enthusiastic response, I cocked my head. "You like it?"

"Yeah, it's a decent paying job. Especially for someone with a record. Work can be hard to find sometimes."

His reply hung heavy in the air as I attempted to formulate a response. Was it rude to ask what he'd done? I'm sure in the big house, he spouted that stuff to the rafters. But out in everyday society, was it okay to broach that subject with someone I'd just met?

"I can imagine," I settled for.

We talked some more, mainly him asking me what I did for a living. When we boarded the bus, Rich made no moves to sit next to me, which I was thankful for. He passed me on the way to the back, wished me a good day, and posted up on the last seat with his backpack preventing anyone else from sitting beside him.

What a baffling person. Normally a man had only one purpose in chatting up a woman my age, but it didn't seem like he was interested in me that way. He was just friendly. Even more of a conundrum. Wasn't prison supposed to harden you? It made me wonder even more about what he'd done to get locked away.

The next few days at the bus stop, Rich waved me over. At first I felt obligated to join him. I didn't really want to talk to anyone, but I didn't want him to think it was because he'd been to prison and I was scared of him. Even though I kind of was.

He told me about how he and his family had grown up in the projects of Denver and his father was a firefighter back in the day. He seemed proud of that fact, and his faith.

He was Catholic, and told me how he had gone to church since being in prison and atoned for his sins. I found it maddening that he wouldn't go into detail about those sins, but just couldn't work up the courage to ask.

)X( )X( )X(

It was as nice a day as December would allow. The weatherman said it might get up to fifty degrees. My breath still came out in a fog, but the sun shone and sparse clouds hung in the sky.

I headed down the train station stairs and toward the path I ordinarily took. Then the shuttle caught my eye.

When I first started taking the bus, the shuttle had turned me off. It was more people I would have to talk to. That's how things started off at the bus stop. Then Rich made me realize it really wasn't all that bad.

I took a deep breath and strode to the shuttle. A middle-aged man with a potbelly and thick, brown mustache pushed a button and the doors squeaked open.

"Good morning. Where to?" he asked as I stepped inside.

I rattled off the name of the company I worked for and took my seat. There were a few others already inside, chatting to one another.

I just sat there and every so often smiled at their banter. But, hey, this was socially awkward me, so I said nothing.

)X( )X( )X(

Early spring . . .

I awoke on Wednesday morning. It was darker than usual, and it took me a moment to realize I'd woken up before my alarm. I wasn't exhausted like I'd been up until my car had gotten repo'ed. It was as if the stubby little rat I was had used her teeth to file down the bars of her cage. Sure, losing my car had made a meteor-sized impact in my life—not to mention my credit score—but now I was thankful it had happened.

I stood and stretched my arms out. The ache normally present in my back and joints was gone. It had been for the past week or so.

I showered and dressed, then headed to the kitchen to greet Alanna. She leaned against one of the counters, nursing a mug of coffee. Her hair was piled in one of those sloppy buns, and with the dark circles under her eyes, she didn't look quite as chipper.

"You're early," she said.

I shrugged. "Might as well get a head-start on my day."

"Freak," she murmured.

I smiled and grabbed an apple from the fruit bowl on the counter. Once my winter gear was donned, I trudged through the snow.

At the bus stop, I spotted Rich. His hands were crammed into his coat pockets, so he did one of those chin thrusts as I approached. "Hey."

I glanced around, but saw no one else. "Hey. Where are your buddies?"

He shrugged. "They usually catch the next bus. I'm a bit early today. Looks like you are, too."

"Oh, I guess I am. How are you?"

"I'm good," he answered. "Counting down the days. Just five more months until I'm out of here."

"You didn't get to pick the halfway house you live at? I mean, there has to be a closer one to your job than here."

"Nope, we're assigned them. Wherever there's space."

"That must suck."

He shrugged again. "It's better than being in prison for the past twenty-eight years."

My eyes snapped up to his. *Twenty-eight years? Holy hell, that's a long time.*

He must've read something off my expression, and nodded. "Yep, went in when I was nineteen." He glanced away. "But, you know, I'm not the same person I was at that age."

The last thing I wanted him to feel was that he needed to explain himself to me—even if I secretly wanted him to—so I played it cool. "Nobody ever is."

"I made a lot of stupid mistakes," he continued as if I hadn't said anything. "I mean, killing a man is something I should have to pay for, but I was just a stupid kid back then."

I almost choked. On what, I don't know. Maybe the knowledge that I'd been in the presence of a murderer all this time. I looked at Rich and his lips were thinned to a grim line. Like he expected me to gather the locals for a good, ol' fashioned lynching.

Oddly enough, I wasn't the least bit afraid to be standing at the bus stop in near darkness with a murderer. Maybe because he wasn't just a murderer. He was a murderer named Rich who had befriended me when no one else had.

"Back then, I got involved with the wrong crowd. Gangs. Drugs. You know how it is." He glanced away again, but I could see the demons swimming in his eyes. He must've realized his weakness, and squared his shoulders. "But I atoned for my sins. I did my time. And I'm looking to get on with my life."

I managed a smile that was actually genuine. "Well, you're certainly doing that. You've got a job."

He returned my smile. "Yeah, my boss is great, too."

I didn't know what to say to that, and thankfully I didn't have to. Number sixty-six pulled up and we hustled into it. I didn't blow out my pent up breath until after I took my seat. Just like always, Rich sat alone in the back.

I gazed out the window that had begun to fog from the heat inside. It was a rush to finally find out the reason for Rich's incarceration.

He said he'd atoned for his sins, and his body language very clearly tried to portray he didn't care what I thought of him. So then why had his eyes begged me not to judge him? Why had he waited until the day we were at the bus stop alone together to tell me?

The rest of the trip to work was a blur. When I finally arrived at the office, I had to look up the meaning of "atonement." The first definition I found was "satisfaction or reparation for a wrong or injury." I had a hard time believing he'd made reparations to the family of the person he'd killed from prison, so I scrolled to the second definition. "The doctrine concerning the reconciliation of God and humankind, especially as accomplished through the life, suffering, and death of Christ."

That must be it. Rich said he'd found God while in prison. Had some jailhouse reverend convinced him he would be forgiven for his transgressions in the afterlife? But did someone else saying he was absolved of his sins make it so? If Rich truly believed in this, then why had he tried to defend his actions to me?

I contemplated it more than anyone should. For the whole rest of the day, I was preoccupied with it at work. My coworkers were put-off by my even more introverted behavior. I chalked it up to an upset stomach. If there was a vague inclination that you were having diarrhea at work, people avoided you like the plague.

Later that night, instead of falling asleep easily as my new routine had allowed, I tossed and turned.

✕ ✕ ✕

Saturday . . .

I strolled up to my parent's house, boots sliding on the skating rink that was their driveway. Luckily, there was a train station just a few blocks from their house, so my trek wasn't far.

I didn't bother knocking—this was my family, after all. I shouldered the door open and walked right in. "Hello!" I called out.

"Renee, you're here." My mom rounded the corner into the room. She had a stained kitchen towel thrown over her shoulder, and dyed auburn hair that made her look the ten years younger she'd intended it to.

"Hey, mom. Something smells good."

She smiled. "Hamburger Helper. The cheesy taco kind."

Oh, my wonderful, mid-western parents. "Gourmet" did not limit the inclusion of pre-packaged meals.

When my dad came into the kitchen, we all sat down at the table with our plates. Now was the time to get their perspective on Rich's atonement. Wisdom was supposed to come with age, right? I cleared my throat.

My dad looked up from shoveling food in his mouth and they both stared at me.

"So I met a new friend at the bus stop."

My mom gasped and grinned so wide, I could see the speck of pepper stuck in her teeth. "A boy? Oh, Renee! Tell me all about him. What does he do for a living?"

I wanted to roll my eyes. "I said a *new friend*, not a boyfriend."

My dad went back to wielding his fork like a shovel.

Disappointment emanated from my mom. "Oh."

I trudged on as if I couldn't see her interest in the subject promptly leave the room. "He's really cool. His name is Rich."

"That's great, honey," my mom said, staring at her plate dejectedly.

I pushed around a piece of iceberg lettuce in the pool of dressing I'd heaped on my salad plate. "He lives in the halfway house by my apartment."

My mom's head snapped up so fast, I think I got whiplash by proxy. "What does that mean? Like a place for druggies?" Her tone grated on my ears.

"No, convicts recently released from prison." Like that was so much better.

"What did he do?"

"He, uh . . . well, he killed someone," I blurted out. *Okay, probably could've said that more tactfully.*

The silence that followed my comment stretched on for an eternity. What shitstorm had I just let loose?

"Renee, I don't think I like you taking this bus," my dad finally said. His brow furrowed and his face became a roadmap of hard lines that had nothing to do with his age.

"Dad, it's not like that. He's really nice." The words tasted sour on my tongue. Here I was defending the very man I'd partially condemned.

"He killed someone," he repeated slowly, like I was a few bricks short of a load.

"He said he got in with the wrong crowd and did something stupid when he was nineteen. I was wondering what you thought—"

"How can you trust anything he says?" my mom interjected. Her voice morphed into that on-the-verge-of-hysterics screech she used when she got overly excited about something. "Everything you know about him is from what *he's* told you. How do you know he's telling the truth about anything?"

"If you think he's incapable of telling the truth, then why do you believe he killed someone? He could've made that up, too."

My mom sputtered, and her face turned ten shades of red. She quickly changed tactics, "Are you taking anything with you for protection? You can't trust *those* types."

"I've taken the bus every day for the past four months and I'm still alive."

"You need a bat or something," she murmured to herself.

I jerked back. "A bat?"

"To defend yourself."

"Right. Because carrying a bat to the bus stop with me totally makes sense," I quipped sarcastically.

My mom glared. "At least people would see it and wouldn't think about attacking you."

"Nobody's done anything to me! I'm not carrying around a baseball bat." This was getting out of hand. Why had I even brought it up? Oh yeah, because I thought they'd behave like rational adults and not like, well, parents.

"I wasn't talking about a baseball bat, Renee," she said like I was being the unreasonable one. "I was talking about those extendable ones the cops use."

"A police baton?" I couldn't help the chuckle of disbelief that erupted from my mouth.

"Exactly." She nodded as if the idea of me carrying around a nightstick wasn't completely ludicrous. "Like the riot police use." She turned to my dad who'd resumed eating his Hamburger Helper. "Don, take Renee to the sporting goods store."

He frowned down at his half-full plate. "Right now?"

She ignored him. "See what you can find there and buy it. No daughter of mine is going to hang around a bunch of hoodlums and not have a way to defend herself." She stood up from her seat, scooped up all of our plates—much to my dad's dismay—and stomped into the kitchen.

So that was it. They weren't even going to listen to my dilemma? They were just going to judge him and leave it at that.

I couldn't help my own dismay over the fact that I'd done the very thing they had. Sure, it was before I knew Rich. That first time I'd taken the bus, I was frightened to even walk to the bus stop by myself. I thought for sure someone was going to attack me.

Had I known a halfway house full of recently released felons awaited me, would I have gone? Would I have even talked with Rich? Would I still be the same quiet girl afraid of everyone?

I turned toward my dad for solace. "He really is a nice guy. He told me he isn't the same person he was. That he atoned for his sins."

My dad looked at me a long time, then blew out a breath. "Did he say he regretted it?"

I frowned, thinking back. Well, no. He hadn't. But then, prison was a tough place, where you had to kick someone's ass, or wind up having something unpleasant done to yours. Would he really just admit to a stranger he'd met on the bus how horrible he felt about taking a life? That was a vulnerability no man would reveal, let alone a felon.

My dad got up from the table. "Come on, Renee, let's go before your mother breaks every dish in the house."

)( )( )(

Several weeks later . . .

It had been awhile since the debacle at my parent's house. My dad didn't make me get the riot baton—mainly because you couldn't buy them at the sporting goods store. Not to mention it was illegal for a civilian to possess such a weapon in Colorado. Mom had graciously researched that for me. So I now had a mace keychain. But I left their house with something more than that. I left with a belly full of cheap salad and doubt.

Maybe my parents were right. Had I been too accepting of Rich? Was it because I knew him—or thought I did—that I hadn't taken an honest look at what kind of person he was?

I slept restlessly for many nights after as the conflict took root inside me. Cosmetically, I worried over whether because I "knew" Rich that I had given him a free pass, and would now defend his actions to anyone without really knowing the circumstances surrounding them.

On a spiritual level, however, Rich's supposed atonement festered inside me, too. I couldn't help but feel he'd used religion to forgive himself and what he'd done. But honestly, if I'd killed someone, I'd be looking for any way to make myself feel better about it, too.

More troubling though, was that I didn't know who to ask or what to do to find the answers. The internet could only tell me so much. For now, it was business as usual.

It was a Tuesday and the coldness had been buffeted by a current of warm air from the west. It was still bundle-up weather though. I strode to Daryl's shuttle after an encouraging conversation with Rich. I'd told him the countdown was on with only three months remaining for him. He'd appeared surprised I'd kept track, but a grin had soon formed that was both ecstatic and contagious.

The slide of the shuttle doors parted to Daryl's own contagious smile. It took him a while to crack my shell, but now I'd become one of his chatty passengers.

"Hey, Renee." He seemed in better-than-usual spirits today.

"Morning, Daryl." I nodded a greeting to another passenger.

"What time are you supposed to start today?" Daryl asked me, glancing in the giant mirror above the dash.

"Oh, I'm pretty early. I don't start for another forty minutes."

"You interested in making a donut run with us before I drop you off?"

I paused and stifled the reflex to point at myself and ask, "Me?" Really? They wanted to make a donut run with me? The smile that spread across my face was as warm as the feeling in my chest. "Yeah, that sounds like fun."

Not having a car often left spontaneity to be desired. It was such a hassle to get from A to B, that any meal out was a cherished rarity.

Once another man the others knew boarded, we were off. The aptly named "Donut House" was a tad bit off Daryl's usual route, but it wasn't far from the office.

We all disembarked and entered the café. It smelled of fried dough and brewing coffee. Light jazz music spewed from the PA system.

My eyes feasted upon the glass case filled with colorfully frosted assortments. I picked out an apple fritter bigger than my head that barely fit in the to-go bag. This was the first time I'd been out in weeks, so I might as well make it worth my while.

We paid for our goodies, and the sun burgeoned on the horizon by the time we made it back to the shuttle.

I peeled back the bag until my fritter was poking out, and took a bite. The second I tasted the sugar, my lips curled in a wide grin. Nothing, *nothing* had ever tasted so good.

I watched the others laugh and joke around, occasionally joining in myself without even a hint of nervousness.

That's when the answer to everything I had been struggling over hit me. This whole internal debate about whether Rich was a good person, and his atonement, wasn't for me to decide. I could think and think on it until I was an old lady, but I would never divine the answer simply because it wasn't for me to divine.

Before I met Rich, I couldn't even make small talk in an elevator. All it took was one man to say good morning to me, and here I was, making a donut run with the shuttle driver and two gentleman I didn't even know.

The fact that the man who prompted all this murdered someone didn't matter. Nor did his atonement. Anyone could change the course of someone's life for the better. Strange though, that the one person who should've been the scariest of them all had taught me not to be afraid.

"That must be good," Daryl interrupted my reverie.

"Yeah," I said with an even broader smile. "It really is."

I didn't realize just how closed off I'd felt until Rich made me see the cage I'd been trapped in was one of my own making. And the rat race wasn't really a race at all.

By the time I arrived at the office, the sun was almost fully risen. "Thanks for the donut run, Daryl." Some part of me wanted to tell him what it had helped me figure out, but a larger part said not to ruin it with the depth of my feelings.

"You're welcome. That was fun, wasn't it?"

I nodded and slipped outside. As he drove off, I waved. A feeling of utter contentment with my life filled me so fully, it was as if my body couldn't contain it all. It surged out of me, pouring into the world I wished could feel as I did.

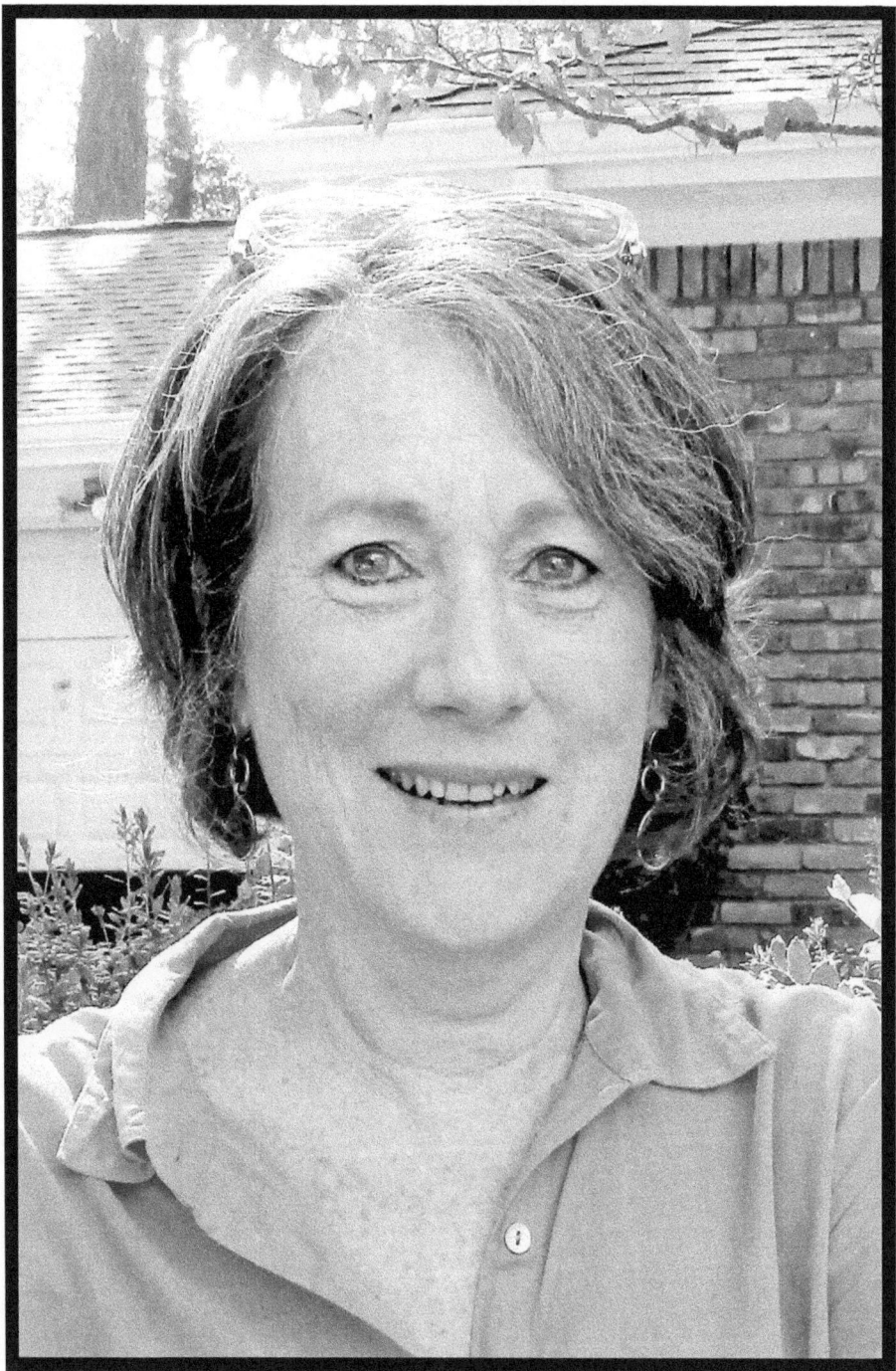

LAURIE KLEIN

BEHIND HER EYES

Airborne over Asia with my husband, I crossed the international dateline where time hiccoughs, then replays itself, a magical moment. But time disrupted my pivotal birthday: I turned fifty. Twice. Then I was one hundred.

Where were we headed? My mate wanted to help a third-world village, and the two-month mission trip to Thailand before us was our chosen opportunity. During our layover, our team sang "Happy Birthday" to me and served bonbons.

Still, should marking one's half-century on the planet really include a red dirt village overrun with roosters and rats? Water buffalo munching the neighbor's shrubs? It felt crazy.

Well, I was crazy about him.

)( )( )(

Bangkok's humidity wilted us. Imagine clouds of hot steam when you lift the lid on a seething cauldron. The atmosphere weighed on our lungs like congealed fat. I was *not* feeling kind.

After a brief orientation the next day, our team bumped along dirt roads for hours to reach a remote village. Tired and stiff, we staggered from the elderly vehicle crammed with gear. The local leader, a kindly American woman and long-time village resident, welcomed us, smiling broadly.

Then she assigned chores.

First we scoured an abandoned building, home to spiders wide as my splayed hand. Then the men on our team moved in with their backpacks and sleeping bags.

Next, we cleaned an upstairs room in the leader's house, where the women would sleep. I had expected housing readied for us since we were the free help. Recognizing my angst as fatigue plus wounded entitlement, I zipped my lip. Fully fifty now, I would be wiser, kinder.

Over dinner that night our leader prepped us for sleeping arrangements. "Mosquito netting *must* tent each group of four people. If you get up in the night, re-tuck it tightly beneath your bag."

Those of us from the Midwest smiled knowingly.

"It's not for mosquitoes," she added. "Netting deters the cobras."

✕ ✕ ✕

Our first days passed slowly. Some of the Thais welcomed our aid. Three computers had been donated for village use, and the youth were eager to learn skills. Aside from the computers and the local co-op, there were few communal resources: no shops or hospital, no post office, school, or laundry facilities. Motorcyclists paid the village cook for gasoline stored in Pepsi bottles, alongside her wok.

By the end of week one we were teaching English and music lessons. We also wired an industrial oven that had been donated. We test-drove the appliance by baking snickerdoodles. The Thais loved them. We began teaching the women our recipes for baked goods; they started selling them at their co-op.

I was fighting depression. Chronically homesick and sweaty, was my limp presence making a difference? My husband's dream was slowly unfolding—albeit like damp newspaper.

✕ ✕ ✕

Culture shock drains you, as does self-condemnation. It's hard to be nice when you feel like you're *doing time.*

In our second week there, I met Yai, a local widow. Aged and stout, her lightless eyes were so dilated they looked black. She seemed to stare straight through me. I looked away. But if I had taken her picture, the answering image of my lens would have shone up in those huge pupils. Of course zooming in on her face would have been rude. Instead, I made the Thai gesture of respect for an elder.

She responded by patting down my privates. Appalled, I pulled away, red-faced and shaking my head.

"It's nothing personal," the leader murmured. "Just go with it."

Go with it? I had recently completed months of therapy for inappropriate touch from a grandparent during my childhood. I'd barely begun befriending the shamed parts of myself. Yai's touch felt wrong.

This was a boundaries issue.

Before I could protest further, the leader, as if sensing my unease, assigned me an errand.

I told myself Yai's greeting was a one-time occurrence. A fluke. Later that day, I noticed two village grannies patting each other's breasts. I shivered.

)( )( )(

Yai continued her invasive behavior, chuckling at my discomfort. I asked the leader to intervene.

"Here in the village," she assured me, "this kind of affection is normal between older women."

"None of the others fondle me," I argued.

"It's her way of accepting you."

Or bullying me.

My time-whacked birthday sealed my status: older woman. Now that I could finally say, "Please don't touch me like that" (in two languages), my message proved moot.

"You'll get used to it," the leader said. "It's not wrong, just different."

No one else on our team received these attentions. Did I look like a victim? Did my dread of offending Thai culture project helplessness, or personal weakness?

Everything about village life felt wildly different. Strange. Husbands and wives never touched in public. Men held hands. Children with head lice hugged us freely, and old ladies took physical liberties.

If I stopped cringing, would Yai leave me alone?

)( )( )(

At our next encounter, I smiled calmly. No side-stepping touch. No blushes. No arguments.

Later that day, she changed tactics.

Gap-toothed and gumming her usual slaw of lime and betel nut (a homegrown painkiller the color of beets), she cornered me near the co-op. Her dilated eyes seemed ready to swallow me as she (playfully?) drew the dull side of her coconut knife across my throat, from ear to ear.

"Oh, dear," my British teammate said. "Love is gentle, Yai. Love is kind."

My eyes must have looked like rising moons. Yai cackled.

Fellow teammates shrugged off the incident and led me away.

I wanted to believe Yai was play-acting but sensed something I didn't understand. I felt wronged. Threatened.

)( )( )(

Over the next week Yai often grabbed my hand, then hawked up a gob of betel as if to spit in my palm. Once, she did, then faltered, stepped back as if mortified.

Another day she caught me alone and backed me down the long red dirt road, waving a long wooden dowel fitted with a hooked blade for harvesting tamarind.

Week by week, she taunted me. Only the cutlery varied.

"Her little joke," the leader said. "They only tease the ones they like."

My teammates enjoyed Yai's antics, but then, she never picked on them. They laughed at her. At me. Then they looked away. At least, that's how I remember it.

As to the villagers, other than respectful greetings acknowledging Yai's age, I didn't notice them treating her with special deference. Was she a valued elder? I didn't know.

One day, Yai told us via an interpreter that not one of her eight children ever visited her. She said we loved her more than they did. She even smiled a little. And something softened in me.

Still, she continued to single me out, as if she sensed traces of shame from my past.

One day, our gazes locked. And I wondered: had Yai been shamed?

As the days passed, the stories I made up about her in my head began to reflect my own.

"Love is patient, love is kind."

)( )( )(

Thereafter, I resolved to be a blessing to Yai, and each time I did, her wicked sense of fun lost its menace. I wanted meaningful contact. Who was she, as a woman? She had raised eight children. She must have a soft side.

I ate her strange food. When she hunched her shoulders, as if in pain, I rubbed her back. One day, I sang to her. She swayed and bobbed her head in time to the music, then playfully choked me. This time, we both laughed.

Something was shifting between us.

When a traveling market stopped outside the village, I bought her two green hair combs. Gently, I swooped long greasy bangs from her pleated brow. She thanked me, but in the ensuing days, I never saw her wear them.

Meanwhile, we practiced Thai sounds that pretzled my tongue. Her strident voice challenged my ears to discern the language's subtle tonalities. Shoulder, elbow, and knee—I'd point to parts of myself that I didn't mind her prodding, She'd supply the Thai words. She drilled me on these, and she waved her knife or threatened to spit when I mispronounced them.

)l( )l( )l(

The day we said goodbye Yai was wearing the hair combs. No one else was around when she stretched work-worn hands toward my face. Wary, I tensed. She smacked my chest and grunted. I acquiesced. At least she was knife-less.

She traced my ear's cartilage as if her fingers were feathers.

"*Hoo*," she half-crooned, half-murmured. One green hair comb slipped, and she peered at me shyly from under her bangs.

Over each of my eyelids she trailed two pale fingertips, butterfly-light, stroking my lashes. "*Tah*," she whispered, then "*Kontah*."

Sensing affection, I sighed as Yai's hands Brailled across my face: brows, temple, and bridge of the nose. Every nerve ending quivered; I barely breathed. She *read* my wrinkles, my lips, and my chin. She tapped a fingernail against my front tooth and spoke an elongated Thai word: *funn*.

Eyes catching the light, Yai peered into my soul as if loving all she found there, and she called each part of my face by its proper Thai name. Perhaps she was naming *me*, as a doting grandparent might, taking me into her gaze, her heart, her family. Something deep within me stretched itself again, expanding in the warmth of her touch. It felt holy.

Perhaps it's partly the contrast from how things began between us, but I cherish that farewell. To this day, no one has touched me with more kindness.

MURALI KAMMA

BRAHMS IN THE LAND OF BRAHMA

"Steve . . . Steve . . . how are you? Do you know who I am?"

"Narayan."

"Very good. And the music?"

"Brahms. Fourth symphony, third movement."

"Excellent, Steve! I knew you'd be okay. The doctor will be here soon. Don't worry. Everything is under control. Hope to take you home soon."

Narayan's glasses, as he leaned forward, slipped down his nose—and from his brow, before he fished out a handkerchief and mopped it, glistening beads of perspiration threatened to fall on the hospital bed. He must have been drinking hot chai. Every morning at Narayan's home, Steve would see him reach for the fan switch as soon as chai was served. Then, after handing Steve the *Express of India*, he'd sit back and read the local vernacular paper, while they waited for eggs and toast or crispy dosas with chutney.

Why was he listening to Brahms—*his* CD, surely?—and how long had he been lying there? The lively third movement having followed the lovely second movement, now came the Bach-inspired, ingeniously weaving melody of the final movement—his favorite—and as Steve lay still, listening, the familiar music swelled majestically.

"Your CD, my player," Narayan said, smiling, as if he'd read Steve's mind. Clad in a white, loose-fitting khadi shirt, and sporting bushy eyebrows and longish grey hair, he looked like a benign swami who was about to bestow his blessings. "The hospital was okay with it, Steve. Music is a healer, no? Isn't Brahms a great composer?"

Tired and a little annoyed, Steve turned away. Why these questions? And why this pretense that he'd be going back to Narayan's house, since Steve had already given his notice and was going to check into a hotel? While there was little pain, he was still groggy—it was the drugs, no doubt—and he didn't feel like talking. Feeling constricted, he wished he could drift off again.

He closed his eyes and tried to sleep, but then remembering something, he opened them and saw Narayan peering at him, still smiling.

"Ashok . . . what happened to the driver?"

"Ashok will be fine," Narayan said, patting his shoulder. "Don't worry, Steve. He was also wearing his seatbelt, thanks to you."

)( )( )(

If it hadn't been for his friend Rupa, who lived near him in Atlanta, Steve would have checked into a hotel in India—where the company he currently worked for was based—just as he'd done on his first visit. But when Rupa told him about Narayan, whom she knew and offered to call on his behalf, Steve decided to be a paying guest at an Indian home this time, not only because the idea appealed to him but because he knew it'd be more economical and maybe more interesting than staying in a hotel. Narayan lived not far from Info Tech City, where Steve would be working. Now that he was an independent IT consultant, he'd have to be careful with his money until he could establish himself.

After a couple of phone chats with Narayan, Steve arrived in India and moved into his house the same day. At the last minute, Narayan had unexpectedly sweetened the deal by offering his car for Steve's use—and so, it was Narayan's driver, Ashok, who came to the airport to pick him up, holding a sign that read "Mr. STEVE of USA."

"Good morning," Narayan said when Steve, bleary-eyed, emerged from his room the following day. "Our chai is ready, Steve. Would you like to see today's paper?"

Steve wasn't keen on it right then, but as he sat on the black sofa facing Narayan, he politely took the newspaper from him and glanced at the first page. "Gridlock in Parliament," a headline announced. He felt a sense of déjà vu and wondered, fleetingly, why it didn't say "Congress," only to realize that he was looking at the *Express of India*.

"Steve, I wanted to say something." Narayan folded his vernacular paper and took a steaming cup from his housekeeper. "I know you're not married, but if your girlfriend wants to visit, she's welcome to stay here. I'm not as conservative as I may seem to you."

Steve smiled, and sipped his chai. He'd already sensed that, as a host, Narayan, who was retired and had never married, would be sociable and voluble, giving him less privacy than he was accustomed to. But that didn't worry Steve, because Narayan's manner, far from being intrusive, made him feel welcome and less lonely than he'd been for over five months, following the abrupt—and painful—end of his last relationship.

Steve said he was single—and, no, he wasn't expecting any visitors from the States.

"You're single, Steve? Well, who knows, you may end up with a wife here—or, as we say, *bibi*. I run an unofficial matchmaking service; it's called Hurry-and-Marry." Narayan laughed, his belly shaking.

An explosion interrupted their conversation, just as Steve drained his cup. Startled, he stood up and, through the open balcony door, spotted a plume of white smoke curling into what seemed like a question mark.

"Not to worry," Narayan said, unperturbed. "It's only the military doing their testing. Come, Steve, I'll show you."

Standing on the balcony, Steve was surprised to see a vast expanse of uninhabited, wooded land that he hadn't noticed earlier. The government-owned property hadn't been gobbled up by developers, thank god, Narayan said, and the occasional noise of bomb testing, which rattled the windows, was a price worth paying, because no other place outside the few remaining parks in this booming yet congested city had such a luxurious stretch of greenery, making you feel—at least when you looked on this side—that you were in the tranquil countryside, far from the chaos and clamor of urban India.

"Now *this* boom is a boon for us," Narayan added, with his belly laugh.

The metro area had grown rapidly in the last several years as a result of the IT revolution, attracting droves of domestic migrants and transients, along with a growing number of foreign residents. Steve, though, still felt like a visitor, a stranger. Turning left, he got a partial view of Info Tech City's gleaming towers, where the ambiance was ultramodern and the working conditions so efficient—with power, clean water and hot food available 24/7—that Steve felt he was back at his old job, albeit in a tropical setting.

It was a tale of two cities. These islands of calm, familiar to Steve because of his work, were surrounded by the metro's surging waves of humanity, which had come as a shock to his system on his first visit. He'd never seen so many people massed in one place. But now, standing on the balcony, Steve felt as if he'd swigged a bracing tonic, a tonic he knew he could handle in moderate doses. The vast country was fascinating yet bewildering, stimulating but also overwhelming.

Turning right and looking past the alley humming with activity, Steve caught a glimpse of the haze-shrouded main road, which he knew would be crowded with pedestrians and a mix of vehicles, not to mention the odd cow ambling near the busy vegetable market. Shops would be opening, and some roadside vendors would be doing brisk business.

When Steve thought of India, he pictured himself sitting in a jasmine-scented garden, where the chirping of birds mingled agreeably with the strains of a sitar—only to clash with the constant blaring of horns outside. India was contradictory; it was both modern and ancient, with the 21st century co-existing easily, and uneasily, with earlier centuries.

And everything seemed more intense. The sun was sharper, the colors brighter, the sounds harsher, the smells stronger, the pollution greater, the air warmer, the rains heavier, the food spicier, the chai sweeter, and the fruits tastier. Even the television dramas, or melodramas, Narayan watched were louder, unfolding at a higher emotional pitch than Steve was used to, going by what he'd observed the previous evening.

"Come, Steve, let's have breakfast," Narayan said, placing his hand on his back.

✕ ✕ ✕

For earlier generations of American travelers, Steve liked to say when anybody back home asked him about India, the attraction lay in spiritual traditions. For him, it was software solutions. Steve would laugh, but he was only half-joking, because it was true that most of his time—and energy—was spent in Info Tech City, where he sat before a computer screen in a posh office, or interacted with clients and attended to their needs.

Wanting it to be a little different this time, Steve was glad he'd accepted Rupa's recommendation. Narayan, who frequently wore immaculate white clothes that included a dhoti wrapped around his waist and reaching his ankles, was steeped in his country's dominant cultural traditions, judging by his well-appointed home, which was adorned with framed pictures of various gods and goddesses, brass sculptures of elephants and a dancing Nataraja, and paintings depicting classical dancers, temples and sacred rivers, and picturesque village scenes.

And then there was the *puja* room where Narayan prayed every morning after his shower. Steve, not particularly religious, was intrigued by Narayan's deep yet unshowy piousness. It was obvious in the devotional music he enjoyed listening to, the clothes he wore at home, the vegetarian food he always ate, the incense sticks he lit before his *puja* every day, filling the room with a pleasing fragrance.

Steve saw at first hand what he had, until then, only vaguely known— culture in India was often inextricably tied to its religious traditions. This was apparent even in prime-time TV serials, some of which were based on mythological characters from the epics.

Then, of course, there was the newer and younger and more secular India that Steve already knew about and which he began to experience again in Info Tech City, where he worked alongside ambitious, often Westernized Indians in up-to-date office buildings. Narayan's house was also a welcoming island in the pullulating metro, though of a different sort, and at the end of a long day, after riding in Narayan's car on the choked highway leading out of Info Tech City, Steve was glad to be back. Ashok, a competent driver, was accommodating no matter when Steve wanted to leave. But he seemed to think his seatbelt was a luxury—or a hindrance—that he could push aside before starting the car, making Steve nervous. He decided to speak to Ashok about it, gently.

)( )( )(

"What were you listening to, Steve? Yesterday."

"Excuse me?"

They were having dinner, which Narayan's housekeeper, Shanti, had prepared and was now serving. Although Steve hadn't made any requests, she made sure there was one non-vegetarian dish for him at every meal; this time it was a delectably tangy fish curry.

Shanti, a widow belonging to a different community than Narayan's, lived with her daughter and son-in-law close by. She came to the house in the morning and left only after they'd eaten in the evening. Her attachment to Narayan was striking—and yet, Steve couldn't help being aware of the distance between them, dictated by social circumstances that perhaps remained unbridgeable. Always deferential, she never ate in their presence, preferring to eat alone in the kitchen after they were done and she'd cleared the table.

"I heard this beautiful music coming from your room last night,"

Narayan said. "I wanted to ask you about it, but your door was closed. I didn't want to disturb you."

"Oh, you're welcome to knock anytime, Narayan. Yesterday? I was listening to Brahms—"

"How wonderful! Reminds me of Brahma."

"I'm sorry . . . who?"

"Brahma, Steve. He's the creator of the universe for Hindus. But Brahma is less well known than the other two in the trinity: Vishnu, the preserver, and Shiva, the destroyer."

After they finished eating, Narayan took Steve to the *puja* room and showed him a bronze idol of the multi-headed Brahma, resting on a makeshift altar and surrounded by other deities in the pantheon. Narayan said he was a devotee of Brahma, though India had just a few well-known temples dedicated to Brahma. "And you're a devotee of Brahms, so maybe it was fate that brought us together," he added, chuckling.

"I don't know about devotee," Steve said, "but it's true that, lately, I've been listening to Brahms a lot."

"I can see why. The music you were playing was divine. I'd like to listen more, Steve, if you don't mind. I'm ignorant about Western music—of any kind."

"Certainly, Narayan. You're welcome to take my CDs anytime. Perhaps we can listen together sometimes. And I'm hoping you can tell me more about Indian music."

Less than a week later, this pleasant cross-cultural engagement, as Steve saw it, ended abruptly. When Steve got back from work, Narayan would usually greet him brightly and, turning to his housekeeper, say: "Shanti, make chai. Steve is here."

But that evening, returning home, Steve didn't see Narayan and mistakenly thought he'd stepped out. As he was finishing his chai, a glum-looking Narayan emerged from his room and said, "Mr. Steve, I want to speak to you about something."

"Is everything okay, Narayan?"

"I don't know. This morning, after you left, I noticed that you'd accepted my friend request on Facebook."

"Yes?" Steve had been surprised to receive the request, not having seen Narayan use his computer.

"Steve, I hope you don't think I'm nosy. I was browsing through your album and saw some nice photos of your life in America. I was just curious. Then I saw one that showed you . . . and Tom." His voice dropped. "I had no idea . . . Rupa never told me."

Steve bristled. "Told you what, Narayan? You're welcome to look at my pictures, but I don't see why my personal life should be any of your business. Tom and I are no longer together, but that's irrelevant."

"Sorry, Steve . . . I'm old-fashioned. Please don't misunderstand me. It's my mistake."

"Well, seems like we both made a mistake." Steve said, rising. "I'm so disappointed, Narayan." Walking quickly to his room, he closed the door.

He felt a little agitated. Sitting on the bed, he distractedly reached for his stack of CDs.

The opening section of the Brahms Piano Quintet, with its seductive blend of strings and piano, unfolded at a low volume as Steve pondered his next move. A hotel in Info Tech City, where he'd stayed last time, would cost a lot more, but that seemed like his best bet for the short term. Looking for his notebook, in which he'd jotted down local hotel phone numbers and other information, Steve noticed that his camera, which he remembered leaving on the window sill after taking pictures around the house a few days earlier, was missing. It was an expensive new model, and Steve had it only because his brother had given it to him as a gift. He searched the room thoroughly, without luck, and wondered if he was losing his mind. Could he have taken it to the office and left it there?

Not long after the quintet ended with a thrilling flourish, Shanti knocked on the door and said softly, "Sir, dinner."

Steve and Narayan ate quietly as Shanti served them and, like she often did, shuttled between the dining area and kitchen, bringing fresh rotis or filtered water to drink. At the end came a milky, sweet-smelling vermicelli pudding that Steve had never had before.

Thanking Shanti for the delicious meal, Steve asked her, after she took his plate, if she'd come across his camera when she was cleaning the room. As usual, Shanti, understanding only a few words of what Steve said—their rudimentary communication involved a lot of smiles and gestures—turned to Narayan for translation.

"What do you mean?" Narayan said, putting his spoon down. "Why would she touch your camera? She's trustworthy."

"That's not what I said, Narayan." Steve felt his anger rise. "You're being impossible. All I wanted to know was if she'd seen the camera. I'm merely trying to find it, in case I misplaced it. But, you know what, it doesn't matter."

"Steve, don't get upset. Please. Did you look everywhere . . . ?"

Steve had, however, already got up from his chair and was walking away. Entering his room, he shut the door firmly.

)( )( )(

After Steve was discharged from the hospital, he didn't object when Narayan took him back to his house to recuperate. A hotel seemed out of the question, at least for now.

Besides, Narayan insisted, saying, "You're my responsibility, Steve, until you make a full recovery."

Earlier, a day after that unpleasant exchange of words, Steve had given his notice and also mentioned that he'd switch to a cab service for his daily commute.

"Let's talk about it," Narayan said, sounding distressed. "I'm sorry, Steve. I know you felt insulted. That wasn't my intention."

"Not *insulted*, Narayan; *hurt* would be more appropriate. But I know you didn't mean it, and I'm sorry as well. Still, I think it'd be better if I move on."

Narayan accepted Steve's decision, but he persuaded him to stick with his car and driver for the time being. Steve had to visit a couple of clients that day, so he went with Ashok to the city. As they drove back in the evening traffic, it started to rain heavily, when a bus making a turn skidded and hit the car from behind. It happened so fast that all Steve could remember was the sound of crunching metal and shattering glass. Neither Ashok nor Steve had life-threatening injuries, but the medical expenses still added up alarmingly. The bus company, accepting responsibility, agreed to cover them fully.

"Ah, Steve, I see that you have a book about Kerala," Narayan said, as he walked into his room, holding a cup of chai and the *Express of India*. "No Brahms today?"

"Well, I'm giving him a break, I guess." Steve was partially reclining on the bed, with a few pillows to prop up his back. Putting his book down, he took the cup. "Thanks, Narayan. I'm still hoping to visit Kerala later this year."

"I'm sure you will, Steve. You're already making good progress." He paused. "I'm so glad we found the camera. Hope it wasn't damaged."

The camera had been lying on the ledge just outside the window. Presumably, a bird had dropped it there—or more likely, pushed it from the sill.

Steve held up his hand. "No worries, Narayan. I'd been foolish to leave it here, and then make a fuss. The camera is not important, but I won't use the open window as a shelf from now on."

Narayan smiled, and Steve was glad that there was no lingering awkwardness.

"By the way," Narayan said, "Kerala has one of the few notable Brahma temples in India. We plan to visit Kerala, too, after we get married."

Steve put his cup down. "You're getting married, Narayan? This is news to me."

Narayan looked away, and then down, before smiling at Steve. "I know," he said. "It was a sudden decision. I'm still in shock. Shanti and I have decided to get married."

Steve gazed at him, quietly. Like India, he realized, Narayan could be full of surprises.

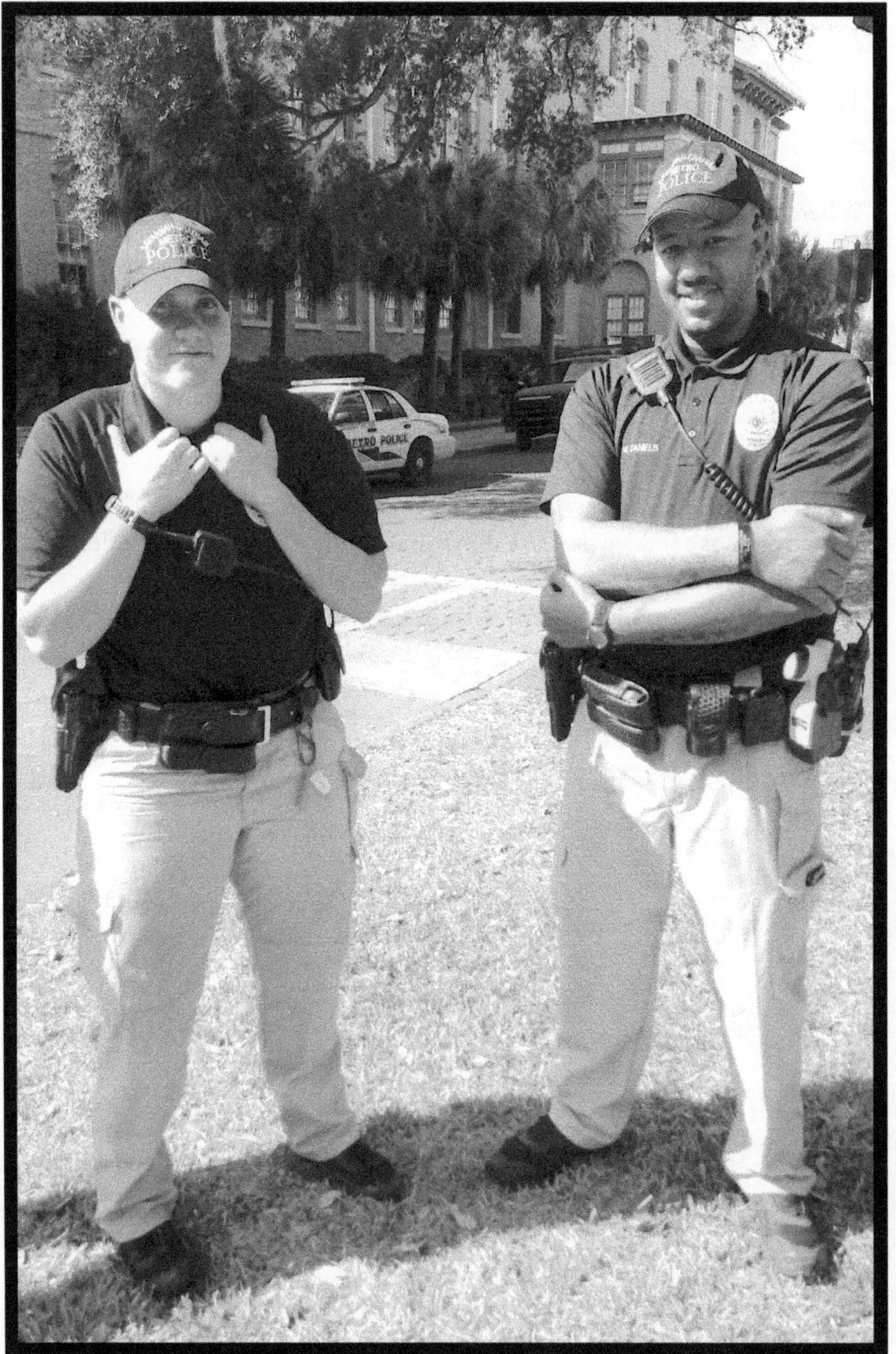

III. HELP WHEN WE NEED IT MOST: ILLNESS & ACCIDENT

SHIREEN DAY

UNEXPECTED STRANGERS

The call came at 4:30 a.m. I had gone to sleep excited that my twenty-year-old daughter was coming home for Thanksgiving. But when the phone rang, my heart caught in my throat. I bolted out of bed to grab my cell phone from the charger on the other side of the room.

Ellie's voice sounded strong and clear as she said, "Mom, I've been in an accident, but I'm fine. I just wanted you to know I'm going to miss my flight."

Nothing in her tone suggested she was bleeding and trapped inside her car on the side of a highway with fragments of glass embedded in her face. All I knew for sure was that it was 6:30 a.m., in western Massachusetts and she was driving herself to the airport in her 1995 Buick Le Sabre.

A chill swept through me. I felt like an undertow was dragging me away. "What happened?"

"I think I hit black ice. Then I saw a black truck coming toward me. I don't know what happened next."

Black ice. Black truck. Black out.

She paused before saying, "Someone is coming. I need to go."

And then she just hung up.

I stood in my bedroom. Silent. Shaking. My daughter was 2000 miles away, alone in a disabled car on the side of the highway. It was dark. She had been hit by a truck.

Someone was coming.

☓ ☓ ☓

Someone.

A million stories of young women disappearing begin inside a car on the side of the road. I had taught her to lock her doors. I had taught her to be wary of strangers. She was a smart young woman with good instincts, but I worried she was defenseless.

I knew too much about being defenseless. When I was a young child, I lived in St. Thomas, in the U.S. Virgin Islands. It was a small community back then and everyone knew everyone else. There weren't many strangers. Tourists mostly. But bad things still happened. Grandmothers were mugged. Drunken mothers drove off cliffs. They forgot to protect their daughters. Only the best of friends offered help.

I'm also one of those hyphenated Americans raised in my teen years by a parent from another culture. My father immigrated to the US from Iran in 1947. During the Shah's reign, I moved to Tehran for a few years. We lived in an extended family household. It was there that I learned that family equals protection. It was there I learned that a stranger is anyone who doesn't share your blood, your genes, or your father's name. Strangers were the men who followed me down a city street or tried to overcharge me when buying the latest bootleg Elton John album. Strangers were people who didn't know my father. The definition was broad, yet precise. It was paired with the idea that family keeps us safe.

As I thought about my daughter, the highway, the stranger, I would have given anything to be with her. She needed her mother, not some unknown person. *How could someone that didn't know her actually help?*

I paced around my bedroom. I didn't turn on the lights. My darkness made an invisible bridge to the darkness that surrounded Ellie in the pre-dawn hours on that icy highway in western Massachusetts.

I called her back. A man's voice answered her cell phone.

"Who is this?" I asked trying to keep my tone light, neutral.

"I'm Bob," he said. "I stopped to see if I could help."

Help. He wants to help. But who is he, really? I had no way of knowing his intent.

"Do you know what happened?"

"No. There are several cars here," he said. "Is this Ellie's mom?"

"Yes." I said. My voice cracked and broke. "How is she?"

He didn't tell me that her car was destroyed and that she had been hit at least three times. He didn't tell me she was trapped and covered in blood. He didn't tell me that he had reached through the glass and given her a bandana to hold her dangling ear in place.

He simply said, "She's a bit spacey. The ambulance will be here soon."

My fists clenched. *I need to get to my daughter.* My legs wobbled. *I'm 2000 miles away.*

It dawned on me that she had probably lost consciousness.

He put Ellie back on the phone.

"Don't worry, Mom. Really. This nice man will stay with me until the ambulance gets here."

Shock gives us time to save ourselves.

The sound of sirens filled up the space between us and then she said, "I have to go now Mom."

She hung up the phone before I could say anything else. Tears ran down my cheeks. Bile surged in my stomach. When my phone rang again, I didn't recognize the number, but I answered anyway. It was Bob, calling from his phone. He told me that the paramedics had arrived. He told me they were moving her to the ambulance. He didn't tell me how hard it was to get her out of the car. He gave me just enough detail to understand the situation was bad without saying how bad.

At the trauma center, the doctor reattached Ellie's ear, closed some small facial lacerations, sent her for scans of her brain and spine, x-rayed her pelvis, hip, knee and ankle. She had bone deep bruising, a sprained ankle, but nothing was broken.

I was in the process of buying a ticket to fly East when the doctor called me and said, "Sit tight. Airplanes are pressurized and she'll heal better at home." He told me he was talking with the airlines and hoped to get her a seat on the next flight. He mentioned a winter storm was on the way.

The nurses let her use their shower. Someone gave her loose fitting scrubs. Her skinny jeans didn't fit over her swollen limbs and she hadn't packed any sweats. When she realized her wallet with her ID was in her coat, and that her coat was still in her car, a state trooper drove to the tow yard to pick them up. Someone else drove her to the airport thirty minutes away, and yet another person took her to her gate.

By the time Ellie finally arrived in Denver, thirteen hours after the crash, my life-long definition of strangers was in tatters.

An airline employee pushed her to the curb in a wheelchair. She wore socks, but no shoes. Her favorite boots didn't fit over the swollen ankle and calf, but she was happy the ER doctors hadn't cut them off her feet. She pulled back a thick lock of curls to show me her ear and said with a smile, "I asked them not to shave my hair and they listened. They put in 18 stitches."

My relief that she was finally home was palpable, but the worst was yet to come. The Buick's steel frame had buckled a little more with each collision. We still didn't know how many cars had been in the accident. Three? Four? Airbags release only once. Every time her car was hit, her neck ricocheted back and forth slamming the soft grey matter of her brain against the inside her skull. The brain, like any other part of the body doesn't swell immediately, but when it does, the signs are unmistakable.

The discharge paperwork from the emergency room said she had a concussion. Within a day, vertigo made standing difficult. She didn't trust her balance. She couldn't sleep. She lost her sense of taste. It was hard to swallow. I kept her warm with heating pads and hot packs. She often seemed far away, as if lost in a soft cloud except that her brain's inability to filter sound turned the tiniest everyday noises into a form of torture. The doctors simply said she needed to rest and she would get better.

For the next three months we silenced the doorbell, the telephone, ate on paper plates and spoke in whispers. Soft food reduced the reverberations from chewing. She was completely homebound except for the acupuncture appointments that helped her headaches.

At the ninety-day mark, she began cognitive retraining. At six months she was finally thinking clearly enough to begin her schoolwork. By the end of the eighth month, she had finished three courses from her fall semester and she began driving, ever so cautiously on dry roads when the sun was shining. She returned to college nine months after the accident, having missed only one semester.

)( )( )(

Throughout her long and often lonely recovery, we have often reflected on who offered help and who disappeared from our lives. We both understand that many have no idea what to do or say when there is a medical crisis. Family and friends became strangers. Strangers became family and friends.

Bob taught us that help could come from unexpected strangers. He didn't have any special medical skills or experience with car accidents. He was a carpenter on his way to work. He talked to my daughter. He talked to me. We both know the comfort of his voice.

Now, when I hear about someone who stops to help an injured woman, finds a lost child, or rescues dog that fell through the ice, I see a version of

Bob. I think about how few people ever take the time to stop at the scene of an accident.

My definition of stranger has become much more nuanced and complex. We are all strangers at some point in time. But it only takes a moment to reach out to someone and suddenly everything changes.

I still have Bob's number written on a scrap of paper towel. It's clipped to the front of a file called, "Accident." When I recently asked Ellie if she wanted to call him, she said, "No Mom, I want to thank him when I feel like myself again."

I understand. Injury makes a stranger of the self. It's been two and one-half years and her brain is still healing. The neurologist told her that it may take up to five years before she feels normal, but, however long it takes, I have no doubt that she will recover and when she does, I know she will call Bob.

As for me, I know that bad things happen in a random sort of way. I know that someone I have never met will help. My definition of stranger includes a newfound trust that someone unexpected will stop and lend a hand.

PEGI DEITZ SHEA

WHO EVER YOU ARE

The Vernon Circle isn't a circle anymore, now
a precisely-timed traffic-lighted, 4-lane intersection
with turning lanes, arrows yellowing way too fast,
north/south 83 bisecting east/west 30
ramping on/ramping off Interstate 84,
strip malls hollering from all 4 corners,
the homeless with tin cans, hoping for gridlock.

Between Cardio Express and Staples,
in a rare spell of green lights and rights-on-red,
God kept me from killing anyone, for only
10 seconds after I parked at Price Chopper,
I fell face down, convulsing on the macadam.
(I don't remember that part.)
In the ambulance, I couldn't remember
my name, or even what the word "name" meant,
or if I was married, what my husband's name was,
and crying because I didn't know if I had kids,
and then exclaiming, "I do!" then sobbing because
I couldn't get their names. What kind of mother
can't remember the names of her own children?
I remember thinking: Why are names
so damn important?

Released from the hospital 4 hours later,
lucid again, I wondered about the people
who saw my seizure, kept a safe ring around me,
called 911, and who, when I finally went limp,
turned me over, checked my pulse,

blotted my bloody face, laid a coat under my head,
another over me, delayed their errands
during a Friday rush hour, and waited
for the police and EMTs. Someone
found my wallet and turned it in; all its contents
intact when I checked that night.

I don't remember any of the kind strangers,
and I'll never know their names,
but they were there for me at Vernon Circle.
Whoever you are, know this:
my prayers orbit your every step.

NORMAN KLEIN

VETS

It was Doctor York who arranged my first meeting with Sergeant Novotny in the summer of 69. I was coming out of York's office, and Novotny was sitting there in his police uniform waiting to go in. We looked at each other, each of us knowing the other was a vet. We exchanged cards, and agreed to have breakfast together the following morning in the diner in the mall.

He arrived with another vet in tow, and the three of us found a booth. "Jack, this is Victor, Victor this is Jack," he said before we sat down. I put out my hand, but Victor didn't notice. He just stood there, and I could tell by his stare, his long narrowing look into nowhere, that he was a vet just home from Nam, a man home but not home.

"Jack, Victor comes here every day for breakfast, don't you Victor?" Novotny said. Victor nodded, and sat down and picked up a menu.

That's how the deal was struck. I'd show up at the diner in the mall at eight to read my paper over coffee and muffins. Sometimes Victor would sit with me. Usually not. He didn't come to talk. He'd put up his hand when he saw me. It wasn't a wave. It was hello, a hand that said he knew I was a vet like him and that's why I paid for his breakfast. He was a vet. I was a vet. I had his back.

Martha and I were living in a one-mall town back then, and behind the mall were five acres of woods where Victor and five other guys were camped out. The non-vets went into town to beg, but Victor never begged and was always alone. Knowing he was alone bothered me. I couldn't help wondering if he was getting three meals a day, if he was seeing a doctor, and could find things like a change of clothes and a toothbrush.

When I first mentioned I would be going to a plumbing supplies conference at the end of July, the first thing Martha asked was, "What about Victor?"

"He'll be okay. He knows I can't be there every day."

"Jack, when you're gone for a week he won't know what to think."

"You're right. I'll leave a note, and arrange for him to run a tab if he wants to."

"That might not be enough. I'll stop by the diner to tell him why you you're not there. Maybe he'll talk to me and let me buy him breakfast."

I warned her that he never talked to me and seldom sat at my table, but it turned out I was wrong. He did talk to her. She was wearing her nursing uniform. That's what did it I think. She called me minutes after I checked into my hotel to tell me that Victor ate lunch and dinner at the Salvation Army Kitchen, and showered and shaved at the Y. The Christ Church Ladies Club clothed him and kept him in razors and toothpaste.

When she called on Wednesday I learned that Victor's wife and little girl lived with her parents in town, but Victor was not allowed to visit them.

"I can't see them until I'm well," he had said.

On Friday, the day before I returned, she asked him if he had a doctor, and he said he didn't, and didn't want one.

"I have to do it myself."

Martha told him the best doctor was Doctor York, and that York had told me two years ago that no vet should ever have to do it alone.

My Martha, what a woman. All that in just a few days. I know, too, she was checking up on me, never telling me not to slip, not to go out drinking with the boys, but knowing that just the sound of her voice keeps me strong.

I'll never forget my first week home, how angry I was when I couldn't find my hammer, and how I stared down the mailman when he wouldn't give me the mail. Martha stayed with me. She was my angel and bedrock. She learned that when I began to slip back to Nam I would shut my eyes, and she would come to me and hold me and kiss my eyes open. In two weeks she had me out laughing with the mailman, admiring the pictures of his grandchildren.

But Victor wasn't laughing. He was staring and hurting, I could tell. Something must have happened. He couldn't talk to me, and my guess was he wasn't talking to her. Or maybe he was self-medicating, drinking, doing drugs, or both. My guess was that he wasn't drinking. I hadn't seen any of the telltale signs.

When I returned from the convention the following day I thanked Martha again for all she'd done for me, and for Victor. But right before we nodded off that night we agreed that she had done everything she could for

him, and we should leave it at that. She had done it just right while I was
gone, but you can't push a vet, and you can't do things for them.

A couple of weeks later Victor called Martha at home to ask if she would
meet him at the hospital the next morning so he could ask for a doctor. She
said she would.

When I came home from work that night and heard about the call, my
first thought was that it was good news, and then I couldn't help thinking
that it wasn't right for him to be calling her but still not be speaking to me.

"Where did he call you from?"

"The Y."

"How did he get our number?"

"From the phone book. I didn't give it to him. We agreed we were not
going to go out of our way to help him, remember?"

"But you just did."

"Jack, Family Services is ten steps away from my office."

"Okay, but if he calls again, let me speak to him," I said.

Three days later he sat down with me at my table and we had breakfast
together. "How did it go?" I asked. That was the first time I had spoken to
him.

"Good," he said, and showed me his appointment card with Doctor
York.

When I handed it back to him he looked me the eye for the first time
and nodded. I nodded. There we were, two Vets nodding. Two Vets getting
the job done, knowing it wouldn't be easy.

A week later, we talked again. He placed his breakfast opposite me, and
then still standing said, "Doctor York said I should sit with you and talk to
you. Good . . . good morning."

"Good morning, Victor," I said, and we did the nodding thing again.

Two weeks later he joined me at the table and said, "Thank you, and
please thank Martha too." There was a pause and then he whispered, "I never
would have gone to the hospital if she hadn't been there."

"You don't have to thank me, Victor. We're Vets. We know what it was
like over there."

He didn't want to hear that. He didn't know what to say. It made him
uncomfortable. "Will you thank Martha?" he asked.

"Yes I will. I promise," I said, and he nodded and I nodded.

By the end of September his good mornings included my name, and he would give me news from the Y or the Salvation Army Kitchen.

"Bad news, Jack. Tim Bothner died. We played checkers at lunchtime."

"Was he your friend?"

"Yes, but he wasn't a vet."

Come the first cold snap in mid-October it was the weather he wanted to talk about.

"Another frost last night. Not a killing frost. That's okay," he said.

"Victor, where will you go this winter?"

"Three old guys from the woods got the last three beds at the senior center. The two younger ones sleep at the jail."

Maybe his not having a warm place to sleep is what caused what happened at the diner the next morning. Right after we found a table I made a quick trip to the men's room and when I returned there was a cup of coffee on our table, but Victor was gone.

I went to the register and there was a new girl there. I asked her where he had gone.

"I don't know. He saw a woman he knew and ran after her, and I went after him because he didn't pay for his coffee. Security nabbed him before he caught her."

I told her I'd be back, and ran to the security office, and there was the security guy seated opposite Victor in the back room. I knocked and went in. He told me to wait outside take a seat and he'd be out in twenty minutes. I told him I could explain what just happened.

"I don't think so." he said and turned his back on me.

"Do you know who Sergeant Novotny is?" I asked.

"Sure."

"I'm going to call him. He'll want to hear what I have to say."

"Look, this bum stole a cup of coffee. You want Novotny to come down here and arrest him, that's fine, go ahead."

"No, first you need know who introduced me to this man four months ago. It was Novotny. He's a vet. I'm a vet, and this man you called a bum is a decorated Vet. I bought him the cup of coffee you said he stole. What do you say we tear up that report and let Victor and me return to our breakfast."

The security guard hesitated then tore up the report.

As we walked back to the diner Victor told me he'd seen his wife and ran after her to tell her he was talking again. Then the security guard had grabbed him from behind and spun him around. He shouldn't have done that. It made Victor so angry he couldn't talk.

"I have to stop being angry," Victor said.

"He made me angry too. Could you tell?"

He smiled and nodded. Before I left the diner I told the new girl who Victor was, and showed her the envelope in the cash register with fifty dollars in it and Victor's name on it.

She apologized. She said her boss had showed her the envelope, but she didn't know what he looked like. It wasn't her fault. I walked away thinking what every vet knows: that nobody can protect everybody all the time.

As soon as I got home that night I asked Martha if she knew of any other winter housing options for Victor. She said she didn't, but maybe her friends in Family Services would know. The Y came through with a position as a volunteer security guard. All he had to do was keep the entrance lights on and walk through the building now and then.

"They're giving me a place to sleep. Is that what they're doing?" Victor asked me.

"Not exactly, they need someone they can trust. They want a vet, not just anybody."

Then Victor disappeared for nine days. Martha did a little snooping and found out his mother was in town visiting her granddaughter. With the help of Sergeant Novotny, she also made contact with Victor and had breakfast with him several times.

Martha also learned that Victor had walked into the emergency room the night of the sleet storm. Knowing that, Martha and I put our heads together and decided to offer Victor the use of our summerhouse for the next several months. It was nothing fancy. There was a 20 by 20 main room that served as the kitchen, dining room, and living room. The one bathroom featured a sink and toilet, but no tub or shower. It sat at the end of a 10 by 15 bedroom.

There was a kitchen sink, a refrigerator, and a microwave, but the only stove was the wood stove. If you stepped out the door next to the stove, you were in the woodshed looking at three cords of dry wood. There were another four cords stacked outside under a tarp.

"Victor will like keeping the stove going and cooking on it, I'm sure," Martha said, "but what I'd most like to see is that wife of his dropping by to tell him how well his daughter is doing in school, and how much they have missed him."

"Don't get ahead of yourself, Martha. And don't be thinking we'll invite him over every Friday night for dinner."

"I know, Jack. Victor doesn't need help, and we won't be offering any rides downtown. It's only a mile to the Salvation Army Kitchen, and he'll insist on walking."

Victor did like keeping the stove going, heating the water he needed to bathe. He told me one morning he had found the book *Walden Pond* in the bookshelf and read some of it. He didn't like it.

"Why would a man go live in the woods if he didn't have to?" he asked, and I had to tell him I'd never read the book.

He seemed fine right through Thanksgiving. He told me he had just bought Christmas cards, and asked if it would be all right to send us one. I said sure and asked Martha to put him on our list.

We knew Victor wasn't going to be with his wife and daughter for Christmas. He wasn't well yet. We'd see him at the kitchen sink for hours on end washing his clothes and sheets, then twisting them clean with his powerful hands. When his chores were done he'd pace talking to himself, banging his fists on his arms. York had told him he was making good progress, and Martha and I agreed with him. So did Novotny.

But on the Saturday before Christmas, at a few minutes after 10:00 p.m., a figure walked up our driveway and approached the summer house. At first I thought it might be his wife pulling the laundry cart, her hair up in a bandana, but when the figure pushed through the door without knocking I could see in the light it was one of the homeless guys wearing the bandana and hauling all of his worldly goods behind him. I could also see he was drunk.

I watched as he pulled a bottle out of the cart and offered it to Victor. Victor returned it to the cart and took the man's arm and pulled him toward the door. The man pulled away yelling, then grabbed a bread knife from the table. Victor stayed calm. He pulled up a chair for him to sit in, but that enraged the man and he came at Victor. Victor took several steps back, gesturing to the man with both hands trying to calm him down. He backed all the way to the door of the woodshed, opened it, and grabbed the axe he used to split wood. Seeing the axe, the man raised the knife in his right hand but before he could bring it down Victor swung the axe and landed the blunt end on the upper part of his left arm. The man fell screaming.

I hurried over.

"Victor, I saw what happened. Just be sure you don't touch that knife."

"I think I broke his arm."

"Don't worry, I'm going to take our friend to the hospital. Grab his cart. I'm going to take it with me."

On the way to the hospital I made clear to my friend in the front seat that if he went to the police I would testify that I'd seen him try to kill Victor.

"Look what he did to me. All I wanted to do was sleep one night on his sofa, and he tried to kill me."

"I saw the whole thing. You tried to kill him. We have the knife to prove it."

"He told me I couldn't stay because I wasn't a vet."

"He's a Vet who doesn't drink, and you're a drunk who got kicked out of the Senior Center."

"How'd you know that?"

"It doesn't matter. Think about what I said. I'm doing you a favor."

I left him with his cart at the entrance to the emergency room, and drove by the police station, but Novotny wasn't there. I was surprised to see all the lights out in summer house when I returned. I knew he was gone, but went in to check. Everything was clean and in its place, except for the bread knife. He had left it on the floor, just as I asked him to.

I couldn't sleep that night. I wanted him to know I had his back, but wasn't sure I'd done the right thing. Martha said I did, because he had to stay out of trouble. If he didn't he might never get a job.

Martha whispered me awake at ten the next morning to tell me there was no smoke coming from the tin chimney of the summer house. She had hoped he might come back. I told her he wouldn't. He was a vet, and leaving was his way of telling us he had our back. That's why he left, and we never saw him or heard from him again.

STEPHANIE HART

AN UNEXPECTED KINDNESS

It was early summer and my body was healing. Cancer had overtaken my life in December of 2015. In a metallic voice over the telephone the doctor had given me the diagnosis. This led to two surgeries to remove uterine and ovarian tumors as well as six rounds of chemotherapy. I suffered nausea, deep lingering fatigue, the indignity of hair loss, and the menacing fear that the cancer would run unchecked throughout my body. I would look in the mirror at my pale face and bald head and feel as if I had lost a part of myself.

My long-time live-in partner, David, bolstered my spirits by making me simple meals and regaling me with his wit. My friend and neighbor, Ruth, encouraged me to walk with her in the long hallways of our building. As I gained physical strength, my will to fight for my health returned. I had an optimistic oncologist, who pronounced, "I never want to see this disease again." Chemo nurses reminded me of how much courage I had to endure this rough regime as they administered treatment. Finally, in late spring, I emerged, according to scans and blood tests, cancer free.

As if I had just broken out of a cocoon, I felt both stunned and grateful to have a new chance at life. Although my legs ached from nerve pain, an after effect of chemo, I could still walk. While I feared for my future health, I wanted to embrace the moment. I loved the feel of my feet on the pavement moving forward. Since it was such a pleasant evening in Chelsea, Ruth suggested that we have dinner out. This happened to be the evening of the annual Gay Pride Parade in Manhattan. Our neighborhood was alive with color and activity. Men and women wore headdresses and brightly colored outfits; they carried banners announcing their newly granted freedom to marry. They held up signs, showing solidarity with the lost lives in the Orlando night club. They carried rainbow flags. The spirit of liberation was manifest on every block as we navigated our way toward Sixth Avenue.

The restaurant we chose, like so many others in the area, was teeming with customers. People were talking, and laughing, and enjoying the festivities. There were placards on tables saying *Heritage* and *Pride*. Yellow balloons on long strings were tied to chairs and bobbed proudly in the air. A rainbow banner had been hung across a window, saying *We Support Gay Pride*.

Luckily Ruth and I were seated right away at a small strategically located booth near the door. Set apart from the crowd, we could survey the patrons.

Six young men occupied a rectangular table across from us. The young man directly opposite me had intense blue eyes, high cheekbones, and wavy brown hair; he looked at me and smiled. He seemed to recognize me, but his face was not at all familiar to me. Perhaps he was looking at my red and white scarf, designed to camouflage my bald head. Perhaps he was a student at the college where I taught, or someone I had met briefly in the neighborhood. He smiled more broadly, and I smiled back at him.

Our waitress, a young woman with curly dark hair looked harried but eager to do a good job. "We are so busy tonight," she explained. "Service may be slower than usual."

Ruth and I said we understood. We ordered ice tea, omelets, and fruit salad and then sat back and tried to acclimate ourselves to the electric atmosphere.

Ruth unfolded her napkin and placed it on her lap. "It's great to see you out and about," she said in her determined way. Her eyes were bright and purposeful. "We are going to be doing a lot more of this," she admonished with a laugh and the characteristic growl in her throat which meant she wasn't kidding. I smiled and nodded in assent.

The young man across from me smiled at me again. There was something comforting and serene about his face. I nodded and acknowledged his smile.

Always an alert and keen observer, Ruth asked, "Is that someone you know?" I shook my head. "I think he is just friendly and happens to be facing my way."

Our omelets came and Ruth and I savored the buttery eggs and melted cheese. "It's so good to be part of the human race again," I said. Ruth touched her napkin to her lips and agreed. "Things will get better and better," she promised. "Right," I said, wanting to believe her. Next came the fruit salad. Slices of melon, mango, and strawberries were cool and delicious. Three weeks away from chemo I was getting back my sense of taste.

A while later our waitress approached with surprising news. "Your bill has already been paid," she said.

With an edge of New York skepticism, Ruth asked, "By whom?" The waitress pointed discreetly at the young man who had been smiling at me. He was currently engaged in conversation with the blond man next to him. Ruth and I looked at each other in amazement.

"I'd like to find out what this is all about," she said.

"Sure," I agreed. I too wondered what was motivating him.

Taking assertive strides, she walked over to his table. While I couldn't hear what they were saying, I did intuit a pleasant interchange. I found myself both curious and excited about what was going on.

Ruth returned to our table with a sheepish look on her face. She said, "This young man just revived my faith in humanity."

Reassured about his intentions, I went over to him myself. "Thank you so much," I said. "Would you like us to leave the tip?" "It's been taken care of," the young man replied. He was looking directly at me. "I want you to know that I had cancer, and I got well, and you will too." Then he stood up and hugged me, and I hugged him back. I felt the sincerity of his words and the genuineness of his good will. There were tears in my eyes. I was aware of a warm glow in my chest as if a light had just been turned on inside of me. For the first time, I had the certainty that I would be well and thrive.

Back at our table, Ruth and I marveled at the young man's kindness. We found it extraordinary that a stranger would reach out and inspire someone who had a common experience with him. When the young man was leaving the restaurant, he stopped by our table, and he and I hugged again. "You're going to get well," he said.

On the way home I watched the early evening sun sparkle across Fourteenth Street. I was happier than I had been in a long time. I was glad to have Ruth beside me.

In the months that followed I thought about the transformative power of a simple act of kindness among strangers. I remembered the times I had made an effort to smile at patients in the chemo suite, especially the ones with circles under their eyes and somber expressions. They always smiled back. I wondered if I had helped improve their moods and suspected that I had. At a time when I was feeling frightened and vulnerable, the young man in the restaurant had given me hope and faith in the future. By connecting with me on common ground, he had lifted my spirits and touched my emotions. He forged a connection between us that normally would not be there, and in so doing, I believe, enriched both of our lives. We were now part of the same community of people who had suffered from and survived cancer, permanently linked through time.

NORITA DITTBERNER-JAX

UNIVERSAL DONOR

The pin prick hurts more than the needle
The nurse checks and re-checks
my answers and my name.

No one will get sick from my blood.
I have the best blood, prize blood,
O negative blood.

I started donating when my brother
needed pint after pint,
although he didn't get my blood.

I can donate every 56 days
and sometimes I think
I've given enough.

It's fine to be a universal donor
but it's not as if I'm helping
my brother, I'm just adding

to the walk-in refrigerator with units
of blood immaculately given
and sorted by type.

The room of the gurneys is quiet today,
the nurse relaxed as he swabs
my arm with iodine.

I start rolling the gauze back and forth
in my hand helping the flow
along; the nurse talks easily,

he tells me that my blood
will be used for newborns.
The movie projector in my mind

starts rolling: I've had three newborns, I saw
their spidery blue veins, I know
they were born too soon, even full-term,

too delicate for this world.
I watch the bag filling,
the bag of my blood

so like the shape
of the heart
pumping, pumping.

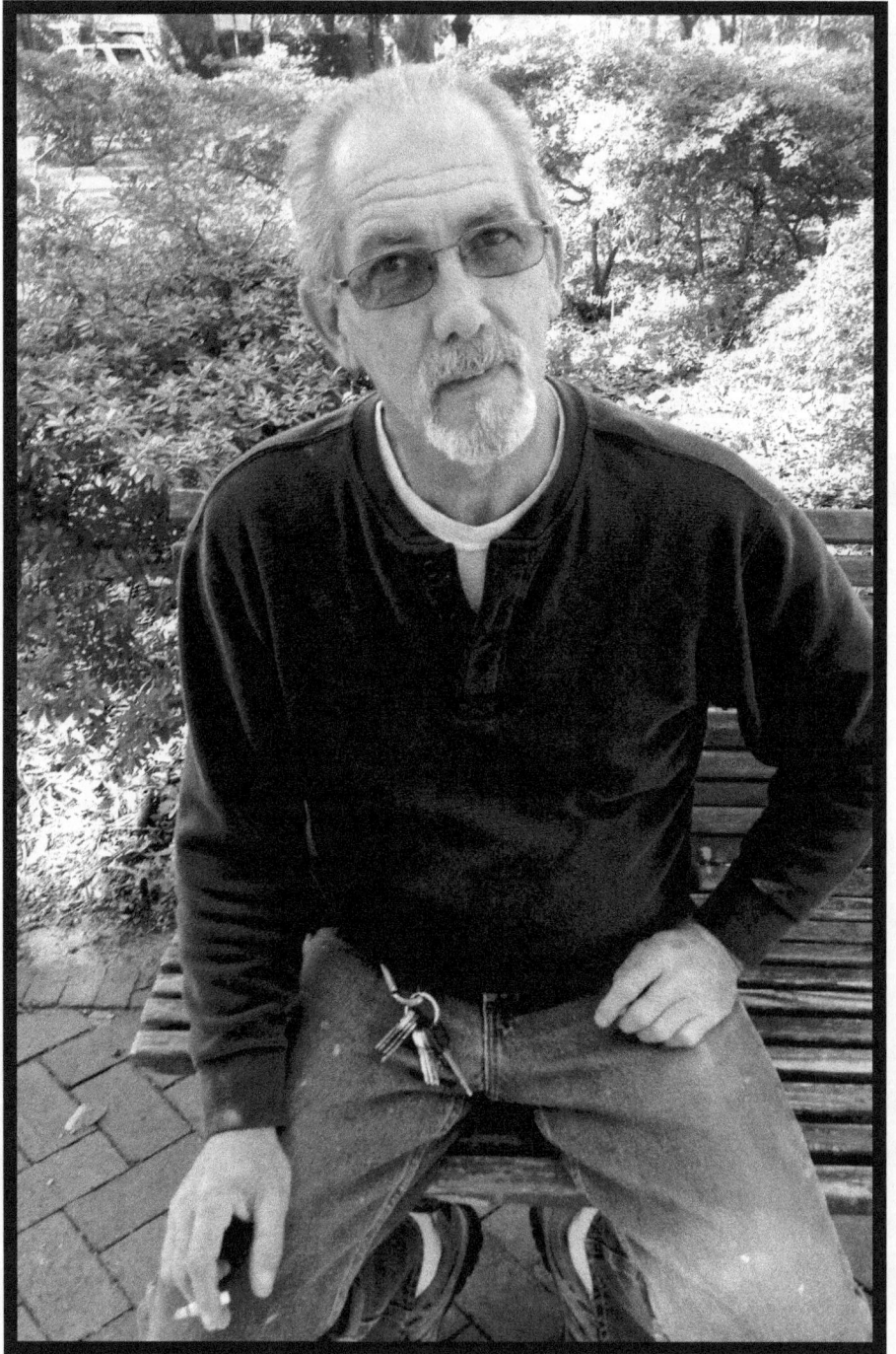

PATTI SEE

TO GIVE AWAY: ONE USED KIDNEY

I had that little orange organ donor sticker on my driver's license since I passed my test on the second try back in 1984. Twenty years later, my interest was piqued about living organ donation when I read a *New Yorker* article about millionaire philanthropist Zell Kravinsky who walked into a transplant center and offered his kidney. The staff thought he was crazy. Months later I saw an ad for a kidney in the local paper. My blood type didn't match that woman-seeking-kidney, but I was compelled to do more research. On MatchingDonors.com I was drawn to tag lines from ads seeking living kidney donors: "Please help me to live" . . . "Let's meet on this side of heaven" . . . "Life Desired—Age 23" . . . "Baby needs healthy kidney."

At that point I allowed myself only to read ads for patients with a blood type different than mine, ones to whom I couldn't donate even if I wanted. There were creative pleas—"Looking for Kidney Angel" . . . "Got kidney?" . . . "Wanted: 1 Used Kidney"—mixed with the polite—"Appreciative of Kidney" . . . "I'm in need of a kidney, please." The desperate—"My family needs me"—and the universal —"Please help me."

Research shifted my central question from "Why should I donate?" to "How could I not?" I am extremely healthy, and statistics show I'll continue to be even with one kidney, since the other grows larger to compensate. My family history shows no risk of kidney disease—which affects both kidneys anyway—or even hypertension or diabetes, which might damage either kidney.

This was easy math for me: over 60,000 people are on the waiting list for a kidney in the U.S., and seventeen of them die each day. Healthy people can live normal lives with one kidney, and some research shows kidney donors actually live longer than the general population in part because they are more health-conscious before and after donation. In 2005 when I donated, there were fewer than 200 non-directed donors—also referred to as

"Good Samaritan," "anonymous," "altruistic," or "benevolent community" donors—since transplant centers began accepting them in 1999.

After the most thorough physical of my life and a 567-question psych exam (no, I don't hear voices or tease small animals) I became the thirty-third non-directed donor accepted into the University of Minnesota-Medical Center's world-renown transplant program. My kidney went to the next person on their waiting list, and I was told only the age and gender of my recipient: a fifty-year-old man from Minnesota, Wisconsin, or one of the Dakotas.

All medical costs are covered by the recipient. Laparoscopic surgery means a small incision just below the belly button, a two to three day hospital stay, and a short recovery time. All federal employees and state employees in some states can take up to six weeks of paid medical leave; other states offer tax incentives for donors. Since I teach at the University of Wisconsin-Eau Claire and was given a paid leave, my donation essentially cost me three days of my time so someone else can live.

A few weeks before my surgery, when I started to tell friends and colleagues about my plans, I most often received the following reactions. 1) "Well, that's sure nice of you!" In Wisconsin, this is our standard response to just about anything—dropping off a casserole or giving away an organ. 2) "Well, I could never do that." Certainly my donation doesn't mean I check out everyone I know and expect the healthiest looking ones to give up one of their kidneys.

Fellow donor Father Patrick Sullivan says, "Deliver a box of antibiotics to Baghdad and you will save more lives than by donating a kidney. Discover a vaccine for Malaria and you will save more lives than all the transplants in the world. But organ donation is a work of mercy."

Days before surgery I told my son about my donation as we were driving to the video store on a Friday night. We sat side by side in the front seat, both of us looking straight ahead. I pitched the surgery as safe and routine as having my appendix out.

"Okay," Alex said. At fourteen—the summer before high school—his mom's experiences weren't quite on his screen. Though later he asked, "What happens if you don't donate a kidney to this guy?"

"He keeps waiting for one or he dies."

"Oh," he said.

My decision to donate was based on science and ethics, both of which were challenged by a little voice that frightened me with what if's throughout my six month screening process: *What if your remaining kidney gets damaged? What if someone you love needs a B positive kidney? What if the recipient doesn't care for your organ?*

Research helped me make a rational decision, but it really came down to a spiritual choice. Could I make this leap of faith? Put my life in the hands of a transplant team, trust that the risk of losing my remaining kidney was minimal, hope the recipient would commit himself to a healthy lifestyle? Or—most troubling—believe I was making the right choice, one I wouldn't regret? Eventually, after much prayer and meditation, my fearful what if's disappeared.

My surgery went smoothly, and I had very little pain afterward. Two days out of the hospital, I was off of pain medication. Eight days post-op I was back to an exercise routine, minus the stomach crunches. Except for my incisions and much needed afternoon naps, I felt as good as before. Twelve days after surgery I told my parents and my siblings what I'd done.

I've always been blessed; my donation was a way of sharing that good luck, good life, and good health with another. What I've received in return may not be as tangible as a new organ, but it is just as life-changing. Preparing for kidney donation made me revisit some significant questions—*How will you make your life extraordinary? What is your rent for being in the world? Where will you spend your time?*—and it renewed my commitment to a purposeful life.

I used to think of my kidney's new owner every day; I used to celebrate him on the anniversary of my donation each July. It's been over a decade now. The two of us are still unknown to each other though we are forever linked by something so small it would fit in the palm of his hand.

DOROTHY OLIVER PIROVANO

THERE WHEN HIS BODY FAILS HIM

Larry falls.

When people ask how many times a week or month he falls and he says anywhere from one to three times a day, they ask again, thinking he misheard the question. He is extremely lucky he hasn't broken anything and the warnings that *someday* a fall will land him in a wheelchair have yet to come true.

Parkinson's disease—nineteen years' worth—is what's tipping him over, but he is among the fortunate whose disease is progressing slowly. He seldom has an obvious tremor, although his left foot thumps uncontrollably at times. Only in the last few years has he suffered significant change, going from hiking trails to using a cane, to two canes to a three- and now four-wheeled walker.

There always seems to be help around when his body fails him. If it's just Larry and me, we size up the situation and see which armpit I should be circling to help hoist him up. A physical therapist taught us a few tricks: for him, rolling over, crawling to something he can grab onto, digging his toes into the ground to gain leverage, using that arm strength. For me, steady his walker so it can be something for him to grab, take hold of his belt, bend with my knees, don't hurry.

The prospect of the next fall is haunting. It has happened in the middle of a busy intersection, on downtown sidewalks, in restaurants and parking lots, in and out of elevators, in every room in our house—the venues are too numerous to mention but are recorded in a notebook he keeps in the section called Falls.

People kindly rush to help, especially young ones. As he went down in front of his barbershop the other day, two young women ran up to lift this man who weighed more than the two of them together. They took one side, I took the other and we popped him upright. Ponytail bobbing, one showed him a tiny cut on her palm and reassuringly told him how she just fell and knows just how embarrassing it is. "You remind me of our granddaughter," he said and she gave his arm a little hug.

If he's within sight of a police officer, help comes rushing over. They always call him sir. They always ask if he is hurt. They always linger as he walks away and watch him as he continues down a street. Sometimes they'll shadow him for a while as though they need to go exactly where he is going.

We got our wires crossed when I was to pick him up from an appointment and after not being able to reach me, he decided to take a bus home. When he answered my frantic call we agreed he'd get off the bus at a specific intersection and stay put until I arrived. I was on the wrong side of the street when we caught up with each other so he grabbed his walker and hustled to cross with the light. Hustling is never a good idea. Down he went as the light changed and cars started moving toward him. At my own version of lightning speed, I ran to put myself between him and the cars but was beaten out by a well-dressed man who must have seen the drama unfolding and was instantly at his side, one hand out to stop traffic, the other under Larry's arm. Thank you just doesn't suffice.

I sing in a community choir and we performed the national anthem at a professional women's basketball game, our first performance in front of a crowd of thousands. Larry came with me and we found seats before the game fairly close to the court—a spot where he could easily see us. The choir assembled, then walked out onto the court for our proud moment. While the color guard presented the flag, I scanned the crowd. No Larry. We burst into song and I peered around our director for another scan. No Larry. As we reached "the land of the free . . . " I could see a commotion by the players' bench across the court. "And the home of the brave . . . " we sang as I saw him, sprawled on the floor, cell phone camera in hand to capture my big moment, with a half dozen alarmed team assistants helping him up. I took off when the applause stopped, reaching him as the team doctor was assuring herself that he was not injured, and being assured by him that he thought he got the shot before he hit the floor.

Help is not universal and there is no one type that avoids him as he stumbles and falls. It is unusual enough that we talk about the instances—the man who hustled around him as he was losing control, the woman who kept looking backwards as she walked away, the few who stop, stare and move on. Sometimes he literally springs up with no assistance and a particularly kind person will not only ask if he is okay but will stay nearby for a while to make sure.

We spent our thirty-ninth wedding anniversary walking around the zoo, one of our favorite destinations, and decided to walk a few more blocks to a hotel that boasts the best open-air rooftop bar and grill in the city. The walking caught up with him and we were glad we brought the four-wheeled walker that had a seat. It's a relief to be able to sit wherever and whenever you need, even if it is just for a minute. One of the cautions with this walker is that it is not to be used as a wheelchair. If someone is sitting in it, they have to face backwards as it is being pushed and we've been warned by others with first-hand experience that it can flip over.

Anxious to get to the rooftop views, he centered himself on the seat, lifted his feet and I pushed him forward, very carefully. It was working quite well right up to hitting a small pothole in the pavement that caught a wheel, which sank down into it while the rest of the walker tilted and then crashed over backwards. Trying to stop its descent, I held on and went over too, landing on top of him, face to face, legs tangled, arms cushioned by his big shoulders rather than hitting the sidewalk.

To our rescue—a young, long and lean jogger, a third our age, who whipped his ear buds out and assured us he would get us out of this tangle. "Let's get you up first," he said to me, a logical first act as I was on top trying to figure out how I could extricate my leg from between Larry's and roll off around the handlebar that was holding me firmly in place. Sufficient tugging and pulling were working and more help arrived to hold down the walker and begin to address Larry's predicament when this wonderful husband of mine said, in all seriousness, "Gee, honey, I thought you were going to try and make this look like an accident." No one could stop laughing—except of course, stone-faced Larry who manages to make life more livable with his dry sense of humor and a tenacity that astonishes.

Once upon a time, he and I were so busy keeping up with the day-to-day of our lives we didn't think much about the future, beyond dreaming of trips we might be able to take when the kids were on their own. That would be the idyllic time for two people who combined their five pre-teen kids into one family on their wedding day, who both worked and juggled schedules that included volunteering, homework oversight and cheering for our budding athletes at their games. We had never lived as just the two of us.

Our nest finally emptied when the youngest went from grad school to a full-time job ninety minutes away. A year later we sold our suburban house and moved to a new life downtown, starting up an urban real estate practice for him and eliminating the commute from my life.

The idyll had begun and true to its definition, threatened to stop abruptly seven months later when we sat in a doctor's office and the words *Parkinson's disease* entered our lives. At home, we sat on the bed and cried and didn't tell anyone, even our kids, until we could get a handle on our future. We met with a specialist who reassured us he would never be sitting in a wheelchair in a nursing home drooling and dying from this disease. Medicine had advanced too far for that specter to come true, she said. Go live your lives and I'll see you every three months forever after.

So we lived and worked and traveled and appreciated what we had. We danced badly at our children's weddings and welcomed grandchildren. We retired, signed up for classes at the nearby university, started writing and volunteered as tutors, reading with kindergarteners. We saw the doctors, added pill after pill, and worked hard to deny the unsteadiness, diminished handwriting, sudden weakness and other signs that Parkinson's was intruding on and changing our lives.

It has and it will, but as long as we are able, we will maintain a united front. It will be made easier knowing we are surrounded by people who take time to show you they care. They emerge from out of nowhere in a moment. We are forever grateful.

JOEL WACHMAN

THIS IS GETTING OLD

Near the end, my mother checked herself into the emergency room as often as some people go to the gym. There was nothing dramatically wrong with her, and she needed a lab-coated medical professional to tell her so. The first few times we all responded as if it were an actual emergency. My brother Josh left the kids at the skating rink and drove the minivan as if it were a getaway car. I squirmed out of meetings, deflecting my colleagues' offers of help. On her third visit in as many weeks, I put down the phone, took a deep breath, and finished my sandwich. It was Josh who texted the news. He was changing planes in Charlotte and wouldn't be in Boston until after dark, so it was up to me to look after Mom. I think "Charlotte" was his way of saying he was tired of canceling the rest of his day to get her back to the assisted living complex where she belonged.

Poor Josh was always the first one to get bad news. When our father was taken to the hospital in respiratory arrest two years earlier, I was visiting my in-laws in Ottawa. His text message, "Dad admitted. They're doing some tests." was distressing enough. As the situation worsened the text messages became less intelligible. They arrived garbled, comically auto-corrected, typed under stress and sent un-edited. The one where he misspelled "respirator" was a real hoot. Eventually the text messages stopped and he started to call. The last call came at 5:00 a.m. I didn't need to hear what he said, but I answered anyway because I knew he needed to say it.

Some people might think it was heartless for me to stop for coffee on the way to see my mother, but those people don't have a parent who thinks a jaunt to the emergency room is a diverting way to spend a Thursday afternoon. What was heartless was the fact that I didn't bring any for her. I stopped bringing her coffee when she began to forget whether she drank decaf. Last time I gave her the one with the little orange plug in the cap and she challenged me. "Is this decaf? Why did you bring me decaf?" It was because the time before that when I had brought her regular coffee and she had remarked, "Thank you dear, but I can't have caffeine."

It was difficult to tell what she was thinking as I stood awkwardly between the hospital bed and the heart rate monitor, surrounded by drab curtains that hid her from her neighbors the way a cookie jar hides a cookie. I bent down and gave her a kiss, breathing in her perfume, the same she had worn since I was six. Her signature odor. She was dressed to go out. A bright blue blouse, a ceramic brooch in the shape of a Scottie dog. Despite the wires and tubes connecting her to the EKG and saline drip, her appearance was familiar and comforting. Until she spoke.

"The doctor. I mean the . . . girl. The girl doctor who—she isn't really a doctor—anyway, she has a dog like the one I have on my sweater. She said I have the same one. I said to her, 'you show me mine and I'll show you mine.'" She interrupted herself, frustrated. "I'm getting all confused. What were we talking about?" We were supposed to be talking about her emergency room habit, but I didn't have the heart to confront her.

Wordplay had come easily to my father and brothers. In my childhood, our conversations often devolved into contests to see who could make the most clever pun or oblique literary reference. While my father acquired English as a second language, it was my mother who spoke like a recent immigrant from Albania. Her sentences were Frankenstein monsters of syntax, sewn together from clichés and remnants of advertising slogans. We learned to infer her meaning. We had to. She was the one who knew where the Pop-Tarts were hidden. Things had become worse lately. Her mind would wander in the middle of a sentence. She would start off strong, like, "There's something I want to tell you." A few words later she would get lost in the weeds, mixing names and metaphors.

The ER nurse showed up to check my mother's levels, speaking with the no-nonsense sincerity of someone who grew up in Southie and went into the healthcare biz with her girlfriends from the neighborhood. "I was telling your mom that I have a terrier that looks just like her pin."

"Oh, a real dog," I said out loud to nobody in particular. The nurse gave me a puzzled look.

"She has a little clot in the back of her knee, but some aspirin every day should help break it up." As she spoke she slipped her hand under the hospital gown and lifted a leg gently, with a gesture that, in any other context, should have been preceded by dinner and drinks. The leg came out pale and splotchy as a hunk of raw pork, and as lifeless, since my mother had given up trying to move it on her own.

"Are you taking her home or would you like me to call a chair car?"

"Do you mind going in the chair car, Ma? I took the bus."

"Of course, doll," she replied. "I don't mind."

The chair car was a miraculous contraption that would ferry my mother back to the assisted living facility strapped safely into a wheelchair so I could be back at my desk by lunch time. I wheeled her to the exit and gave her a kiss goodbye. The man who operated the service, be-turbaned and cheerful, kept up a stream of palliative chatter while he hoisted her into the back of the van and locked her into place. "We are going to have a fine time. You're my only customer right now, so we'll get you directly home. Tell me what kind of music you like. I have an iPod with a hundred playlists."

Before the sliding door closed she waved and smiled, "You were very good to come down and rescue me. Go and be with your family. I'll be okay. I have always relied on a little help from my friends."

Without my father around to be demanding and judgmental, my mother's life had no purpose. Her grasp on reality had become fragile as her physical condition worsened. With the few hours left to her day after dressing herself or commuting to pick up the mail, she sat at her kitchen table scrawling illegible notes on scraps of paper, making phone calls to distant relatives and falling asleep in the chair. She had been fighting Parkinson's disease and arthritis for years and used a cane. At first the cane made her look dignified, even jaunty. Recently she turned it in for a walker, which completed her transformation into an old person. The little ribbons and stickers affixed to the rubberized handles did nothing to cheer it up. A cane can be a stylish accessory, a statement of devil-may-care insouciance. A walker is a prosthesis, and no amount of Hello Kitty can change that.

Once my mother lost the ability to putter on her own, she hired an aid to do the puttering for her. She was there in the mornings and evenings, composing and cleaning up breakfast, moving the laundry from one place to another, even answering the phone when it was too far across the room for my mother to reach. I met this woman for the first time on a Friday night. My wife and I brought a dinner of roasted chicken, carrot *tsimmes*, and potato kugel. This was not nostalgia for the Sabbath dinners of my childhood. I simply wanted to protect my family from the dry portions of paper-flavored Soma that passed for food in the communal dining room.

When we arrived the aid was seated on the sofa, knitting in the corner where my father used to do his crosswords. In lieu of an introduction, my mother issued a dismissal.

Me: Hi Mom. Who is your guest?

Mom: That is my helper, Mulatto. She's from Africa.

Me: Her name can't be Mulatto.

Mom: They pronounce it differently there.

Me: Will she be eating with us or will she just sit in the corner like that all evening?

Mom: She doesn't eat food.

In the middle of the meal, while my mother cooed over my teenager, my wife set a plate on the coffee table.

"She said you weren't going to eat, but I'll bet it has been a long day."

The woman nodded gratefully. "Actually, I am hungry. Thank you. You know, she's a very sweet person. I have gotten to know her over the past week. She loves her sons. Her grandchildren. Doesn't stop talking about them. And she's funny. You know? Really funny. We laugh together."

A forty-ish black nurse from Cameroon and an eighty-year old Jewish widow from Queens. To me that sounded like the set-up for a joke, not the punchline. I assumed she was just being polite. Besides, what kind of person chooses a career that involves doing menial tasks for strangers twice her age? Maybe the job is like caring for children (which I can do for about eight minutes before losing patience), the common denominators being that the very old and the very young tend to be emotionally volatile and occasionally incontinent. At least children are cute and, anyway, they look up to you. And, in general, they become better with age. Caring for an old person suffering irreversible decline is not my idea of fun. Yet the stranger on the sofa, taking a break from being my mother's crutch, was able to find satisfaction and humor in it. If I am too squeamish to help my mother with her pressure stockings, does that mean there is a hole where my heart should be?

I've decided the thing that made me cranky about my parents aging was their loss of independence. In their mid-seventies my parents moved from their four bedroom house in the suburbs to a two bedroom unit on the other side of the same suburb because the upkeep on the house was too exhausting. It's not as if they did much of it themselves any more. They had already delegated the physically intensive chores. They had a yard guy, a plow guy, a guy to install the air conditioners in the windows. They had a house cleaner and a laundry service. It was like they were running a small Yorkshire estate. By the time they moved, it had been a year since my father had taken out his own trash. He continued doing small repairs, though. He could fix anything with epoxy or duct tape. He just couldn't bear to raise a sweat.

I think they imagined life at the assisted living facility was going to be like being on a cruise, except they'd get a stateroom with a window and there was only one way off. Once aboard, though, they discovered that the kind of pampering they were hoping for was reserved for the incapacitated and infirm. They earned that status eventually, but not the way any of us expected.

The transition became complete when they sold the car. The 1990's era Honda was their connection to life off campus. It was a cheap and squishy ride as compared to the classic Saab my father had traded in when he no longer had the attention span to drive a standard. They only used it for three reasons: to get across the highway to the supermarket, to drive around my block eighteen times hoping to park in front a house that looked like it was owned by white people, and to help in their quest to visit every doctor's office within twenty miles of Boston.

When my father stopped driving, my mother was stranded too. I do not recall ever seeing her behind the wheel, although I assume she must have driven at some point. Come to think of it, I spent a lot of time on my bicycle when I was a child. They could have taken advantage of the in-house car service, or a network of volunteer drivers, or the fleet of public buses that passed by their facility on an hourly basis. My father wouldn't hear of it. Unaccustomed to sitting in the passenger seat, he became so irascible and controlling any rational volunteer would be tempted to let him off at the nearest intersection. Only a family member would possess the necessary restraint. As soon as my parents gave up driving Josh and I were on call. The phone would ring and it would be my mother.

"Doll, I have an appointment—it's down near the water, you know the place, the doctor who looks like your cousin what's his name—anyway, it's at two o'clock. Can you drive me?"

This being at one-thirty.

"Can you ask your neighbor, Mrs. Belcher, if she can take you?"

"I wouldn't want to bother her. She's got a grandchild with alopecia."

These calls were so frequent and unpredictable I think she was using them as an excuse to spend some more time with me. Quality time. In traffic. It could be worse. Many old people who don't have family nearby take the bus. They have to get up at dawn to get to a bus stop by eight, then wait for ages. It can take all day to run a single errand that many of us could do on the way to the gym.

This is about the time my mother began her regular visits to the emergency room. When the pain her leg got bad she was convinced that a spring or a rubber band had snapped and that if only someone could reach inside and reset the mechanism the pain would go away and she would take up her top hat and cane again. She didn't call me or Josh for these jaunts. She ordered an ambulance.

Two weeks after the absurd conversation about Scottie dogs I got another call. My brother was exasperated.

"Something about the pin inside her leg coming out and rattling around," he said.

"She doesn't have a pin in her leg, right?"

"What do you think? Can you go be with her? I've been there since seven and have to take the kids to a bar mitzvah."

This time, she was sitting in the examining cubby with her pocketbook and a manila folder on her lap. There were forms to be signed, a wheelchair to be requisitioned. This being an inner-city hospital, the car had been parked by a valet service and had to be recovered. It took nearly two hours to relocate ourselves from the ER to the street, a mere fifty yards away.

"This is getting old, Ma," I gently chided as we waited for the car.

"I know, doll. Being old is terrible. But it's better than the alternative."

Back at her home, men and women, residents and staff, approached the chair and crouched slightly to touch her as if receiving a blessing. Every one of them expressed sincere concern for her health and profound relief at seeing her upright and fully operative. "How are you, Barbara? Will you be in the dining room tonight? We'll reserve a table." "So happy to see you're back, dear. When you feel up to it Mrs. Abramowitz wants to have the four of us to her apartment for tea."

My mother returned this adoration with considerate and surprisingly grammatical replies, as if she were calling on a supply of supportive phrases. She may have lost her ability to walk and dress herself. Her cognitive capacity was fading as quickly as Charlie Gordon's in *Flowers for Algernon*. But she had the retained her emotional intelligence, and was still able to turn those high beams on anyone who approached her, making them feel loved and important.

Lydia, a diminutive staff nurse whom my mother called "my young friend from an island," slid through the crowd and placed her hand on my mother's shoulder. It was so compact it looked like something you'd put on a toasted bun.

"How are you, my dear," she asked.

"I'm alright," my mother replied. "I think it's time for the—my—that thing you do. I hope I'm not too little too late."

"Not at all," she replied, her little handcake patting my mother's arm. "Come on."

She eased herself between me and the handlebars of the wheelchair and before I could do anything about it, they were rolling toward a vestibule in the hallway. I tried to follow, but the woman put her head in the door, saying to my chest, "We'll be out in a minute," and closed the door firmly. This left me on the wrong side of whatever was going on in there. It's not that I actually harbored a desire to take my mother's blood or clip her toenails. It's just that, having spent most of the afternoon with her, I felt a strong sense of propriety. It was my responsibility to care for her, not some hourly health worker, regardless of how sweet and tiny.

While I stood in the hallway thinking about going for a jog just to make sure my own legs still worked, one of the residents approached me. A once-famous professor from Harvard who had retreated to the quiet surroundings of this suburban rest home to write books. Whenever my parents spotted him in the dining hall they would elbow me, whispering and pointing as if he was an exotic bird. With a crooked smile, one eyebrow raised, he extended his hand. I took it, and he held on gently while he spoke.

"It is okay that you didn't go in with her, you know. She doesn't want you to take care of her that way. It's not what any of us want from our children. Just be with her. That's enough."

Later, as my mother and I sat waiting for her dinner companions, I observed the residents shuffle into the lounge. Some arrived in pairs, some on their own. They gathered in cliques arranged by demeanor, dress, and level of physical fitness. This was cocktail hour in purgatory. Only here, purgatory had the social dynamic of a high school cafeteria, with the same social divisions, insecurities and personal dramas. The ex-jocks and beautiful people were surrounded by admiring laughter and no small amount of flirting. The eternally nerdy were still shunned. Young and healthy staff stood along one wall with their arms crossed, vigilant lesser deities, watching for a moment when they would reach out to their assigned mortals to administer a restorative touch. Looking more closely I could see the pride in their eyes, an almost parental sense of ownership. I wound your key, their expression said, and I will be there again when your spring has gone loose and needs winding again.

When I am lying on my final fainting sofa, in a place, I hope, where I can see the mountains and buy an authentic *pain au chocolat*, I imagine seeing credits roll. The stars will be first: parents played by Wallace Shawn and Carol Kane, reprising their roles as Vizzini and Valerie from *The Princess Bride*. Emma Thompson as The Wife. And introducing Troye Sivan as the Sullen Child. Next the text changes to small type, listing crew members with undecipherable titles: phlebotomist, psychiatrist, psychiatric social worker, kinesiologist—the unheralded many who attended to me so sympathetically as my body began to fail. I will thank them, too, as they will be there to hold my body together so my mind and heart can find peace.

As we age we become more and more like our true selves. If we don't eat ourselves to death, aren't demolished in a cycling accident or murdered by cancer, for those of us who live long enough to simply wear out, this is the way it goes. As we become less physically adept we tend to become more emotionally honest. As my father got older his internal systems failed one by one until, finally, he was unable to leave his Barcalounger. That was fine with him. He had finally given up pretending he wanted to see anyone.

My mother's persistent quality was her empathy, her tendency to treat everyone with honor and grace. The last time I saw her she was sitting next to the entrance to the dining room, negotiating for a larger table as grown men and women crowded around her, hungry for her attention. Now I can see her daffiness as a charming quirk that could not hide the light inside her. While she appeared to need me less than ever, I realize that I had been misreading the line between her decency with her helpers and housemates, and our sincere relationship based on love and history and family. Even at the end—perhaps especially so—my mother exhibited qualities that I never acquired: compassion, patience, the belief in the value of helping others. It is a good thing she was surrounded by people who were just like her.

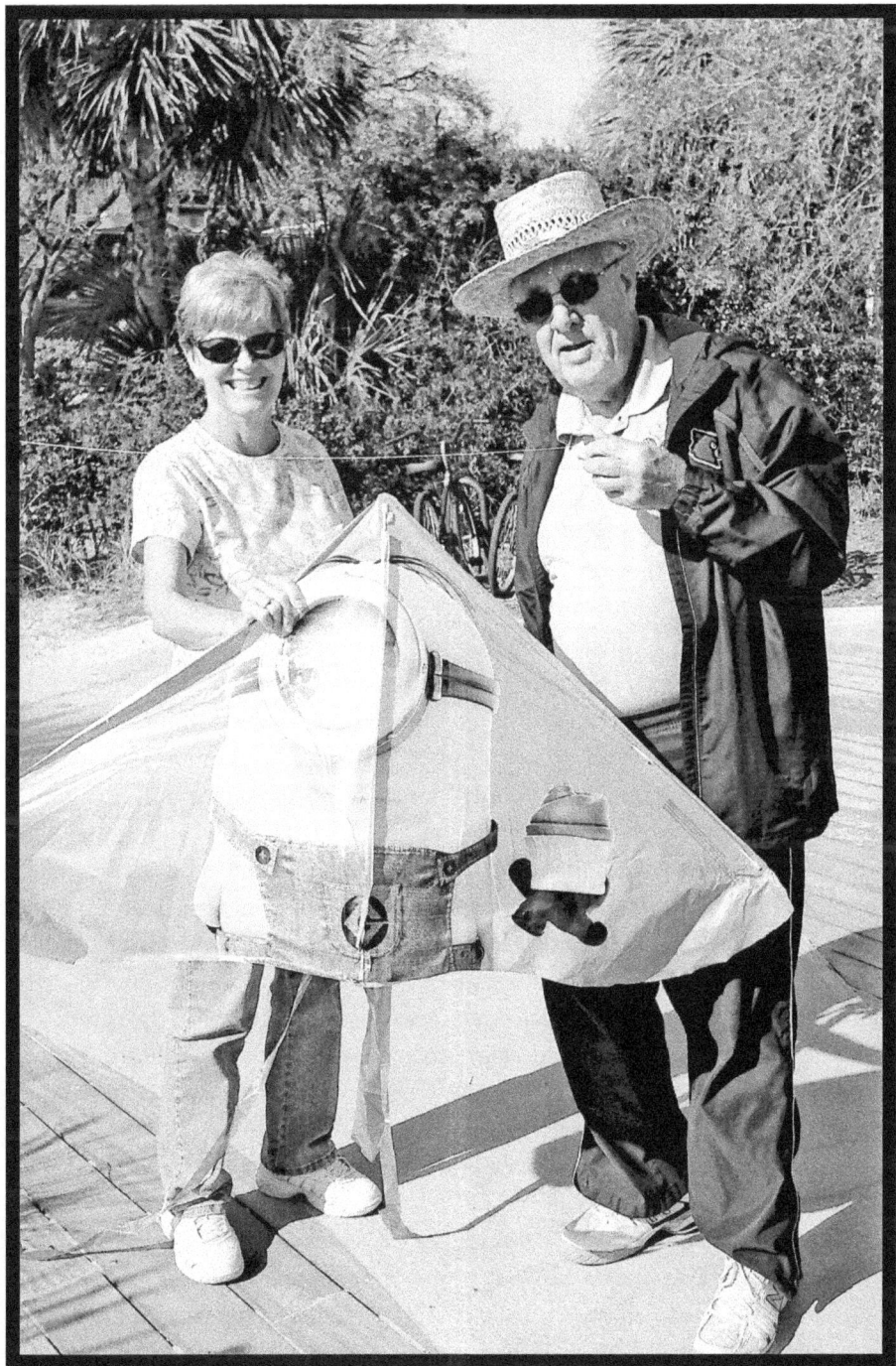

KEN STALEY

MISSING

The Aunties were sisters separated by less than two years and always a staple in my life. I can't remember a day in childhood that I didn't see them. I never really thought about why they were living together, or what happened to their husbands. I don't recall anyone ever mentioning the uncles. From late summer until after Halloween when cold weather stepped in, the two sisters picked us up from the house and walked us down to Uncle Ed's store to wait for the school bus. In my mind, they were, and still are, sitting in their cedar rocking chairs just to the left of a dust encrusted screen door.

Just fifty feet up the lane from a really bad curve in old Highway 41 squatted KENDALL GROCERY, its clapboard a blistering white-wash and its tin roof streaked with rust. The place pleaded for attention that never came, at least to the exterior. Kendall Grocery Store was not only the best place in the Hollow for a school bus stop, but a sort of social and economic hub for the region. To us, though, it's always been just Uncle Ed's Store.

In the late summer evenings and early spring mornings, the two Aunties perched outside on the entry porch on old, cedar rocking chairs. As they got older, shawls, old comforters and seat cushions joined them, but in my memory, every school day began with a walk to Uncle Ed's with the Aunties. Uncle Ed called them his cigar store Indians, but never in their hearing. He wasn't far wrong as Auntie Mabel always claimed we had Cherokee blood in our past.

Auntie Ruth may have been a bit older, but it was the same, for all that. She braided her hair with colorful bits of cloth, the tresses hanging almost to her lap. Ruth went grey very slowly.

"See, it's kids that do it to ya," she said one September afternoon when it was too hot to stay inside the store. She let a handful of her tresses fall across her face like a theater curtain. Cross-eyed, she singled out the grey strands. "I paint them fresh every morning just to remind me."

"Really?"

Dakota, who still believed in Santa and the Easter Bunny those days, crawled into her lap to examine those hairs closer.

"This'n here is Eddie Earl," she said. "This'n here is my first grey hair. My son, Elbert, give it to me when I was still babyin'. He gimme lots and I still get a new one now and then from El."

"Which one is mine?" Dakota asked seriously. That got him hugged and brought a great peal of laughter from the Aunties. Auntie Ruth little girl's laugh tinkled like a high giggle, and she tried to hide the sound behind her hand whenever it erupted. Auntie Mabel's classic, witch-like cackle was the butt of many jokes from the gathering of old salts around the wood stove inside.

"You two tryin to lay eggs again?" Uncle Ed often called from inside the store when he heard her laugh.

"He's the one," Auntie Mabel said of Uncle Ed. "I turned grey all at once and it's all his fault!"

Auntie Mabel once had lovely chestnut hair. Now she wore it in a tight bun pulled severely away from her face. Now, instead of rich brown streaked with grey, she closed in on silver streaked with lighter brown.

"Time was I had a friend who chased all the grey away," Mabel explained to Dakota, who was still examining Ruth's hair closely.

"Really? Where did she go then?" He asked without looking up.

They laughed again but Mabel wasn't quite ready to give it up just yet.

"Why her name was Miss Clairol," Mabel told him. "She lived in a bottle."

"Oh she didn' neither," Dakota lisped with his own bashful smile. He was still missing his two front teeth at the time.

"I swain, right hand afore God," Mabel lifted her left hand. "She lived in a bottle and used to come out about four times a year just to make your Auntie Mabel look pretty."

She cocked her chin to one side and up, batted her eyes at him, and put her hand behind her head, striking a 'glamour pose'.

"Did the bottle break then?" Dakota asked, now taken in.

Mostly, the Aunties taught us about life, in their own fashion. They sat in those chairs, day in and day out, and inspected every visitor to Uncle Ed's store without comment—well, mostly without comment.

"That's Daisy Richardson," Mabel hissed to Ruth one spring afternoon as a large woman went in to do her shopping.

"No!" Ruth said and turned for another look, but the dust that caked the screen door didn't allow much more than a peek at her silhouette. "What happened to *her*?"

"Kids," Mabel leaned back, assuming an air of deeper insight, "and that no account man she shacked up with so long. She done had eight by him before he disappeared. You remember. 'Twas in all the papers for awhile, him just up and missin' like that. Not a word, not a hint. There's them that say she did him in, but I don' believe it none. She warn't big enough to swat a fly and he was huge."

"But she got so big," Ruth said. "I 'member her in high school as this little bird of a thing."

"Still would be, too, I'm guessin'," Mabel said. "But she got the women's problems and swelled up like a balloon. I heard tell she been seein' that doctor up to town, but don't look like he's helped much. She shoulda stuck with Aunt Fenny."

Another day, another visitor; a man this time, with a funny lurch and almost a hesitation in his walk. He came to the door, tried to peer through the dirty screen and opened it cautiously, like someone was about to scold him for just being there.

"Rory the simple," Ruth said after he stepped across the threshold and closed the screen gently, without letting it slam. "He rode the other bus when I was in school. Nice enough boy but jumped outta his skin at any loud sound."

"What's wrong with him? Is he a retard?" Dakota asked.

"Hold your piece!" Ruth scolded and reached out to flick his ear. Dakota yipped loudly. "God done scrambled his brains good when he was born. Ain't no call for you to be remindin him he ain't all there. He knows that already."

It was a mild October, I remember. An Indian summer crept up the hollow. Dakota disappeared inside that day and I sat on a free spot on the rail, fanning myself, trying to get cool. That was the day the Aunties became all too human. Auntie Ruth reached into her pocket for the small linen bag that held her fixins. Until that day, I never paid her no mind at all, it was so routine, such a normal part of her. Every day as she walked us to school, first thing she'd do, right after fetching coffee, was bring out her fixins and roll a cigarette for her and Mable.

She carefully laid two thin papers on her lap, took her pouch and lightly sprinkled in the fillings, then deftly rolled the whole thing, slipping it into her mouth to seal the paper as a last move. Time was, she let Dakota or I light her smokes. I guess I was just too old for that treat now. I must have been a teenager by then, or very close, because that day, what had always been Auntie Ruth's fixins, took on a whole new meaning. I always believed what Auntie Ruth and Mabel said; they always rolled their own smokes because "the cost of store boughts is too dear." That they could get them cheap from Uncle Ed never entered my mind.

Truth was, Auntie Ruth's 'home grown' consisted of half tobacco and half home grown sinsemilla. Shock at that discovery must have registered on my face. Ruth and Mabel laughed almost as loud as I'd ever heard them.

"How the mighty slip from their pedestals, eh Mabel?" Ruth said as she gasped for air, their first puff blue cloud filling the covered porch. "Would you like some, Janey Sue?"

"I would not!"

I'd heard the horror stories. I'd seen the burned out husks at my school, generally boys from bad families, whose lives already threatened to waste away as they blasted their minds with home grown day after day. A few years passed, and a child or two came, before the Aunties recipe of morning coffee and smoke tempted me. I never looked back.

About the time of my highest indignation, Dakota brought out our Dr. Peppers, still dripping water from Uncle Ed's chest cooler and filled with peanuts. As he settled on a chopping block, Ruth farted. It was a gentle thing and *should* have passed without notice—only slight embarrassment—but Dakota was there and still thrilled with bodily functions, the way young boys can be. With a snort, Dr. Pepper squirted from his nose.

"You farted!" he called when his coughing spell broke and he could speak again.

"Why Dakota Edward James, I never," Ruth exclaimed indignantly. "If you please, sir, women *do* not fart."

"You did so," Dakota said. "I heard you."

"That warn't no fart," Mabel said.

"Was too!" Dakota said, a bit miffed at being called out.

"No it warn't," Mabel said. "That couldn't have been a fart. Ruth didn' go no where or raise up at all. Now this is a fart."

With that, she leaned over and passed gas—loudly.

Dakota howled with laughter. Ruth blushed just a bit, then leaned over and tooted two or three times, only to be answered by Mabel's trombone one note. While I remember being terribly embarrassed, I also remember smiling. The whole thing was just too funny.

Our laughter brought Uncle Ed to the door this time, something he rarely did during business hours.

"She farted," Dakota said as he pointed at Ruth, "then *she* farted. They been havin a battle of the farts."

"Musical assholes, huh?" Uncle Ed snorted and returned to his circle of friends. Laughter from inside showed that he'd shared the news. My guess is those old boys inside did their best to match the Aunties, but they had a long, long way to go.

)( )( )(

Auntie Mabel went first, so slowly we hardly noticed for a few years. Ruth noticed.

"What's wrong with Mabel?" Uncle Ed demanded. "I swear she'd forget her head some days."

"She just missing sometimes," Ruth said one day with a smile as Mabel picked at the front of her flowered dress. "Seems like these missing streaks get longer and longer. She just sort of takes off in her mind someplace. Wish I knew where that was."

Eventually, they had to take Mabel in for a physical. The news was very grim, so grim that they couldn't tell me or Dakota—but I knew, in my heart, I knew.

"You just keep a special eye on Mabel when she's around," Uncle Ed said to both of us a few days later. "You make sure she don't go wandering off somewhere."

"Why would she leave?" Dakota asked.

"Never you mind. Your job is just to make sure she don't go alone."

Ruth followed close on. Sure enough, another trip out of the hollow, another grim diagnosis.

I was in high school by then and nearly at the top of my class. I'd done some research by then. My dear Aunties had early onset Alzheimer's. Worse, for all they did for me and mine, there wasn't a thing I could do for them— but be there, I guess. I had a long talk with Uncle Ed about it.

"I can make it up next year," I said as I offered to stop school and sit with the Aunties every day. "Really, Uncle Ed, I can go down to the junior college over in Macon. That'd bring me home every afternoon and I could watch them."

"No," Ed said flatly, and no argument I could muster changed his mind at all. He was firm enough about it, but, as was his way, very gentle. "Look, honey, they could be like this for years and years. The doctor don' know himself how long. You finish that high school and get your scholarship, you hear? We're all proud of you—them two old girls is almost as proud as if they was your Mamma. If you quit now, you're going to make a lot of people sad and angry. My sister's will be just fine as long as they remember where their chairs are out front."

Although Ruth started later, her deterioration came on much more rapidly. Within a year, whatever there was that made Ruth—Ruth, evaporated. Eventually, to keep Ruth steady and 'home', Mabel walked her to her chair every morning on a kiddie leash. When I sat with them, day after day, I would have to introduce myself every time. Ruth forgot overnight. Most days I read stories for them. Sometimes Ruth demanded the Bible, although she rarely, if ever, attended services that I recall. She did so love the *Psalms*.

Mabel slipped away quietly, slowly, but much further. Ruth seemed to have some deep seated understanding of where home and hearth was and stayed right close to Uncle Ed's store. Mabel always wanted to be somewhere else, somewhere pressing and urgent called her; places to visit demanded her attention and she'd make ups stories about living in places she'd heard about but never seen. One Saturday, when I caught her just as the roaming bug bit her, she had an old grass suitcase, filled with flowers and two jars of molasses, and had started up old Highway 41.

"Paris," she said when I finally caught her and asked where she was going. "Are you going on the train to Paris, too?"

"Why, yes, I am," I assured her as I took her arm. "Why don't we just sit in the waiting room they have here. It's ever so much nicer than standing out here in the rain."

Ruth was given to fits of crying, which usually brought tears from Mabel as well. According to Uncle Ed, Ruth cried over people that she'd never known, men she'd never met.

"Oh Cal, Cal," she wept bitterly one day from her bed. By then she was so far gone we had to keep her in her room most of the day. I sat with her whenever I could pry myself away from life. "Why did you go Cal? Where did you go? Why didn't you take me with you Cal?"

"Not that I know," Uncle Ed said that evening when he stopped by. "She dated lots of guys, true enough, but I don't recall a Cal."

It took three years—three very long years—before they were completely missing and unable to communicate at all. I just couldn't take that last ride down the hill to the home with them. I wanted to. Uncle Ed seemed to want me to go, but he understood, too. I think, if he'd had that choice, he'd have stayed behind as well. It was all too much, their having to leave. I just couldn't face taking them down the hill and leaving, knowing the only time they'd come back was in caskets for their own funeral.

Ed's decline followed shortly on, although he's not completely missing just yet. We've put him in a home now. How I wish I had time to sit with him as I did with the Aunties, but life presses on without relief and Ed needs more attention than I can give. I visit him several times a week. According to the nurses, he still gets up every morning at five and dresses for work, putting on the same starched white shirt and khaki pants he wore to work in his store every. He sits now, going over lists of items and produce he needs to order for the grocery. He's convinced that one of the visiting nurses is his produce supplier and makes sure she takes his list with her, which she does. She gives them all to me.

"You keep these, honey," she said one day. "You'll want to remember him and these will help a great deal. He's a kind, gentle man and deserves to be remembered like that."

Now he sits in a soft chair near the fireplace and has conversations with long gone friends, laughing at their stories only he can hear. Still in all, he's sprightly enough for someone in his eighties.

Scooter Davis and his brother, Big Al, now run Kendall Grocery. It's still standing, much as it always has, at that sweeping corner just off Highway 41. A small group of regulars, mostly friends of Scooter and Bobby Ray, gather around the old stove every day. The state re-paved and widened the shoulders of the old highway now and the school bus still stops at Uncle Ed's store— even Scooter and Big Al still call it that—how could it be any different? My kids meet Bobby Ray and Junie's kids to wait for the bus. Some days, Junie and I sit with coffee in those cedar rocking chairs and share one of the Aunties home-rolled specials.

"I sure do miss 'em," Scooter said one hot August as we waited for the first bus of the new school year. He and Big Al sat in the Aunties' chairs.

"They be missing, sure enough," Big Al said. "When you suppose they comin back?"

I had no answer for him. They weren't really missing, not truly. When things get too tense or too heavy, when life just seems too oppressive, one of us farts. Dakota and I still break into uncontrollable laughter when we're together. Or even when we're alone.

And it's their fault.

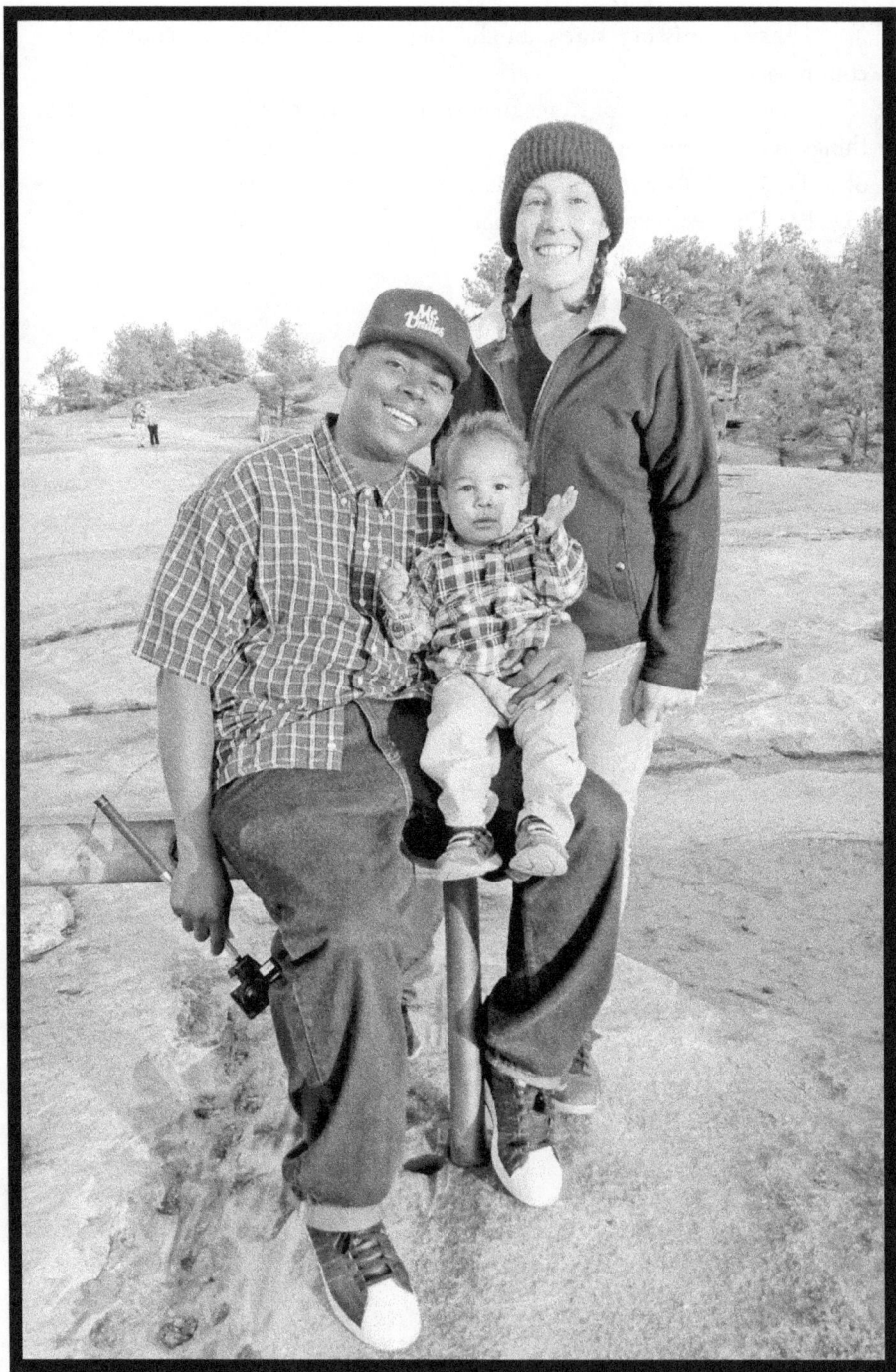

IV. WEAVING A NEW FABRIC

MARGARET HASSE

AND ALL POINTS WEST

Her silk blouse sticks to the plastic chair.
She's going away from home
and never coming back
the same girl. She's bunched
like leaf lettuce between two large men
whose hairy forearms lie on armrests
to the left, to the right. A gray transfer
station in Utah. The sign on her new bus
will say "Reno, Nevada." The announcer
will add, "And all points west."

Already, she has given ten dollars
to a woman who said she had no money.
Cigarette smoke drifts through the air.
In a washroom in Omaha, she removed
the ribbon with her boyfriend's ring
strung around her neck like a cowbell,
stuffed it in her purse.
As graduation gifts, she has a new watch
and a new suitcase with an alarm clock,
wallet, shoes, clothes she sewed for 4-H,
underwear from a store in Sioux City,
and a novel that all freshman are to read:
Manchild in the Promised Land.

She stands to stretch. A soft clatter.
On the floor, her Timex. One of the men
scoops up the metal and its unbroken face
like a handful of dice, turns to the girl
who lifts her wrist as if he will check
the pulse in the runnel of her veins.
As his big paws fasten the buckle,
he says, "I do this for the wife."
He fumbles with a second clasp
on a safety chain. All her life
she will think the stranger blessed her,
opening one delicate gold loop
and linking it to another.

LINDA MAXWELL

THE BUSINESSMAN'S TRUTH TABLES

Little sisters, seven and eight,
Never suspected that
Peter, Paul and Mary's *Leaving on a Jet Plane*
Was written by John Denver,
And they sung it repeatedly
For weeks
After their mother bought those coach tickets,
And claimed they were first class.

What did they know
(That morning of Trans World Airlines Flight 351,
Departing from Albuquerque)?

He was one of those businessmen:
Coat, tie, smooth-cornered brief case
Like they had seen on *That Girl*,
Silvery pen in hand,
Reading typewritten papers of great importance.

Noticing their youth,
He surrendered his window view
To Callie and Grace
Who glanced at their mother and big sister
In the row behind them (embroidering),
Before deciding Grace would sit in the middle
Because she was taller.

Over the fading Rio Grande,
The businessman now in his aisle seat
Heard Callie and Grace wish for a *Weekly Reader*
And their mother promptly tell them to shut up.
"Do you ladies like puzzles?" he asked them,
And opened the pages
Of the glossy magazine whose name they'd try to remember
Millions of skymiles later.
Maybe *Highliner, In-flight, Wingwords,*
Compiled for selling upgrades, watches and luggage.

But the puzzle was missing, so he asked for another, then let them read
The Brainteaser, Project Logic, Five Men and Four Cabins
Another title lost over Texas.

On the back of his papers, he drew perfect blue boxes,
Then listed the clues that Callie read
Aloud, because she was the oldest.
"The American wears a red hat and shoots the teal,"
Which let them cross out the useless threads:
The snipe, coot, duck and goose lies
And distill spectrums of truth:
Red, blue, gold, white—pure white,
All with the businessman's shared pen
All with the businessman's shared heart.

Grace didn't remember solving the puzzle,
Nor what the stewardesses served for brunch—
Or what aunt they visited in Dallas that summer
Or even what happened to the TWA tote bag
She and Callie bought immediately at the airport gift shop.
So they could resemble the businessman: smart, kind, generous.

Her math professor called those puzzles
"Truth Tables"
Grace's first day of college.

And now degrees, children, arrivals and departures later
Professor Grace produces her whiteboard pen
For her freshmen's first flight.
Communally, patiently, kindly, they filter out destructive deceit:
The distractions about weapons and waterfowl,
The falsehoods that prey on ignorance
And innocence.

Callie tends her Truth Table too,
Combing hair, creating beauty
Encouraging kids who can't shut up.
At night, she opens the puzzle book
That Grace sends to her salon
And misses them both:
Her sister and the businessman
Forever flying coach to Love Field.

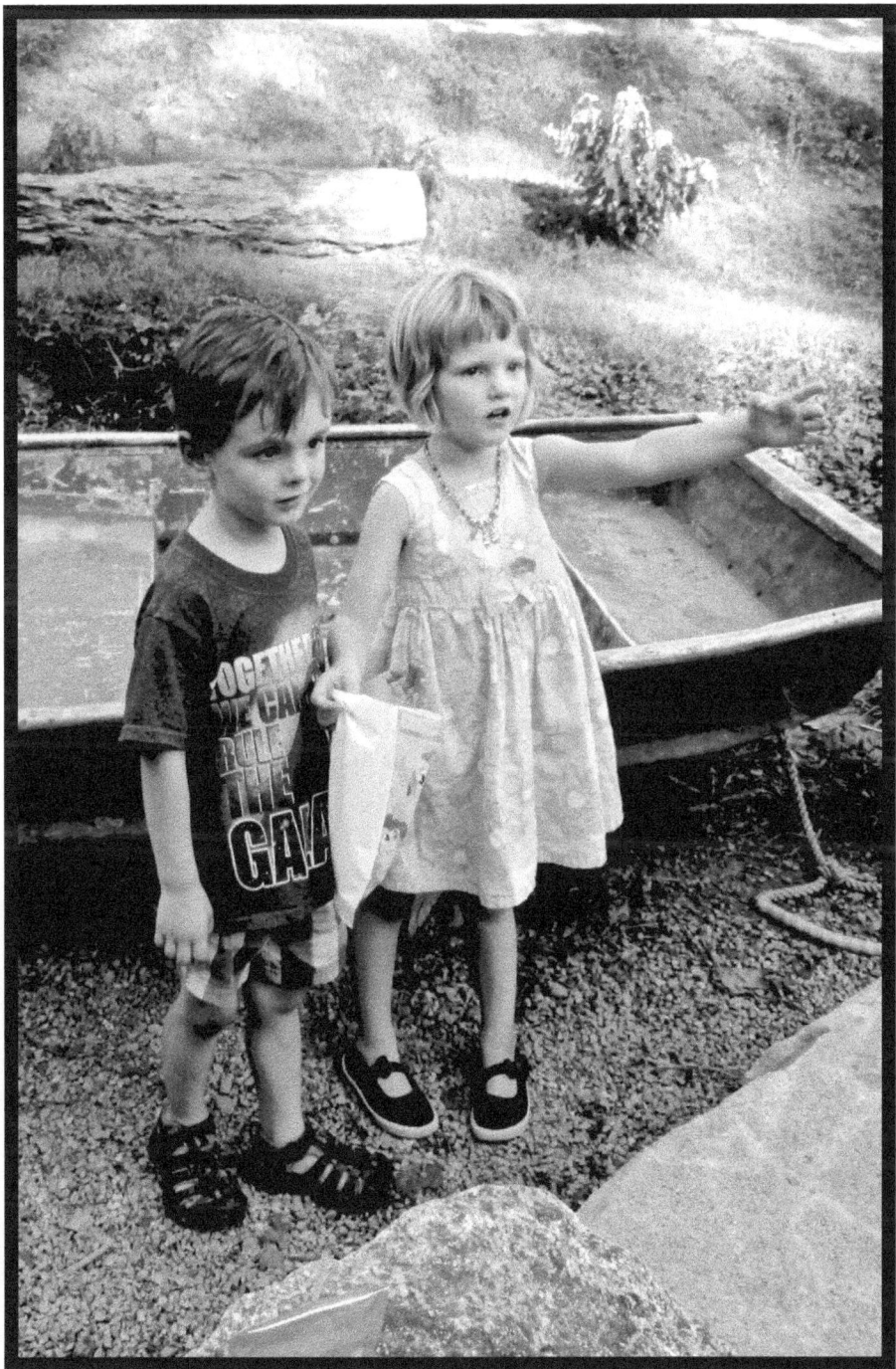

JENNIFER L. THORNBURG

ALL SOULS

Daddy hung the plastic pumpkin over the porch light so its bright orange glow lit all of the porch and part of the night. "Go out my little goblins!" he said. "Don't come back without the witch's broom!" A ghost, a pirate and a bum trooped solemnly down the steps and narrow sidewalk where leafless lilac branches transformed into gnarled, reaching hands. I looked back at my father who stood in the circle of light, his white shirt gleaming orange, his black hair shining, and wished he would come with us. Anything could happen on a night like this.

No street lights graced our corners, beaming out safety, as they did farther up Third Avenue. It was dark where we lived, all ten of us Vosens, on the south side, almost out of town. Our hundred-year-old house stood, implacable, its three stories towering above cracked sidewalks. It endured the seasons' howling arctic winds, torrential rains, and baking summer heat, eaves rising to a pinnacle in the cool autumn air. Across the street, the abandoned China House loomed, its turned up roof corners suddenly strange and leering, its boarded upstairs windows staring blankly. And though we had explored each aged room, climbed each dusty staircase, yes, even though we had thrown the rocks that left the windows jagged, this Halloween night the house turned sinister, lurking in its weedy overgrown field. Shivering in the night air, we hurried down the gravel road toward the paved streets several blocks ahead where bright houses stood in rows, bathed in the light of street lamps. We wanted to trick-or-treat in the nice part of town.

In those days we lived on the South side of the railroad tracks in Glasgow, Montana, enduring the inevitable small-town judgment of a family whose father drank too much. Once, walking home from school with a friend, I saw my father across the street, stumbling toward downtown. My friend pointed, "Look at that man. There's something wrong with him. He's not walking straight." I froze. What could I say? She would never, *could* never, understand.

Her father worked as a carpenter in town, steady paycheck, steady life. Instead of acknowledging him and trying to explain about my father's disease, how he wanted to stop drinking but couldn't, I pretended I didn't know him. That he was not my father. I turned my head, hoping he wouldn't see me. He didn't.

By the time I turned twelve, his eyes were focused solely on the next drink. My father disappeared into the bottle for months at a time. I'm not sure how old I was when I realized this was not normal, that other people's fathers worked steadily and took them to baseball games and provided money for clothes, new clothes, not dresses from the second hand store or coats made from old curtains.

I look back now and see that such times weren't isolated events without repercussion. A slow poison seeped into my being, coloring how I saw myself in the world. I felt the disapproving glance of our neighbors, the sting of their "no" when we asked if their children could play at our house. Shame burned in my cheeks when I stood in line for free lunch at school. Early on, I suspected that if we lived on the other side of town, maybe we could have a different life. But the possibility of things changing seemed unlikely to me, and so I took the opposite tack: fierce loyalty to our house, to my family, and at times, even to my father. And so we floated just outside the hub of "normal." But on Halloween, behind our masks, we drew nearer the center of that glowing circle where the good people lived, the people who had enough money to live. Their houses stood close, nearly identical, bearing colorful paper pumpkins and leaves in the windows. They looked bright and clean and somehow *right*. But to partake in the bounty of the rich people, first we had to get to that desired place, that well-lit part of town.

My younger brother, who was six, and older sister, ten, held hands with me as we walked along in the dark, our empty pillowcases swinging between us. We'd traveled these streets in the daylight hundreds of times while walking home from school. But things looked different at night. Ragged, black clouds scudded across the moon, obliterating its glow. Prickles of fear inched along my neck as I peered at every shadowy shrub and parked car along the road. I thought of the gruesome scene my teenage brothers, Mark, David, and Greg, had created in their "haunted house" in our basement: the weathered tree stump, the hatchet driven deep into its surface, the ketchup dribbled over it to look like blood.

We covered the inky expanse quickly, holding onto each other, holding our breath as we ran. Stepping up to the first well-lit door, I noted the coffee grounds etching a bum's beard on Mike's chubby face. Mom had first applied Vaseline to his cheeks and chin to make the grounds stick. I thought it looked like a real beard, felt proud of my mother's endless creativity. She'd sewn a headscarf and sash for my pirate costume too. As for Mary Lynn's ghost costume, well, snip snip. She made it herself. Together we knocked on the first door, our pillowcases open wide like the gaping mouths of baby birds.

The door flew open revealing a lady with black, birdnesty hair. At first I thought maybe *she* had on a costume, but on closer inspection it was just a bad wig.

"Trick or treat!" we sang, hopeful.

"Oh my, my!" she gushed. "What have we here? Some little ghosts and ghouls! Well, lets see, how about some Tootsie Rolls and Smarties?" We nodded vigorously, mouths watering. She carefully placed one of each in our cavernous bags. One.

"Thank you ma'am . . . " we said, trying to hide our disappointment. But the next place really paid off. It was Johnny Sisson's house—the neighborhood's volunteer fireman. He grabbed great handfuls of shiny-papered toffees, Tootsie rolls, and pink bubble gum and thrust them in our bags. "Thanks, Johnny!" we cried, and this time we meant it. So it went, feast or famine as we visited house after house, crossing street after street, our spooky sojourn taking us farther into town. We encountered mostly kind and generous people, a couple of old grumps, and a few who scared us at the door with fangs and werewolf masks. Finally, after two hours of trick-or-treating, fingers numb with cold, our pillowcases weighing heavily on our shoulders, we turned toward home. The only way to get home was to run the gauntlet— the unlit blocks before our house. We hesitated there in a tight circle, under the last streetlight.

A tall white Victorian house loomed to our right, its paint peeling in curled fragments. It looked a little scary, but since we weren't quite ready to plunge into the even scarier darkness ahead, we agreed that we'd stop there, too. We tramped up the walk to the door and knocked. A faint light shone through heavy curtains. There was a long pause, then shuffling steps. The door cracked open. An ancient man with a dried-up-apple face peered out at us. His shaggy eyebrows winged over eyes the color of cornflowers. Deep furrows wrinkled his brow as he kneaded his forehead with a trembling hand.

"Trick or treat!" we sang.

"Eh, what? What is this?" He groped for the delicate wire rim glasses peeping out of his woolen shirt pocket. He fumbled as he put them on, hooking them carefully behind his ears. "Oh . . . Oh!" he said. His face lit with recognition as he scrutinized our costumes. "My, my. Is it October? Well, let's see if I have anything for you. I must have something here for children." He shuffled back inside.

We giggled on his doorstep, amazed someone could forget that it was Halloween, *that it was October*. When he returned, his hands held large, red and white-striped candy canes. "I hope you don't mind," he said. "Do children still like candy canes?"

"Sure," we said, as he handed them to us. We were used to making do. "Thank you sir," we chorused, "And a Happy Halloween to you!"

He smiled and gently shut the door. His scuffling footsteps faded like the falling leaves of autumn as he retreated into his solitary world. We looked at each other, we three. Then Mike piped, "And a Merry Christmas, too!"

Wanting to be grown up like my sister, I shot Mike a stern look. But my frown broke into a grin and with gleeful abandon I sailed off the steps onto the grass shouting, "And a Hap-hap-hap-py New Year to us all!"

"Shhh! You two be quiet," my sister said, "He might hear you and feel bad. He gave us all he had." And that was Mary Lynn, always alert for potential suffering. When I picture this old man now, a lump rises in my throat. In his age and isolation, he, too, stood outside the circle of light we longed to be part of.

Properly chastised by our older sister's reprimand, we continued down the block, first walking, then breaking into a run as light from the streetlights receded. We were nearly home when I remembered Mom's admonition to visit our neighbor, Steve. We didn't need more candy; our bags brushed the ground. But I could see down the street, past our home and near the dike, that Steve's light was still on. I knew he would be waiting.

We trudged past our house, its lighted windows winking through bare elm branches. I stared at the front door, aching with longing. Oh, to thaw our frozen fingers, to dump our cache of candy and separate it into gleaming piles, to sift sweet treasures through our fingers, to feel the weight and splendor of them. I so looked forward to planning how we would make our bounty last until Christmas. But that would have to wait. On we traipsed toward the dike that ringed our town. Into the deepening darkness we walked until we stood at the doorstep of a tiny clapboard cottage. There sat Steve Sieveshenko, like an old bear, perched upon a stool near the open window. His face leaned toward the book he read as he waited to dole out treats to the few trick-or-treaters who came his way.

"Hello, Steve," we called.

His great bespectacled head pulled back in surprise. "Oh, yes! Ze chiltren are here. I haf vaited for you. How are you on zis fine eef-nink?"

"We're fine," we answered, cowering before his huge presence.

"Vell, now, here iss ze apple and ze orange," he held them out to Mary Lynn and Mike. "And vould you like ze banana?" he asked me.

I looked at the brown speckled fruit, then nodded. Mary Lynn took off her ghost-sheet, but he already knew who we were: children from down the street. He smiled, no hint of judgment in his broad face.

We knew each year that Steve would give us fruit. He'd explained that he preferred to give something healthy, from God's good earth. He'd seen too many desolate winters in the Ukraine Valley. Fruit gleamed at the apex of all that was precious to him. Steve's house was not our favorite stop for treats; we'd rather have had candy. Besides, his enormous size and thick accent made him strange to us. But he was soft spoken and showed interest in the rag-tag lot of children that was our family. When I stood in his presence I felt the balm of his kindness.

He carefully nestled the apple, orange, and banana on top the heap of candy in our bags. I didn't say a word about the mostly brown banana. We accepted the fruit as we accepted Steve, with the unconditional regard of children. We hesitated at his door, perhaps unconsciously wanting something more.

"Plees, come in, come in." He motioned with a huge, paw-like hand.

We had been to his door briefly before, when Mom sent us with bowls of warm oatmeal or soup to comfort him during a recent illness. Stealing sideways glances at each other, we stepped over the worn, wooden threshold and into the soft glow of his dwelling. Now we'd get to see how he lived. The room smelled of chicken soup and Mentholatum, and of age. His swept floors shone while a fire crackled in the potbellied stove. Old-fashioned wallpaper graced the walls with a delicate climbing floral pattern. The roof had leaked— evidenced by a water stain around the stovepipe. Here were signs of a bachelor who lived within this den-like room: a real old-fashioned ice box, piles of clothing, a shelf of canned goods, orange-crate bookshelves overflowing with books in Russian and English.

"Sit, sit." He motioned to a single wooden chair and the edge of his bed, which sat low to the ground. Woolen blankets draped the neatly made bed, and an old patchwork quilt, plus two pillows covered in blue and white striped ticking. We huddled together, stretching our fingers toward the nearby stove. I elbowed Mike, pointed to two wooden crates that held yellowed newspapers. They were covered in black, cryptic symbols. Curious, I stared at the angular Russian letters. They spoke of a whole different world outside our little town. I imagined bear-like people wrapped in fur coats reading strange words and nodding to each other as they huddled before their fireplaces while the wind blew snow past frost-patterned windows.

Steve noticed us staring at the newspapers. "You read zem, eh?" He smiled.

We shook our heads.

"From my Mudder-land," he said, and with that I saw something I did not expect to see. His eyes grew red and watery. But he did not cry.

I was curious enough to overcome my shyness. "Where are they from?"

"Ze Ukraine," he answered. And he spoke as if "The Ukraine" was capitalized, as if it were the only place in the world. Steve Sieveshenko invited us in from the cold, that night so many years ago, to tell us of his homeland. He called it "Mother Ukraine" as if the country were *his* mother. He said he'd ordered a newspaper from that faraway land so he would not feel so alone. So he would know what was happening back home.

He told us about winter in The Ukraine, how cold it was, and how his family had traveled in horse-drawn sleighs. His mother had warmed hot rocks in the stove and put them beneath her children's feet, then covered them with a horse blanket on trips over the frozen Steppe. Our winters in Glasgow were harsh, too. The water in the Christmas tree stand had frozen the previous winter. We didn't have electric heat like the modern homes in our neighborhood. A single gas heater struggled to warm our entire house. On winter mornings we lined up, all eight of us, pressed together, legs straddling the floor grate, anxious to feel warmth so we'd have the courage to run back to our chilly bedrooms and dress for school.

Steve told us about the fruit his family grew, the traditional blessing of the apples and honey on the Feast of the Transfiguration, about the tall plains grasses—*this high*—he held his hand level in front of his nose, to show us. We marveled at the life of this enormous man who had once been a boy on the Steppes. Had he really been small? It was hard to imagine. He seemed like a giant, with his denim bib overalls stretched tight across his barrel chest and round belly.

Steve had written notes in English on the newspaper margins, his handwriting the most beautiful I had ever seen, like ballet on paper. The evenly slanted loops of his L's, the perfect sweeping F's and P's inscribed a grace and nobility that made me think of fairy tales where frogs turned into princes and lovely queens who were really old hags underneath. You know, how sometimes people are different than what they seem.

I look back on this brief window of time and see that it was perhaps my first awareness that there were other people who didn't fit. There *were* other people in the world, strangers in a strange land, lonely and displaced, people who longed for a homeland. And somehow, we found each other. I know, now, that we all have strangeness in us. That we are all longing for home.

Steve asked Mike to hand him a log, then opened the door to his potbelly stove and slid it in. The fire crackled and flared. He lifted the cast iron teapot off the top of the stove, steam rising from its blackened snout. "Are you wanting some of zis hot tea?" he asked, his brows making furry tents over his eyes. He had taken some dried herbs from a Ball jar, sprinkled them in the pot. The smell of mint and chamomile flavored the air.

I looked at Mary Lynn, noted the wrinkle between her eyebrows, saw that she was weighing the situation. I knew what she was thinking: he was clearly not rich. Would it be rude to drink up his tea? Might be rude to refuse, too. She nodded to Mike and me. We each accepted a steaming cup and sipped away. I don't know how long we sat there, a half hour, forty-five minutes. We were three lost children finding home in the momentary solace of a gentle man, a man with his feet on the ground. A man who didn't drink. For though we loved our father, his drinking made him a stranger to us.

"Okay chiltren," Steve said. "Your mudder will be wanting you." Thanking him, we reluctantly pulled ourselves away from the warm fire and gathered at the threshold of his door. Steve looked down on us with kind eyes, eyes that said yes.

"Yah," he patted our heads. "You are *goot chiltren, veddy goot chiltren.*"

We turned away from that great hearth-of-a-man and stepped back out into the night. A host of stars glimmered in the blackened sky, like the tiny rhinestones on the velvet of our mother's only evening dress. The radiance of that huge night shone down on a ghost, a pirate, and a bum.

It was a night for all souls.

Like moths we fluttered home, up the sidewalk and toward the amber light of the glowing pumpkin. A lamp bloomed in the window where Mom and Dad watched, waiting. The air swarmed with change; a weight had lifted. The gnarled hands of shrubs were just lilac branches again, waiting for spring. I hefted my bulging bag up the porch stairs and smiled, hugging the simple praise of the Old Russian to myself. We were *good children*, he had said. Maybe you didn't have to live on the right side of town to be good. His blessing rang in my ears, and though I carried a pillowcase heavy with that evening's plunder, I have carried Steve Sieveshenko's words all my life.

RUPERT FIKE

TUTORING MOHAMMAD MOHAMMAD

After a few homework sessions I'm seeing
   the boy's most important questions
come when the textbooks are closed,
   for he is the English-speaking prism
through which the rest of his family
   experiences this newness, this America.
So yes, he looks to me for certain answers,
   like, did Bill Gates really drop out of Harvard?
He wants to know what Hari Krishnas *do.*
   And on this particular Tuesday afternoon
he asks, as though a friend is in trouble,
   "Mr. Rupert, is it true Lil' Wayne's in jail?"
I respond with the full truth which, of course,
   brings his next question, "What's Rikers?"
And it's somewhere during my description
   of that ancient island prison out in the East River
surrounded by New York City yet apart from it,
   this is when the Head-Tutor-Woman is at our back,
wanting to know *what* we're discussing
   at such great length with the textbook closed.
And even though I try to give Mohammad
   the universal let's-keep-a-secret look,
the *Ix-nay* on *Ill-ayne-way*, the boy replies
   with the most charming guileless lilt,
"Lil' Wayne's on Rikers. Mr. Rupert told me."
   Which I think is smart because it shows
he understood that Rikers is an island.
   But the Head-Tutor-Woman is not pleased.
She's giving me the look that conveys we'll soon

be having a discussion about this,
the look that suggests she'll likely be
    reviewing my background-check file.
So okay, okay, we open the Psychology textbook
    that dulls the boy's eyes like silver polish left on too long,
and as we're flipping to chapter review questions
    he sticks his arm out, *wham*, a human bookmark
at this picture he showed his mother last night.
    It's that famous photograph of Konrad Lorenz,
the German behaviorist, swimming in a lake,
    a line of six ducklings right behind him—
Imprinting—these newly hatched ducks
    think the swimming man *is* their mother,
the argument for nurture in *Nature versus Nurture*.
    Mohammad looks to me, "Is that man still alive?"
And in this long moment it no longer
    matters how disparate our worlds are—
our dreams are common—we both want to be
    the swimming man in that picture,
we both want small animals to love us hard.
    And even though I've been told *not* to,
I open my laptop, "We'll Google him and see."
    "Yes," Mohammad says. "Google."
Ah, he died in 1989, but poor Konrad Lorenz,
    what a life he led, a doctor drafted by the Nazis
then captured by the Russians, six years in Siberia.
    "Why the Russians?" Mohammad asks.
The boy, it turns out, does not know
    who was on whose side during World War II,
so we *have* to discuss *that*, we *have* to discuss
    how the swimming man with the ducklings,
oh, how he must have suffered in those prisons.
    "Like Rikers?" Mohammad asks.
"Yes!" I nod, give a thumbs-up. "Yes, like Rikers."
    "Hitler," the boy repeats after I say the name.
"He had the crazy hair, and stuck his tongue out?"
    "No, no! That was Einstein. Hitler had the moustache,

but Einstein was a Jew, afraid of Hitler
    so he escaped to America, taught at Princeton."
The boy tries to take it all in, so much information.
    I see this could go on forever—Eisenhower, the fifties,
Cold War, Hula Hoops, Civil Rights,
    Dr. King, Elvis, the Infield Fly Rule!
"But Einstein made the bomb." Mohammad says.
    "Well, I think that was more Robert Oppenheimer."
I spell the name as Mohammad taps the keys
    then hits *Images* faster than I thought possible,
which brings up a schematic diagram,
    lines, numbers, colorful equations filling the screen,
a picture of a centrifuge, which is when
    the Head-Tutor-Woman is again at our back,
"What are you showing him? What are you showing him?"
    And then she's acting like I have done
a really bad thing, like it's some kind of huge
    deal to show Mohammad Mohammad
detailed instructions for building a nuclear weapon.
    And though I try to point out that she might
be over-reacting, I am done. This is it,
    the last day in my short history as a tutor.

OUR LIBERIAN STREET PREACHER, MISS EDNA, MAKES HER ROUNDS AT SIX A.M.

Actually she screams more than preaches,
"You must Pray! Pray! Pray!"
words that destroy all hope of more sleep,
become part of your first-blink check-list
for the coming day . . . pray . . . yes. I must pray.
And now she has set off the neighborhood dogs,
fox hounds who will never see a fox,
who instead bay at this too–loud woman
shaking her black book on the reggae beat,
the one and the three, not the two and four,
what I find genetically impossible.
And this is how one wakes up in Clarkston—
pray, pray, bark, bark, pray, pray, Jesus, Jesus, woof, woof—
Miss Edna marching on into her day
where there is no alternative
but to spread the word just as Matthew 28,
that most activist of verses, said:
"Go ye therefore and teach all nations . . . "

But wait. Didn't I, a Methodist teen,
give the collection plate extra quarters
after the Congo mission slide show?
Yes, and here they are coming back at me,
slapping me upside my sleeping head,
for if you're serious about the Godless,
what better place to start than America
where *Temptation Island Wife Swap*
is bounced off satellites, a warning,
to the world: "Don't end up like us!"

Miss Edna a Christian Bodhisattva
living those vows: *The lives of the unsaved
are innumerable. I vow to save them,*
"them" being us between thread-count sheets,
upscale pillows wrapped around our heads.

RICK KRIZMAN

CANTALOUPE ISLAND

It drove Oliver bananas when his sister used his washcloth; the last time he found his face covered with black streaks, which only made sense when he saw Melissa heading out the door with Reno, her eyes dark with mascara. Now he folded the dampened rag in half, then again, smoothed it down just-so next to Melissa's sink, and grabbed a fresh one. As he washed his face, Oliver tried to ignore the detritus of cotton tubes, parabolic reflectors, tweezers, paint brushes, curling iron, hair rollers and the rest of Melissa's beautification-industrial-complex tossed around like post-Godzilla Tokyo. He scrubbed the washcloth up and down, left to right, up and down, imagining his fear ladder; the lowest rung, stable; the next one, a little creaky—he felt a hand on his shoulder.

"Save some skin for tomorrow, okay?" his mom said. She had his saxophone case and her car keys. "Go on and get your books, you're late."

He wasn't late. He couldn't be late if he tried.

)( )( )(

Right at the bell Oliver took his seat in the front row of the Pacific Coast High School jazz orchestra, opened his case, and pried the segments of his alto saxophone from their crèche cradle. Emily Mink was already there to his right, sax assembled, eyes half-closed, chewing her lip, looking at her music, thinking about god-knows. She was thin and pale, with lipstick that matched her pink cheeks, and straight, luminous hair that went on forever. *Supersax*, the boys called her. (Julian, first trumpet, claimed that her perfect white teeth were fake, and that she'd take them out before she'd go for your *spit valve*, by which he did not mean kissing.) Oliver lined up the gooseneck of his alto, sneaking looks at Emily moistening her reed. Unbelievably, they'd gone out once; two months ago, the winter formal . . .

Oliver half-glanced at the chart for "Cantaloupe Island" while he polished his spatula keys with a cloth diaper and worked a Q-tip into the spring hinges. *New day, clean start.* He could sight-read better than anyone in the ninth grade (if not the entire orchestra) and scanning the first sixteen measures of neat, black, notes, he thought *easy-schmeasy*, but then he hit the next page, blank except for one word—Solo—and he felt his breakfast start to bubble like a vinegar volcano.

To his left, Ethan was fooling around on his tenor, blowing nervous riffs that Oliver had never seen on any page, which wasn't helping. Then Mr. Tyler walked in, demanded a note from the piano, and suddenly everyone was tooting and squawking while Oliver, already in tune, closed his eyes and touched each mother-of-pearl key from the top to the bottom of his alto, then again, until things quieted.

)( )( )(

Ten minutes later Oliver was in the guidance office, sitting in front of an imposing man who had a question mark stamped into his large, actorish face. "I guess I didn't want to play a solo," Oliver said.

Terence Franklin was middle-aged but solidly built, his chest almost bursting Hulk-like from his blue suit jacket, gray hair clenched into a ponytail, clearly a man who would not be defined by his position as School Counselor, who's been a few places and you're lucky to have him for now. Rumors abounded: CIA, double agent, assassin; that he'd once killed a man for calling him "Terry." The girls were nuts about him. He looked at Oliver as if his thoughts were too large for their capacious container.

"A man goes on a journey," he said, *intoned*, in a smoke-and-whiskey voice. "He carries a map and a compass." He raised one knowing eyebrow at Oliver, *compadre*. "But the map and the compass do not *determine* a man's direction." Oliver's ears were still buzzing from his own embarrassment. He'd played the chart down perfectly, everything hunky-dory until bar seventeen when he stared at the blank page, at *Solo*, placed his lips around the mouthpiece, fingers poised, then . . . nothing. Next thing the music had stopped and he was on the floor, looking up at Emily Mink.

"It's no big deal," Oliver told him, "I probably just fainted."

Mr. Franklin narrowed his eyes into tiny points, and Oliver could almost feel them tunneling into his forehead.

"Sonofabitch," Mr. Franklin said. "Son. Of. A. Bitch."

"Excuse me?" Oliver said.

"That, my friend, is *exactly* my point." He leaned forward, hands folded over his lips. "A sonofabitch . . ." he said, "a real sonofabitch never looks for an excuse. Do you know what a real sonofabitch does?"

"No sir."

"A real sonofabitch," he stage whispered, *"Does. What. Needs. To. Be. Done."*

"I don't—"

"Stop." He held up one finger. "Here. Now. This moment."

"So I should be a, um, what you said?"

"Not *should* be but *are*. You *are* a sonofabitch. Say it."

"Son of a bitch," Oliver said.

"A real sonofabitch. Again. Like you mean it."

"Sonofabitch. Um, a *real* sonofabitch."

"Good. Now go, and do what a sonofabitch does." Oliver stood and Mr. Franklin leaned back and crossed his arms. "Just between us. One sonofabitch to another." He winked and Oliver got out of there.

Everyone was too busy packing up to notice he was back except for Emily Mink, erect, hands on her lap. Oliver shrugged at her—half apology and half "sheesh" —then bent to disassemble his alto, opening his case upside down, reeds spilling everywhere. One had fallen under Emily's chair and he reached between her feet for it, her bare, white leg just inches from his face.

On the way out Mr. Tyler pulled him aside. "We'll try it again tomorrow Oliver. Don't think so hard. Just play whatever you feel like." *What I feel like playing*, Oliver wanted to say, *are notes stuck tight to the bars and spaces of a music staff*, and as if reading his thoughts Mr. Tyler added, "You can even write something out ahead of time if that helps."

)( )( )(

The first sign that all was not well had occurred a year ago in Algebra. Oliver was already uneasy with the idea of "solving for x," some unknown thing that could only be made known by juggling numbers and letters around in a way he couldn't get the hang of. He tried to explain to Ethan about this jumble of variables spiraling to infinity, not just x, but y and z, the unknown-times-the-unknown. "Dude, you're so philosophical," Ethan had replied, but Oliver knew the problems were real; if you didn't solve for x your rocket would end up on Pluto instead of Mars. That day he'd been trying to decipher the equation Mr. Fitzsimons had scrawled on the board, but as x kept slipping past his mind's grasp, Oliver was first fascinated, then distressed, by the off-kilter numbers and chalk scrawls. He looked down at his textbook, with its rows of tidy script, but when he tried to raise his eyes they wouldn't obey, and suddenly he was wheezing, not enough air in the air. Mr. Fitzsimons rushed him to the nurse, where they both crouched and made rolling-forward motions with their hands, telling him to *breathe, just breathe,* demonstrating with their own gasping inhalations, until he got the hang of it and they sent him home.

"You know, I'll still love you if you don't get an A in everything," his mom said, covering him on the couch and pressing her hand to his forehead.

"It's not the grade, Mom." But what *was* it? He saw a Dr. Spaetzle, who prescribed a twice-daily dose of Metaformyecin, and something else that often made Oliver feel like he was continually stepping into an elevator shaft. He endured weekly cognitive behavioral therapy sessions with the grandmotherly Mrs. Russet, who'd crack open a cabinet door, then stare at a stopwatch until Oliver couldn't stand it anymore. After a year he'd gone from ten seconds to almost a minute and a half.

"I'm so proud, and you should be too," she said, peering over the top of her reading glasses, but they were slightly crooked and he had to sit on his hands.

)( )( )(

That night Oliver kept his mouth shut about fainting in class and about Mr. Franklin's pep talk. At the upright after dinner he faced a blank sheet of music paper, all the possible notes bouncing around his brain like lottery balls. He counted seven books next to the piano, then went seven letters down the alphabet. He would have preferred an even number, but moved his pencil past that thought toward the "G" on the staff, making a small circle which he filled in, then widened into an oval, but too big, so he erased the edges, which left a smudge. He rubbed out the entire note, but there was still a trace so he took a fresh sheet of paper and sharpened his pencil. Twenty minutes later he was using a ruler to draw a vertical stem attached to a perfectly-ovaled G when the lead broke, leaving a dark slash. He put it away and went to bed, where he dreamed of an army of mice in matching uniforms, charging into battle with saxophones instead of rifles.

The next morning he took a longer way to band class, but must have walked faster because he arrived right at the bell, sliding in next to the ever-ready Emily Mink. Everybody was horsing around, Ethan making duck calls with his detached mouthpiece, while Oliver stared quietly at page two of "Cantaloupe Island" with an itchy, anxious feeling. *Sonofabitch.* Was he a real sonofabitch? Probably not.

This was the same antsiness he remembered from the night before the formal. He'd only had the courage to call Emily Mink because he was sure she was already spoken for, but No she didn't have a date and Yes she'd go with him. His mom had driven them, he and Emily in the back, glued to their respective doors. She looked and smelled better than he could hardly stand, with her china-white skin and waterfall of hair. She was too shy to dance, which was okay with him, except for the slow songs, but even then everyone would see she was a few inches taller, so they sat on folding chairs, drinking their punch. Oliver had worried about what they might talk about, but it felt okay to just sit there quietly, and she seemed fine with it as well.

Over by the punch bowl Ethan was clowning around with a couple of sophomores. Oliver took Emily's glass for a refill.

" . . . his ass popped up in the air, lighting his farts with his Bic, when Fish walks in," Ethan was saying. "Fish" was Mr. Dobbs, European History, jowls and tiny, puckered mouth like a two-hundred-year-old goldfish.

"Ho ho, this guy," Ethan wiggled Oliver's shoulder. "So who's 'getting the ride' tonight? *Supersax Express.*" Oliver hadn't thought about getting the ride from Emily, if it meant what he thought it did, hadn't imagined much past the fact that he was here with her at all.

"That's right," said one of the sophomores, a heavy, crew-cut guy named Shake. "Somebody's gonna get his reed wet. Just make sure she takes out her teeth first." He laughed like a donkey and wiggled his tongue obscenely. Then, like idiots, they all turned to look at Emily Mink, who'd been watching the whole deal, now biting her lip and squinting at Oliver with something like heat-ray vision. She rose and spun away, any possibility of the ride disappearing out the door with a backward wave of her perfect hair.

Now, as she sat next to him, about to witness his demise, Oliver clenched and unclenched his fingers, but felt the cement hardening anyway. Mr. Tyler arrived and the room went quiet.

"Right here," he said, tapping his baton. "Horns on my cue, solo at seventeen," nodding to Oliver, "and three and four and . . ." at which point the band dug into the tropical funk groove of "Cantaloupe Island," beginning the dreadful countdown. Mr. Tyler approached him with a concerned look, still conducting with one hand, a sheet of paper in his other, which he slid in front of Oliver. The number Seventeen was written large at the top, followed by ten stanzas of perfectly-lined music paper dotted with black notes. At bar seventeen the other horns dropped out, and Oliver began to play the written music, sight-reading what he recognized as the piano solo from the record, getting most of it, and in his immense relief not worrying about the occasional flub.

"Dude, you are one real sonofabitch, aren't you," Ethan said as they packed up. Oliver looked at him strangely. "Yeah, I've had the SOB talk," Ethan said. "'Go. Do. Be'."

"I sort of cheated," Oliver said, and showed Ethan the written solo.

"Hey, parts is parts."

A couple of senior trumpet players gave Oliver an upward nod, and Steiner, the pianist, offered a "Yo, Herbie" high-five. Oliver looked around for Emily Mink but she was gone.

✕ ✕ ✕

Burlington Hall was packed tight for the spring concert. Every ensemble in the school district, starting with the fourth grade choirs and ending with Oliver's band, would be performing in what promised to be a long evening.

"Too bad I won't be there to see you crash and burn," Melissa had said at dinner the previous night.

"Oh, you're going," their mom and dad said at the same time. "No buts," added his dad. Melissa whispered *you're so dead* to Oliver as she sulked away from the table to call Reno, and Oliver went off to rehearse his solo.

Now, waiting in the cafeteria to be called onstage, Oliver closed his eyes and practiced his measured breathing, telling himself, You've got this, you've got this; *You've got this, you sonofabitch.*

As their first few tunes rolled over the tired crowd, Oliver watched his dad and mom in the third row nodding to the beat, Melissa lost in her phone. Mr. Franklin sat a few rows back, chin on his knuckles, staring at the band as if deciphering the Rosetta stone.

"Cantaloupe Island" was the night's capper, and the warmed-up ensemble slid easily into its funk groove. Oliver moistened his reed as he opened the music to his written solo, but it wasn't there. He flipped the pages forward and backward. Nothing. He looked desperately around, saw

Melissa staring at him with an odd smile, holding up the sheet with the big 17 at the top. Suddenly his sax felt like a ticking bomb and he wanted to throw it down and run for cover, but no way would he get far enough with bar seventeen racing toward him at a hundred and twelve beats per minute. With six measures to go he looked at Mr. Franklin and decided, *I can do this.* Four to go, and his fingers jittered across the keys. Then two. *Solve for x,* he told himself. At one, filled to the brim with anger and resolve, he rose from his chair and looked out at a thousand expectant faces.

Bar seventeen hit and everyone dropped out except the bass and drums. Oliver closed his eyes, fingered a G, and blew, then listened in horror as the sax seemed to take on its own life, squeezing out a flatulent *blaattt* that cracked into a pterodactyl-like squawk. He opened his eyes and saw Mr. Tyler looking at him with bewilderment but continuing to wave his baton, the song surging relentlessly onward, so Oliver took a deep breath and blew another note, this one coming out low and moaning, staggering around like a brain-hungry zombie. He was running out of air, wondering what the hell he was going to do, when to his right he heard what could have been the tortured cry of a trapped animal, rising and wailing, but it was Emily Mink, eyes squeezed closed, her face red, her cheeks puffed out as she stood up and blew into her alto like it was a field horn, and as her note squiggled up and turned into cackling parrots Oliver gazed at her with grateful astonishment. As the drums and bass pounded away he blew into his own horn again, humpback whales now, then harder until they seemed to be lurching up and down on a roller coaster. To his left he heard the see-saw bleating of a foreign ambulance, but it was Ethan, rocking from foot to foot and flipping his Elvis hair back and forth in time with the alternating notes, adding medical emergency to the crying feral beast and roller-coasting humpbacks. Behind Oliver the trumpets had started making duck sounds with their plunger mutes when Mr. Tyler waved the whole band to its feet, and as he pointed here and there, the air of Barnham Hall shattered with the cries of trombone elephants, clarinet monkeys, vibraphone doorbells, crashing pianos, and chicken clucks from the lone bassoon player (not so different from how he usually played). Mr. Tyler thrashed his baton and the trombones became a herd of distressed cattle, the clarinets went from monkeys to myna birds, all of it a crazed circus train ready to jump the rails, then when everyone had found their way to their highest, lowest, or loudest note, Mr. Tyler whipped the baton down and the melee stopped all at once, leaving only the echo of God-knows-what ringing out over the shocked faces of the audience.

"Ladies and gentlemen," Mr. Tyler said into the microphone, "the wild beasts of Cantaloupe Island," even as he was marking time, shouting to the band, "three, four" and with a quick pickup on the snare the wild beasts of Cantaloupe Island launched back into the melody, everything in synch, Oliver now harmonizing perfectly with Ethan and Emily Mink, the trombones and trumpets counterpunching, the drums and bass driving down a funk beat like a locomotive. The only animal sounds were coming from the audience, on their feet, clapping and hooting and whistling. Oliver saw Mr. Franklin relax back into his seat, smile at him, and mouth four syllables.

)( )( )(

Afterwards the cafeteria reverberated with the sound of wacka-wacka birds and animal grunts as the Cantaloupe Islanders packed their things, Ethan wandering around slapping his arms together and barking like a seal.

Oliver approached Emily. "Thanks, I guess," he said.

She snapped closed her case and squinted at him. "I know how it feels," she said, and looking at her perfectly aligned hair and thinking about her always ready and erect in her chair, Oliver thought he might have a new idea about Emily Mink.

"That thing at the dance," he said. "I'm sorry."

"I know. They're morons," she said.

Oliver tucked his alto away and ducked out the stage door, relieved to escape the chaos. Outside, the perfume of night-blooming jasmine blended with the sea air, suggesting a faraway tropical place. He stepped to the edge of the palisades overlooking the beach and pier. Fog had come in from the water, muting the colors of the ferris wheel into spinning pastels and haloing the car lights inching up the coast highway. Out of the gloom beyond the pier came a deep, homesick moan—*foghorn*, he told himself, *or a beckoning ship*. He inhaled a lungful of thick air, rounded his lips, and blew out a low, spooky tone, like the wind on a dark and stormy night. He stood a few moments, waiting for a response, but there was only the sound of moisture dripping from the magnolias, and the power lines buzzing in the damp.

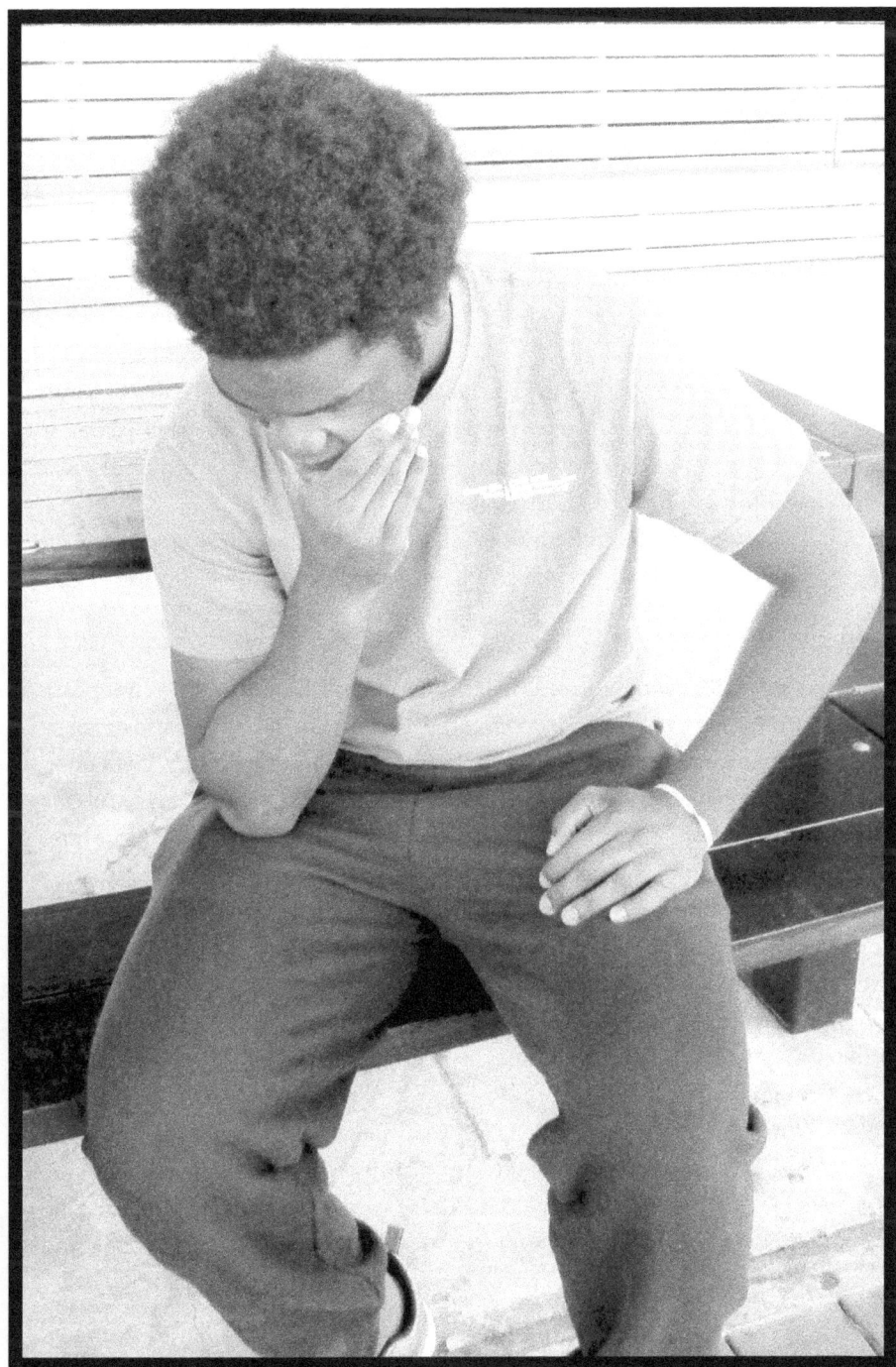

FRANK HABERLE

ROAD TO HAINES

A cold mist blows over the tips of the pine trees. It coats Eddie's anorak and soaks his boots. He stands shaking for an hour. A Winnebago passes. It pulls over and stops on the shoulder. Pink lace curtains flap from a tiny rear window. They must be lost, Eddie figures.

The camper honks. A fleshy, sleeveless arm waves to him from the cab.

"This here the road to Haines?" the driver calls to him.

"Yeah," Eddie says.

"Well, get in!" she says. "We're not going to bite you!"

A side door swings open. Eddie climbs up and sits in a plush velvet chair. He's surrounded by beige and brown carpet and paneling, cabinets and drawers. He glances over his shoulder. A low toilet peeks from behind a very small door. Two elderly women smile at him from the front seats. A huge, white, plastic crucifix hangs from the rear view mirror. The smell of perfume overwhelms him.

"You look like you need a nice glass of iced tea," the passenger says. She gets up and waddles past him to the tiny kitchenette. "Yes sir," the driver says. She turns the camper back out onto the highway. "You sure look like you've been out here a while." Eddie sits in his soft armchair. Gripping the counter with one hand, the elderly passenger hands him an iced tea, then a paper plate filled with Oreo cookies. "No fancy china, sorry," she says; then pulls herself back up into her seat.

"I'm Rosemarie. Corinne here is my co-pilot," the driver says. She brushes back a mane of white hair. She holds a camcorder in her lap with one hand; the other pins a dog-eared book, the *Alaska Highway Milepost*, against the steering wheel. She cranes her neck to squint at maps she's ripped out of a book and taped to the ceiling. "How far are you going?" she asks.

"Haines Junction," he says. "I'm meeting a friend there."

"Well," Rosemarie says, flipping through the *Milepost*. "We're going toward Haines, but a little slow. If you want to jump out and see if you can find a faster ride, you just let us know."

"How about some homemade popcorn?" Corinne asks. "Or I can make some nachos, if you like them. You like nachos?"

Eddie looks out through the lace curtains. The dark forest rolls slowly by. "Oh, yeah," he says. "Nachos would be great."

Hours pass. The sky darkens. Sheets of cold rain sweep against the windshield. Outside, the soaked tundra shimmers silver and green, punctuated by angry dead trees. Rosemarie turns the heat up. She tells Eddie about the little town in Illinois they're from, the church where they run the youth program, the axle they broke in Alberta.

"When that axle broke, we had half a mind just to turn around right there, didn't we Corinne?"

"Oh, yes," Corinne says.

"But like I said, imagine what the pioneers would have done. Would they have turned around and gone home?"

"No, sir."

"It's like I always say, when life gives you lemons . . . "

"You make lemonade," Corinne says quickly. Rosemarie takes a long look at Eddie through the rear view mirror. Eddie stops trying to stuff strands of oily hair up under his baseball cap. He scratches the thick stubble on his neck. He looks down at his hands; his nails are black. When he looks up again Rosemarie's eyes are back on the road.

"Are you going to be roughnecking up here?" she asks.

"What's that?"

"She wants to know if you've got work on the pipeline," Corinne says.

"Who, me? No."

"Fishing boat?"

"No, nothing like that."

"Canneries? You going to work the canneries?"

"I don't know." Eddie starts scratching again, this time all over. "I'm going to get work, as soon as I hook up with my friend. She's coming up to meet me, up from Phoenix."

"That's some drive," Rosemarie says.

"I think we can still get work, I think, up in Kenai."

"Supposed to be really something out there."

"Yeah, it's really beautiful," Eddie says. He brushes salt off his drying anorak. It leaves white flecks on the upholstery. "At least I hear it is. I hear there's lots of work out there, this time of year. Canneries, tourist stuff. You name it."

X X X

The snacks keep coming: corn chips and pretzels and soda. Eddie starts dozing. He half-dreams, half remembers calling Kate from the pay phone on Fourth Avenue; only in the dream he's together, standing erect. His voice is low, confident. Everything's okay now. He's got a plan. She's coming for sure.

Eddie wakes up to an oncoming horn. Rosemarie pulls the camper back into her lane.

"Do you know how they built this highway?" Eddie says, fighting to wake up.

"I can't imagine," Rosemarie says. She rubs her eyes and squints at the maps. Corinne snores by her side.

"I'm reading a book about it. It was the beginning of the war. The Japanese took a couple of Aleutian Islands. So we built this highway. So we could ship supplies up. So we could counterattack. In the Aleutians."

"You don't say."

"Yeah. But it was a black division, from Alabama. They had to build the highway. They got stuck out here in little canvas tents. Freezing cold. They worked through the winter. All hand tools. They built bridges, cut embankments. They finished a year ahead of schedule."

"Well now, ain't that something."

"What's that?" Corinne asks suddenly.

"Eddie's telling us about a book he's reading, about the Negroes who built this here highway."

"The what?"

"The Negroes!" Rosemarie yells. "They built the highway!"

X X X

A town appears suddenly—first cabins, then little houses, then stores. Rosemarie drives the camper down a strip of one-story buildings. Eddie peers through the curtains at glowing beer signs in windows: Labatts, Molson, Anchor Steam, Budweiser. Rosemarie pulls into a gas station. A large woodcarved lumberjack waves from the porch. Taped to his axe is a sign: "12 pack $8.99."

"This is the place!" she yells. "We fill the tank, they let us camp out back for free!" Rosemarie climbs down from the drivers seat and enters the store, leaving Eddie and Corinne alone in the camper.

"Ain't she something," Corinne says.

"Yes she is," Eddie says.

"Her chiropractor told her don't do it. Said she couldn't take it. She broke her neck, you see. Four summers ago. In the accident. Broke her dang neck."

"Wow," Eddie says. "She's lucky."

"Hardly," Corinne says. "She's hardly that."

"Oh."

"The lord giveth and the lord taketh away. It's not for us to question why."

Rosemarie reappears. She's smiling. "Good news!" she says as she pulls herself up into the drivers seat. "There's room out back, one more spot for a camper. And the man says you can set up your tent right back behind there. You have a tent in that backpack of yours, don't you?"

Eddie peers out at a sea of industrial waste scattered under the trees. "Yeah."

"Well, we turn in early. We're just a couple of old ladies. I guess we'll see you in the morning. Do you want to ride with us in the morning?"

"Yeah, that would be great," Eddie says. "Thanks." He grabs his backpack and climbs down, closing the screen door behind him.

)( )( )(

Eddie wakes up to the wild buzz of camper generators. He lies in the tent for a while, trying to remember what he told Kate. It was two weeks ago. He was pretty hammered. He thinks he convinced her he was sober. She was pretty sure she was coming up. He remembers telling her he has jobs lined up, places to stay. In the fall they could work their way back down land, follow the coast. Maybe get home by Christmas. Eddie climbs out of his tent, set up between two rusting, abandoned meat freezers. He gathers his beer cans and tucks them behind one of the freezers. Rosemarie's camper sits nearby, the lace curtains drawn shut. He walks to the general store, buys a cup of coffee, and returns to his tentsite. He perches himself on top of one of the freezers and re-enters his book. While the troops fight through the winter to finish the highway, a team of pilots stationed on a makeshift airbase on the Aleutian Islands makes raids on the Japanese positions. The weather's terrible, their weaponry is outdated and they have few supplies. The isolation starts to get to the pilots. They turn violent, murder each other, have nervous breakdowns. They fight over the privilege of flying suicide missions.

Eddie gets up for another cup of coffee. Half way across the parking lot he hears "Hey! Hey you!" He turns to face a creased old man, grinning in his pajamas.

"You, now, son, you want some coffee? C'mere with me. I'll get you some coffee."

He waves Eddie toward his Winnebago, a smaller model than Rosemary's. "C'mon now, I won't bite you. You just come on over here." Eddie follows him into the compact vehicle. He fits himself into a tiny kitchen booth across from the man. A red-haired woman in a nightgown squints through huge glasses. She puts down a pot of coffee. The old man fills Eddie's cup, then his own.

"That's my wife Barbara," the man says. "I'm Eugene."

Eddie takes a sip and winces. "Wow," he says. "That's some coffee."

"We drove up here from Bakersfield," Eugene says.

"That's a long ways," Eddie says.

"Drove all the way up, far as we could. Drove all the way up to see that big old pipeline, up where the road ends."

"That must have been something," Eddie says.

"That ain't nothing," Eugene says. "Nothing but a load of crap. Them goddamn oil companies think they got it all figured out. They don't know nothing."

"You want some more coffee, hon?" Barbara asks Eddie.

"My old man worked twenty years for the Standard refinery up there on the north slope. Didn't have no pipeline then. Twenty years, never missed a day sick. One day a jack came down, smashed his hand flat. They let him go that day. No pension. Nothing."

Somebody bangs on the screen door.

"That's my hitchhiker," Rosemarie calls in to Barbara. "You can't have him."

Barbara laughs. "Well, if you're ever in Bakersfield," Eugene says, "be sure to stop on by. We're in the trailer parked behind the Bible Baptist

Church."

)()()(

Rosemarie twists her head around to squint at the new map she's taped to the ceiling.

"Haines Junction," Rosemarie says. "Here we come."

"Almost Haines," Eddie says. His head is throbbing.

"Now, did you say you're going to Haines, or Haines Junction?" Corinne asks.

"I'm going to Haines," Eddie says. "I think. I'm meeting her in Haines."

"Now I would have sworn you said Haines Junction," Corinne says.

"Haines, Haines Junction," Rosemarie says. "Can't be much distance from one to another. Do you need more air conditioning back there? Do you need me to turn up the air conditioner?"

"No thanks."

"Maybe you need something to drink," Corinne says, not turning. "Like some water."

"I'm okay, thanks."

"You know now, if we're going too slow for you, you can get another ride. If you have to get to where you're going in a hurry."

"Thanks," he says.

"Would you like some chips? Is it too early?"

"No, not at all, thanks. I'm grateful for the ride."

Corinne's silent, staring ahead at the long caravan of Winnebagos. "Because we sure enjoy the company," Rosemarie continues. "It sure is nice of you to keep a couple of old ladies company."

"Chips would be great, thanks," Eddie says. "Never too early for chips."

)()()(

In the middle of a treeless wilderness, signs and flags mark the approach of Canadian customs. Rosemarie starts rubbing her neck. "Now this should only take a minute," she says.

"Unless, of course, someone's carrying drugs," Corinne adds.

"Hello," the Mountie says as they pull up.

"Just a couple of old ladies out for a drive, officer!" Rosemarie says. The

Mountie leans in Rosemarie's window and peers at Eddie's backpack, then directly at Eddie. "You folks all got a driver's license?" The Mountie asks. His voice is deep but his face is young, covered in red freckles.

"Hand him your driver's license, Eddie."

"I've got a passport."

The Mountie glances at the pack again. "No driver's license?"

"I don't drive."

"Huh," Corinne says, staring straight ahead.

"You don't drive?" the Mountie asks. "You've never driven?"

"No," Eddie says, scratching. "I'm a lousy driver."

"How do you know if you've never driven?"

Eddie shrugs. Rosemarie and Corinne tuck their licenses back into their handbags.

The Mountie glances at the passport and hands it back in to Eddie. "You have a great visit to Canada," he says to Rosemarie.

X X X

They drive along a winding river. Dark clouds cling to the top of stark mountains. At six o'clock, Rosemarie pulls over, next to a beautiful glacial lake shining through the windshield.

"Let's stop for dinner, gang," she says. "We can push on to Haines Junction after dinner. This spot here's just a little too perfect not to have dinner."

Corinne silently prepares a tuna casserole, potato chips and orange soda. She hasn't spoken all day. Eddie stares out at the lake, then jumps up to help unfold the little dining table. Moving much more slowly, Rosemarie reaches into a drawer for forks and knives.

"Let me help you set the table," Eddie says.

"No sir. You're our guest here," she says, swiveling her head from side to side and grimacing. "Be it ever so humble." They sit down around the table. Corinne and Rosemarie hold hands and reach for Eddie's. Their hands are clean and weightless. Eddie realizes how grimy he must feel, how badly he must smell. They don't seem to notice. Rosemarie takes a deep breath. "Dear lord," she begins, "we thank you for this wonderful day and for seeing us through another day's journey in safety. We thank you for helping me with my neck, from keeping it from going out again. We thank you for keeping Corinne's bum leg from swelling up. Thank you, lord, for keeping the generator running. Thank you for the new axle which is just humming right along. We thank you for the road conditions, much better, I'd say, than yesterday, but nobody's complaining about yesterday. And dear Lord, I'm sorry and I'm praying for that squirrel I pegged. Lord, I thank you for taking Marty back into your heart and for sending him once to me, to enrich my life. And dear Lord . . . "

She grips Eddie's sweat-soaked hand a little harder.

" . . . we thank you, last and not least, for bringing this young man into our lives, and for the friendship and comfort he's providing to us, and we hope too that you help us to help him find his way, to Haines Junction, or Haines. And dear Lord, we hope you help him find his friend, and himself, and a purpose for this journey he's on."

"Amen," Corinne says.

Eddie bites into a spoonful of casserole. "Was Marty your husband?" he asks.

"Marty was my boy," Rosemarie answers. They chew in silence for a while.

"She must be very brave," Rosemarie says.

"Who's that?"

"Your friend you're meeting. Coming up here, all that way, by herself. That's some long journey for a young lady, all by herself. She must be very brave."

"Yeah."

"Here," Rosemarie smiles, passing a red plastic bowl. "Have some more chips."

)( )( )(

In the middle of Haines Junction there's a huge signboard with mileage signs and arrows pointing to every possible destination. Anchorage, New York, Quebec, Moscow, Buenos Aries. The light fades behind distant blue mountains. They stare up at all the signs.

"So is it Haines or Haines Junction?" Rosemarie asks Eddie. She's holding her head with both hands and wincing.

"It's Haines, I think," Eddie says, staring at the signpost for Haines. "I think I said I would meet her in Haines."

"Well, we're going to drive down a little farther tonight, toward Haines. We're just going to camp on the side of the road. We'll find a good spot where you can pitch your tent. Then in the morning, we'll make sure to get you to Haines to meet your friend."

⟩⟨ ⟩⟨ ⟩⟨

Rosemarie pulls over in a gravel turnoff boxed in by huge granite peaks. Eddie climbs up a little hill, just out of the sight of the camper, and pitches his tent. He rolls out his sleeping bag and lies down to read a last chapter of the book in the fading light. Supplied by land, from the highway, and by sea, the U.S. mounts its first amphibious assault of the war, against the Japanese soldiers on Kiska Island. The landing craft crashes into coral reefs a thousand feet from shore, drowning hundreds of men. The first soldiers to make the beach are run over by their own tanks. The men fight through snow and rain, inch by inch, to take the island. A hundred have their feet amputated for frostbite. The last group of Japanese soldiers makes a surprise bayonet charge into the field hospital. They kill a dozen amputees; then pull grenades out and blow themselves up. It's too dark to read any more. Eddie lies still in the tent. The highway builders spin into his head, steam blowing from their nostrils, driving pickaxes into ice and dirt. The Aleutian pilots, the Kiska marines, Eugene's dad. They had to come up here, he thinks. They did what they had to do. He hears a lone car pass somewhere out in the woods, on the distant highway, the road to Haines. What if it's Kate? What if she's driving back and forth between Haines and Haines Junction, looking for him? What if they came this close and couldn't find each other? A shiver passes through him. Kate's not going to be there, he thinks. She didn't sound convinced at all. She always knew when he was drunk. She wasn't going to drive two thousand miles up here for him.

It's the first night Eddie's been without a drink since he can remember. The screams of strange insects and birds fill the woods. He starts twitching— first his hands and feet, then his entire body.

"Eddie!" he hears, from the woods. With a flashlight Eddie finds his way back down to the camper. Corinne's silhouette stands at the screen door. She's in her nightgown and robe, her hair in curlers, rubbing her knee with her hand. "It's Rosemarie," Corinne says. "She needs you."

Eddie climbs in. Rosemarie sits perfectly still in the armchair Eddie's occupied for the past few days. Her eyes are closed and she's barefoot, in a long white gown.

"I need you to do something for me," Rosemarie says. Her eyelids flutter. She presses them shut. "Can you do something for me?"

"Sure, Rosemarie. What do you need me to do?"

"I need you to set my neck. I'll show you how. Can you do it?"

Eddie looks over at Corinne, who retreats to her passenger seat, ringing her hands.

"I'm not strong enough," Corinne whispers. "I tried. I just can't."

"I need you to come stand behind me," Rosemarie says. Eddie obeys. "Now I need you to put your arm around my head, like so." She guides his hands to hold her in a gentle headlock position. Her chin rests inside his elbow. Her hands hold tightly to his forearm.

"Now I need you to place your other hand against the base of my skull, like this." he guides Eddie's shaking left hand to the back of her head, against the smooth ripples of her hair.

"Now, I need you to jerk my head up, real hard, as hard and as fast as you can."

"I can't do that," Eddie says.

"You can. Yes, you can. You have to."

Eddie takes a deep breath. Still shuddering, he feels a sudden surge. He snaps Rosemarie's head up as hard as he can. There's a loud crack, then a crunching sound. He releases her. He's sure that he broke her neck. Rosemarie sits still for a moment, then runs a hand up to reposition her hair on her shoulders. She rolls her neck around like she'd just woken from a long nap. She beams up at Eddie.

"That will do it, Eddie. God bless you, and good night."

Her smell is all around him now. She smells so sweet, Eddie thinks. Like flowers.

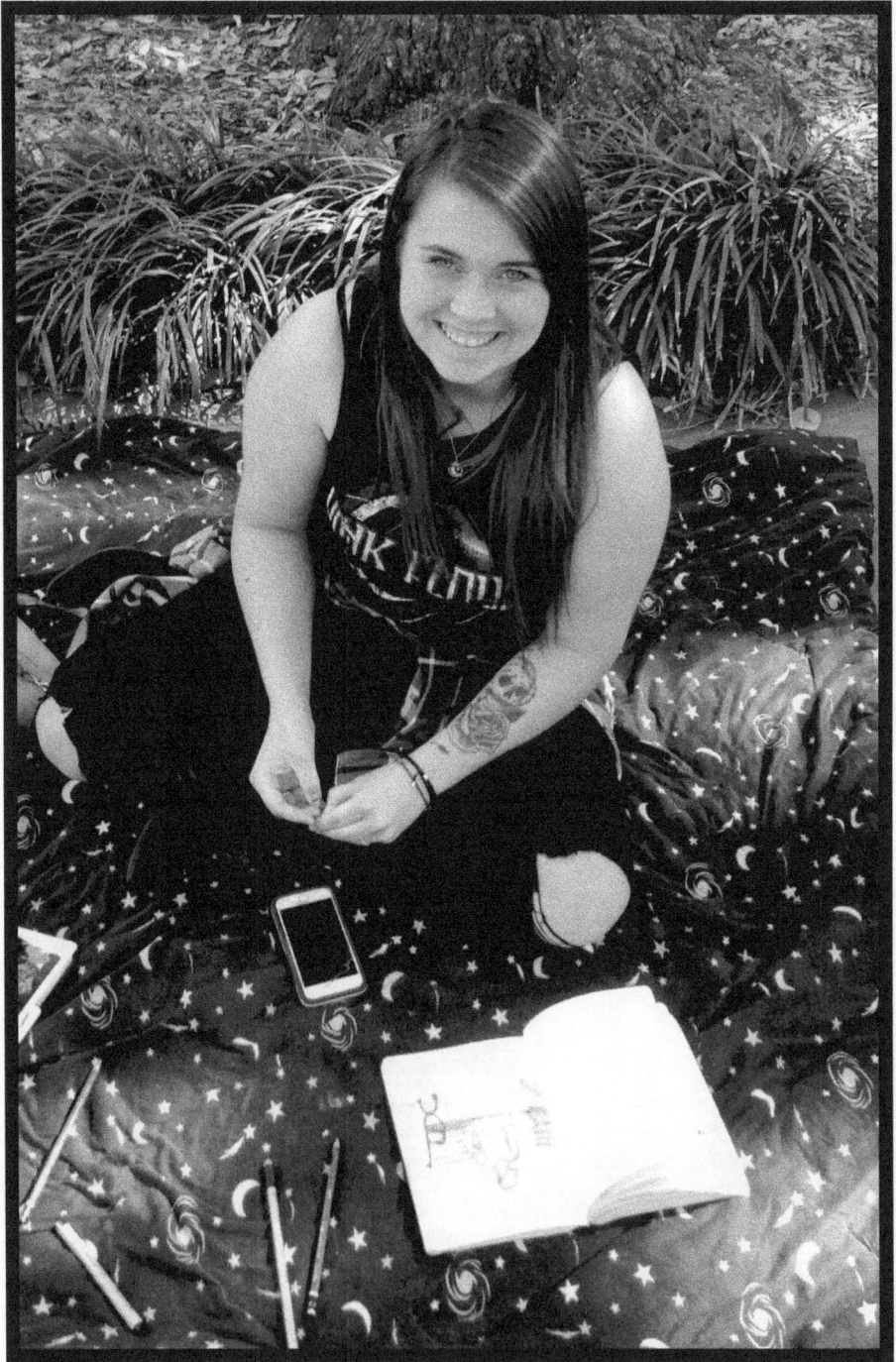

ALETHEA EASON

HOLIDAY COVE

"I'm feeling better," was the first thing my mother said.

"Better from what?"

"I had a little spell."

A long silence.

"And?"

"My heart felt a little strange and everything got black. But I laid down. I'm fine."

"Has this happened before?"

"No . . . only sometimes . . . when I first get up."

She says going to the doctor, "Won't do no good," that she checked out just fine last summer.

There is nothing I can do, but I worried about her all night. I stand at my kitchen sink and look over the lawn the tenants at Holiday Cove share. It is luxuriously soft; I can walk barefoot over it. It extends to a narrow beach, more rock than sand. It has rained off and on for the last month, but the lake is still murky. A crude bridge, some sort of metal contraption on wheels, leans to one side and crosses to a dock shaped like an upside-down L. Karen, my neighbor, is sitting on the bench above where, if any of us had a rowboat, it would be tied.

They took her children away yesterday. She yells at them a lot, unless her aunt's around to run interference, but yesterday the screaming took on a whole different magnitude. I watched her drag Markie by the hair with the baby wailing, purple faced under her arm. She dropped Markie. He landed on his hands and knees in a puddle.

"You fucking goddamned piece of shit," she yelled and kicked him. "I told you to stay out of my stuff."

The baby was practically hanging by his neck by then. I thought he'd choke.

I watch her today. Her body seems as weighed down as mine.

I don't know Karen, and I admit to being prejudiced against her. She lives here because she's the landlady's niece. All of us have complained about the garbage that piles up in front of her door, the steady stream of men with jail tattoos, the neglect of her children. But I watch her now and think about how she played with her kids last summer, throwing a Frisbee to her oldest boy, the little one leaning on her leg. Her laughter, deep laughter for a small woman, carried through my window. She loves her children. She just doesn't have any business being their mother.

I turn on the water, hold my hand under it until it gets hot. Karen doesn't move the entire time I do the dishes. When I'm done, she's still sitting there, staring out at Mt. Konocti or maybe at a duck.

I take my garbage downstairs. Walter, the grumpy old bachelor who lives below me is washing his car. He bends the hose so that I won't get wet as I cross to the cans.

"So, Paula, did you hear what happened?" he asks, his head nodding toward the dock.

"Yes," I say warily.

I don't like talking to Walter, and it's not because he doesn't have teeth. I know he doesn't have the money or insurance. It's just that his attitude is sour.

I take another step, and before I reach the cans he says, "I called CPS."

So, we both called; that's why the social worker actually showed up.

"I caught the older boy playing on the dock by himself again the other day," Walter says. "I took him home. The place was a sty. She was gone off with one of her boyfriends. Left those two all by themselves, a six-year old minding a baby."

Walter hocks and spits. "It'll be raining by this afternoon."

"Then why are you washing your car?"

"None of your damn business," Walter says, uncrinkling the hose.

I walk behind him to avoid getting wet.

A shadow passes over my head. I look up and see a bald eagle flying impossibly low. The eagle looks lazy to me, flapping its wings so slowly I wonder how it stays airborne, too low to be catching an air current. He looks as if he's having a bad hair day. I'm captivated. For the first time in days, I feel a lifting of sorts, as though the bird pulls at my heart. It passes over Karen's head and flies above the lake.

Karen looks up too. The first motion she's made.

Walter says over the spray of water, "Did you know they usually have two babies at once? The stronger one gets all the food and pushes the weaker one out of the nest."

"That's all you have to say?"

"Yep."

Walter sprays another tire. I walk to the dock. It bobs under me as I step off the metal bridge and walk down to the corner of the L. I don't intend to talk to Karen. Let her be in peace with her own misery. I just want to see if I can find the bird again.

The wind picks up. There was a small gap of blue sky while the eagle flew over, but the clouds have clamped together again.

"Pretty bird."

I turn toward Karen. I feel cold and wrap my arms about myself, tucking my hands into my armpits.

"Yeah."

We stare at each other. She's young. Twenty-three, maybe.

"It's getting cold," Karen says. "There's supposed to be a good storm coming." She stands up. She's so skinny. *Meth?* I wonder. "Aunt Juanita don't want me to live here no more."

"No?"

She's twirling a rolled up tissue between the fingers of her left hand like it was a paper baton.

"Do you want to eat dinner with me?" The words blurt out of my mouth like I'm possessed. "It's just warmed over lasagna from last night. And a salad. That's all."

Say no. Say no. Say no.

"Sure, that'd be nice."

I'm afraid she sees how I'm forcing the corners of my mouth to turn up.

The girl eats like there is no tomorrow. She's on her third serving of lasagna, the one I had planned to take for lunch. She tells me about her life in foster homes, her mother's alcoholism. Markie's dad is prison for a long time. Kyle's dad is even younger than she is. He's one of the guys that come around.

When Karen smiles, she's pretty. She asks if I'd like to get high. When I decline, she laughs that low laugh of hers.

"You don't even smoke. No ashtrays." she says, in mock disbelief and then nods to a print of Van Gogh's sunflowers I have hanging on a wall. "That's really nice."

"Where are your kids?"

This must seem like a strange response to her remark, but I've been dying to ask all evening.

"Some lady in Lakeport has them. I get to see them next week." There is silence. I don't know what to say, but Karen starts to talk again before it gets too uncomfortable. "I screwed up. But when I get them back, I won't do it again."

The rain begins to fall. I have a corrugated roof. I love to hear the drumming. It suddenly beats down hard like the sky rips apart. Karen and I could be a thousand miles from anywhere, alone in this little home of mine.

"I should go," Karen says.

I offer my umbrella, but she declines.

"Thanks." Karen stands at my doorway. The light of the porch catches raindrops and for a few seconds they fall like illuminated pearls. A halo forms around her hair. "This was real nice of you."

She pulls her denim jacket over her head. When she reaches the bottom step, she runs across the lawn to where the rain falls invisibly beyond the glow of the light.

Juanita considers herself to be a witch. Her mobile home, perish the thought of calling it a trailer, is filled with dreamcatchers and herbs dangling from the ceiling, decorated with ribbons, feathers and arrowheads. Amethysts as large as fists sit on the top of altars. Affirmations are displayed throughout the house. "I am safe. I do not fear the future," is above the toilet paper dispenser.

Juanita has not kicked Karen out. She says she's working with her, clearing her energy, smudging her apartment twice a week, counseling her on the benefits of a drug-free life, dispensing St. John's Wort which she has picked and dried herself. She has also lent Karen tapes of Buddhist nuns chanting sutras and Navajo flute music.

Karen looks better. Her face has cleared up, so maybe she is off the meth. The only man who is still coming by is Kyle's dad.

It's a cold, clear Saturday in January. My mother calls telling me she hasn't had a spell in almost a month. I hope she's telling me the truth. We play a game of non-disclosure, saving the most stressful events of our lives until the next crisis when we spill our guts. It's too beautiful to stay indoors;

the sky is the color of aquamarine; the lake looks spruced up for winter.

Walter's out there fiddling with his damn car again, but even he won't daunt my spirits. I act as if I can stand the man.

"Good morning, Walter."

"Did you hear about it?" I'm not going to get out of here without hearing him complain about something. "Juanita!"

"What about Juanita?"

"She's going to have one of her covens this afternoon. All that chanting and drumming. I can't stand it."

I bite my tongue. I'm not into evoking either god or goddess, but to each her own, I feel. Besides, she owns the place and can do anything she wants with it. I want to say to Walter, "Why don't you just move if you're so unhappy here?" But I know he can't. He's not going to find a place as nice or as cheap as Holiday Cove.

"See you later," I say instead.

I hike across the lawn, skirting the abandoned houseboat. It would be cute with a thousand bucks or so thrown into it, and if the hole in the side were sealed so that it wouldn't flood. I'm wearing my boots and my feet skim the waterline. I walk to the next piece of property and trespass to get to a path, not more than a deer trail, a swath between manzanita and the broom that choke the hillside.

I feel like I'm on top of the world, even though I'm probably only a couple hundred or so feet above the lake. Down below, I see Juanita and her friends digging out a pit for a fire. I wonder what Walter's reaction will be when he finds out it's not just the usual drumming circle, but a full on sweat. Black Bear, a faux Indian, a white man with a Brooklyn accent who's always dressed in leather and feathers even when I run into him at the grocery store, has arrived.

Juanita is dressed in scarlet, some type of exotic pantsuit. Karen is there. She looks like a puppy next to Juanita, following her about, copying her movements as they dig. I search the sky hoping to see an eagle again and then spy a couple of deer slowly making their way up the hill. They don't see me. Walter calls them big rats. I could stay up here all day, but a pesky feeling of loneliness starts gnawing at me. I wander down, scare the deer. They bound in opposite directions and disappear into separate clumps of brush.

By the time I get back to the lake's rim, I hear the drumming and smell the smoke from the fire. I wave at the gathering and cross the lawn.

"Won't you join us?" Juanita asks.

I want to slink back into my apartment, disappearing from these earnest looking women and the guy from New York whose feathers are drooping.

"I don't think so."

"Oh, come on," Karen says. She looks happy. The social worker was out earlier today with her boys.

I shake my head and back away. I'm adamant about not joining them, until Karen knocks on my door.

An hour later I'm standing naked with a towel wrapped around me, a sprig of wormwood behind my ear. Black Bear gives instructions about how we are to enter the sweat lodge and how we are to crawl clockwise once we are inside. I make smart aleck comments to myself about a bunch of white people playing Indian, but I go ahead and bend in front of the door and ask the blessings of all my relations, crawling behind Juanita's best friend, a large blonde lady who sings like an angel.

It's very dark. And it's uncomfortable; the burlap bags scratch my bottom. I have to adjust for pointy rocks. The space feels very small.

The flap is closed. The singer's voice soars. Water is spilled upon the glowing rocks, and it gets hot immediately. This is just the first scoop I think. I force myself not to scuttle over the naked bodies of the other women.

The third time the flap closes, Juanita begins to talk, and then the woman next to me. They tell two different stories about the past, but the pain seems to be shared. The heat grows. Karen talks of her mother, things I don't want to hear. My head is thick right now; I'm trying to disconnect, but slowly the understanding comes of why Juanita has given Karen chance after chance. The last two women share their stories, but I'm not listening. Juanita pours ladles of water on the rocks. I cover my head with my towel and lie down, putting my nose close to the ground. I poke my finger through the bottom of the quilt that covers the lodge and breath fresh air.

Then the final round begins. The last of the hot stones are brought in. The flap closes; we're supposed to offer prayers as scoop after scoop is poured upon the rocks. It's so hot I think I'll die. I think of my mother, of the things that have separated us, of how we fumble as we try to offer love, of how I begin screaming at her after I'm home for a day, and I feel the fear of losing her as I die in the lodge.

Karen receives her kids back the day before Valentine's Day. She invites me over. Markie is signing his name in a large scrawl, the letters all uneven, the "a" backwards. Tomorrow will be his last day at the school. Juanita said she'd take him so he doesn't miss the party. Karen is smoking. Kyle is bouncing on her lap.

"There's this place on Bear Creek I'm taking the kids. You want to go? It's really neat, I used to party there."

Sure, why not.

When we park, there's a Laotian family gathered around milk crates filled with aluminum beer cans and glass bottles. Karen, with Kyle on her hip, leads Markie and me down a short path. When I see the water, I'm happy. The rocks are eroded, and the scene looks like a postcard shot, the Southwest with all of the color bled out. Right in the middle of the creek is a small island; the water has to snake around either side as it makes its way down to Cache Creek, which in some states would be considered a river. I think that this place would be great to come back to in the summer and skinny dip, but then the sun catches the pieces of glass. The longer I look the more trash I see: plastic rings for six packs and cigarette packs nestled in the crannies of the rock, toilet paper, empty glass bottles. Karen has crossed over to the island with Markie hopping across the rocks right behind her.

The Laotian grandmother and her granddaughter come down the path with the milk crates. Maybe they're Cambodian? Or Hmong? I smile when they reach me, but the look on my face must not be very convincing because they don't smile back.

I cross over to the island. Underneath my feet, the ground sparkles with the shards. The way they shine is almost pretty.

"Too bad they aren't crystals," Karen says.

Markie makes airplane noises. He runs around us in circles with his arms spread out like wings.

I'm wondering who could come here and destroy a place like this, but I say, "This is great."

"It's trashed." Karen turns around in a circle. Markie seems like a moon revolving around her, a satellite out of control. Kyle puts his thumb in his mouth. "I never was here in the daytime, but it wasn't like this back then. We'd walk around barefoot."

"You want to go back?" I ask.

"I think so."

On the drive home, Karen doesn't say anything. Both boys fall asleep. She stares out the window. I want to believe she's taking stock of her life, coming to terms with being a mother, growing up as she sits beside me. I don't trust my thoughts. Who really grows up? But, I know I'll keep rooting for her.

I ease the car up the Holiday Cove driveway. Juanita is talking to Walter. She laughs at something. I think he even cracks a smile. Markie is awake; as soon as the car stops, he's out the door, running to Juanita, but it's Walter who bends over and picks him up.

I get out of the car and walk over to them while Karen takes Kyle out of his seat.

"The eagles were flying overhead just a few minutes ago," Juanita says.

"Eagles?" I ask, and look up.

"They're gone," Walter tells me.

It's getting cold again; the clouds are turning pink from the setting sun. I walk to the dock, sit down on the bench, and wait expectantly.

STEVE KOPPMAN

THE RUSSIANS ARE HERE

"Boris and Ina Weinberg," the social worker said without enthusiasm. "They're both engineers, whatever *that* means." Everyone was an engineer there, even if he only checked the oil. She droned about Ina and Boris like they were used and likely damaged merchandise. "Maybe you'd prefer another family." If they didn't work out, she emphasized, he could always come back for another draw. It was 1991, the Soviet Union was imploding, Russians were a glut on the market.

)( )( )(

The sign announced Hillcrest Manor in old English script. The Weinbergs' two-story semi-circular building was the color of mud. In the dark lobby, their new tutor read names—but no Weinbergs—next to columns of black buttons. A man shouted to come up but disconnected before telling him where to go. He wandered confused into the courtyard parking lot, where voices called in Spanish and Asian languages from windows and open back doors. Then the three of them stood before him, side by side like a family portrait, next to a big red 1960s convertible: A short stocky middle-aged man with square head and black mustache, a green-eyed soft-faced woman smiling warmly, and a pale thin boy of about ten with her features. They shook hands and Boris patted the car's hood. "Jewish Family Services," he said in a thick accent. "Eight cylinders."

Under a red Bugs Bunny paperweight on the kitchen table, food stamps protruded from a pile of supermarket coupons. The one-bedroom apartment was cramped but perfectly kept; nothing was on the floor but rugs. The fresh smell reminded him of mothers at home, dusting, cleaning, fluffing pillows. The big TV blasted but no one else seemed to notice.

Jeff brought his own family album to break the ice, filled with pictures of his twin sons. Ina smiled broadly and nodded, murmuring "nice" and "boy." They showed him the two pictures they had. The rest had been sent from Kiev in a huge shipping container that still hadn't crossed the ocean. The first picture was in a large hall filled with seemingly hundreds of happy-looking people, their clothes familiarly old-fashioned, dancing and drinking.

"Friend," said Ina. Boris looked jauntily into the camera's eye, a cigar held loosely in his crooked smile. There were so many people, looking happier than Jeff had seen anyone in a long time. He missed them suddenly, as if he knew them. The second photo showed the folding chairs afterward, empty yet still celebrant, a cigarette butt on one, a round hat here, a scarf, a wet newspaper. He mused on dancing and talking through vodka into the night, in the morning searching for chickens in empty stores before standing in endless lines to get papers signed. It reminded him of college.

"Hard to leave," he blurted nostalgically. He repeated it before Ina's eyes lit up.

"Can't live for fun only," she said and shrugged.

"House, Berkeley?" Boris asked.

"Oakland, nearby. We rent too."

"Neighborhood nice?" he asked, rotating his right hand back and forth when Jeff didn't answer immediately. "So-so?"

"It's OK. We moved there for the schools."

"There black man?"

"Some . . . yeah . . . a few."

"Drive car work?"

"Just to train, BART station."

"Have to car, this country," said Ina. "I must car. Bus very long. I tired. Go nowhere. Very cost gas." She shook her head sadly and waved her hands. "Don't can speak. Bad language. Can't do thing. Russia, read every time. Now like child. There, library books, rich. Four newspapers. Here, nothing."

Her nice neighbor was friendly but rushed away. Her young cousin from Odessa had even less patience with her English now than the rude people in stores. No one had time here, she understood. She looked disgusted before smiling broadly. America waited for nobody.

"So hard," she continued. "So work." They studied English in Russia but it was all grammar. She held out her hands, eyes watering. "We need every time catch . . . ," making a grabbing motion. "No catch word," she said and laughed unhappily. "Like children we . . . sound like. How say: We . . . like .

". . . primitives. But didn't. Can't give word think."

"I know," said Jeff. "I do know that."

"Every time, 'Good English!' *So good!*" Ina smiled mockingly. "How long in country?"

"People in store, we no," said Boris as he shook his head and held up a hand.

"Understand," she said. "Black man," she added. "And A . . . jen, more worst!" she almost shouted with distaste. "No understand every thing. Every time!"

"Spanish," Boris added.

"Other people," she said.

"That about covers it," said Jeff.

"We Jewish, have much talk, I want talk you. Every time don't speak. Read like three years. In Russia, big. Ideas, all night books. Here like little child," pointing to her son by the TV.

"How do you say his name, Ev-geny or Yev-geny?" Jeff asked.

Boris shrugged tiredly. "America!" he said. "Eugene!"

"I need American boyfriend practice English," Ina blurted. Jeff looked uncomfortable. Boris barked at her in Russian. "I am fun," she said, shrugging and smiling toward each of them in turn. "Itsa joke.

"Why you do this?" Ina continued. "Itsa job?"

"Oh, no, no, no." Jeff shook his head repeatedly.

She smiled. "You like help Jewish?"

The words left him uneasy. He smiled with effort, reminded of pictures in his album he hadn't let them get to, pictures from the Ukraine of all places, recently added brown sepia pages sent by his sick great-uncle in St. Louis, long-dead people who were suddenly supposed to be his great-great-grandparents and their siblings, faces he'd thought lost forever. The men's heads were covered by square black flat-topped yarmulkes, long wrinkled faces by shaggy grey beards, eyes filled with light: passionate, haunted, desperate. The women looked severely into the camera, seeming to judge it from the other world. Their grandchildren never talked much about the old people, the old country. It was so long ago. Who remembered? Who wanted to hear? Even family details he'd heard from his grandmother and each of her sisters were reliably contradictory. Each child in the family seemed to have a different genealogy.

These might be the only pictures they ever had taken, so different from their American great-grandchildren, Jeff's parents' generation, mysteriously born with camera straps grafted into the backs of their necks. Jeff was surprised to see no strong resemblance to anyone he knew; they looked almost generic, inhabitants of legendary Russian Jewish villages, lives fixed now by dates in margins, starting with 1856, names no one living remembered with certainty as they puzzled over Hebrew letters scrawled in margins. He imagined his new forebears around the Seder table at Passover, telling him to eat in loud voices, saying questionable things in Yiddish and snickering.

One of his great-grandfathers in particular he couldn't get out of his mind. Did he always have that half-demented look of dread, awe, anxiety? Now he could never know what it was, in what combination: Was it the fire of knowing, being enveloped in God's presence? Was it fear? Of the smallpox, of not being able to feed those many children, of his sons dragged away screaming for life into the Czar's army, of marauding Cossack *pogromitchki?* Was it being poor, or terrorized, or henpecked? Or was it only the photographer's light?

)( )( )(

His boys grappled across the living room floor as Jeff stepped furtively toward the door one night the next week. Laura yelled from her back bedroom but he honestly couldn't make out her words, maybe berating him for going or something undone. Was he escaping, scaling the Wall, fording the Volga? They would surely stay together longer if he got out more, he reasoned. He smiled at Andrew—looking up because beneath, getting the worse of it, his seemingly oversized head smushed against the carpet—winked and whispered "love you." The boy smiled as Jacob turned from his prey to look up too. Jeff hoped peace would arrive in his place.

He couldn't tell just what had happened to Ina. Despite her pink-purple "Madonna On Tour" T-shirt, she looked disappointingly more like anyone else.

"What happened to your hair?" he asked. Rudeness could always be excused by "bad language."

"You no like?"

The TV blared though none of them could catch the fast words. Yevgeny knelt on the carpet, eyes fixed on the wide color screen, yellow-orange T-shirt glowing "Blonde Ambition" in the dark. Without their container, they'd had to buy new clothes.

"Well, I don't know," Jeff said as they sat down at the kitchen table. "I liked the way you all looked already."

"American?"

"You all look great the way you are."

She shrugged and laughed. "In America, I," she said, patting down her hair. "Do American." He recalled as from a dream the Jewish Federation's stated mission for him: English teaching and Americanization. He was supposed to acculturate the Russians, not they him.

"Free country," she was saying. "Russian grey. Here wash grey," she said and shrugged again. "New country, new hair. New country," she sighed. "Too hard." Her tone grew quieter, and anxious. Boris was out talking with rich Russians in San Francisco. He worried always now about money; they had no job or prospects between them. One day the past week, he'd gone for job counseling, another day to a resume-writing class though only understanding "five, six words." When not at adult school, he talked "business deals." Her eyes conveyed looming disaster. She likes regular jobs; Boris likes business. He started one, selling electronic components, even in Kiev where there were no longer laws. Boris stepped through the sliding back door.

"Where your car?" he asked Jeff. Boris told him more than once to park behind theirs outside the back door. But Jeff left his twenty-year-old green Ford Maverick out on the street. It was hard to explain.

"Park here," said Boris, pointing out back.

"No problem," said Jeff, and Boris' eyes widened.

"No problem," Boris repeated, nodding energetically. "Whatsa big deal?" he continued. "Get it?" They were starting idioms at adult school.

"You talk big deals?" Jeff asked.

"What's happening?" Boris continued. "No way." The phone rang.

"Allo." Ina answered, then was silent several seconds. "Ah . . . no . . . ah . . . no." She shook her head. "Ah . . . no, please." The tinny faraway sound from the other end was insistent. At the hands of telemarketers, they had already changed long-distance carriers three times, been declared winners in two international sweepstakes and won free estimates for several services they could not describe.

"I need go, please. Excuse. Thank you, please." Her face was red. She waved to Boris, who marched over, shoulders hunched, duty in his eyes, and took the handset.

"Hello," said Boris. He was silent for some time. "No . . . I didn't want . . .We didn't." Jeff stepped over to him, asked for the handset, took it from him and closed it into the phone.

She shrugged and smiled with effort. "America."

"Talk business in San Francisco?" Jeff resumed to Boris.

"Ah," said the latter, left hand moving to forehead as he rolled his eyes. He looked at his wife as they shot Russian past each other.

"So-so?" asked Jeff. "Not so hot?"

"Maybe so-so," said Boris. "We see. Maybe deal . . . maybe no."

Boris found things out. An organization brought new arrivals to a few Russians who came many years before and got rich like everyone was supposed to in America. Boris was talking to a guy with 300 people supposedly working for him and an $80,000 Mercedes-Benz. Maybe Boris would help him build a factory back in Kiev where labor was cheap. Meanwhile he was peripherally involved in several enterprises whose nature he could or would not define in any language. "Business America business," he opined, smiling sheepishly. "You business? Have business?"

"What your work?" echoed Ina.

Jeff grudgingly pulled a card from his wallet. It said program specialist. He thought about putting it positively but it seemed too hard. Boris looked at the card without expression. "I work for the federal government. Food programs. We work with state agencies."

He hated more than anything to explain himself. When he thought too hard about it, his life seemed a terrible series of misunderstandings he wished he could straighten out but never actually could. He hadn't meant it but there it was. He'd tried to teach history after college but, longer on theory than patience, hadn't been great at it, nor gotten on so well in the little outposts where he could find jobs in those days when he imagined they would change the world—if only they were bold enough—in large assertive leaps. Later he'd worked his way around the globe, writing travel articles for newspapers, studying in Israel and India, until money was gone. He had offers to work abroad but couldn't decide to stay. The community agency he long worked for finally went under. He went back to grad school and by the time he got out was married with twins on the way. After more than a year looking and many thousands in debt, he'd counted himself lucky to find the government job where he'd stayed.

At family gatherings now, he drifted away from people while greeting them. Cousins were prosperous, doctors and lawyers and noted authorities speaking on public TV about hot flashes and the right to die, incomes at least triple his. He'd seemed the most promising of them as a boy, the first to read at three, the only one to know of Millard Fillmore and Ulan Bator. Now he felt guiltily thankful for his cousin Stan with multiple sclerosis; at least someone was worse off.

"This is the boy," Jeff tutored. "This is his book. This is the boy with his book."

"This is boy with his book."

"This is *the* woman. This is *her* baby."

"This is woman with his baby."

One night leaving their house, Jeff's car wouldn't start. He repeated every useless gesture he knew to get it to go. A drizzle had started. He'd stayed too late; now he'd miss MacNeil-Lehrer at eleven. He couldn't stand the thought somehow of going back to the Weinbergs' apartment. But the alternative was wandering in the dark and rain along the boulevard searching for a pay phone. He sat back in the driver's seat, hands uselessly gripping the steering wheel. Finally he got out, rushing through the courtyard to their back door. Their lights were out. He tapped several times on the sliding glass before sound grew from inside. Ina emerged confused from the dark. She squinted toward the door and called Boris before trying to pull it open herself without success. He came a minute later, in undershirt and pants, red-faced, annoyed, face creased from the bed.

"Car won't start. Need triple-A."

Boris raised his right hand. "I go."

They walked out the parking lot to the street without speaking. The car came into view: Half the radiator grille was missing from a long-ago accident and both sides had big dents. By himself, he didn't notice this. Water leaked in when it rained from rust cracks in the bottom. He'd bought the car after leaving college. It reminded him of everything but he didn't want to give it up. It hurt to see it now through Boris' unsentimental eyes. Boris raised the hood with a tired, knowing look and peered about.

"Battery dead?"

"Guess so."

"New car soon?" Boris asked, smiling very slightly.

He shrugged. "New cars' batteries die too."

Boris shook his head. "More American like new," he said, nodding, then hesitating. "Lotsa money," he added, though it half-sounded like a question.

"Yeah."

Boris put down the hood, smiled and patted it. "Like Russian," he said. "Needed money," and he drew the fingers of his right hand into a point.

)( )( )(

One summer Saturday they went together to the Oakland Rose Garden. The warm tangy air settled over them, a transparent blanket. There weren't many people. They didn't see the young red-eyed black man coming and wondered later how they could have missed him. It was as if one of the small trees started speaking in a strange melodic voice. He was skinny, a couple of inches shorter than Jeff, who didn't know what he was saying at first any more than they did. His thin face looked angry. His hands trembled and he didn't hold their gaze with bloodshot eyes. His arms moved jerkily. The Russians stood behind Jeff, as if in formation.

"You know . . . you know . . . the way to Grand Avenue, man?" he asked.

"You go down two blocks that way," Jeff pointed, "then take a right and it's the next street."

"Thanks, man, I tell you, I just need some money for the bus."

The Russians started easing away. Jeff turned back to them as they upbraided him with their eyes.

"I'm sorry, I can't," Jeff shrugged as he started to walk off.

"Who're your friends? They from around here?" the man walked alongside.

"No . . . no," he hesitated.

"How come they give foreigners the jobs, man? Can you tell me that? We've been here hundreds of years, I still can't find a job."

"They don't have jobs, actually."

"They'll have 'em soon, man. You know what I'm sayin'."

"I know . . . it's terrible."

"Just some money for the bus, man, come on! Came for my mother's funeral, then no place to stay! Had to sleep on the street!"

"We go car," Boris called from up ahead.

"Wait a minute!" shouted Jeff, trotting as the man bounced after them. The Russians were heading for the car, Jeff in pursuit, the man alongside. Jeff pulled out his wallet and handed him a dollar, ignoring a few twenties. The man stopped suddenly but seemed to look at his money in the billfold as Jeff closed it.

"I need twenty dollars, man. Is that all you can give me?" still not looking at Jeff directly.

"Yeah," Jeff said with feigned anger, stuffing his wallet in his pocket as he rushed toward the Russians.

"Why you running away from me?" he scolded them in a low voice.

"Only go car," said Boris with an embarrassed smile.

"No money," said Ina.

"I still wish you'd stay with me," said Jeff.

)( )( )(

Increasingly he found them entranced before the booming television. Their glazed looks lifted only slightly as he passed before them, faces bathed in the band of colored light, dark eyes fixed on rainbow screen, taking in soap opera, basketball game or news program, regardless of language of transmission, with the same devoted gaze.

One night Boris wouldn't stick with his conversational lesson.

"This is Mr. Oliver's house. Listen to *whose. Whose* house is this?"

"Whose house is this?"

"Queen is Mr. Oliver's dog."

"Whose . . . Queen . . . is . . . Mr. Olivyer."

The TV's noise distracted Jeff. He wasn't sure momentarily if Boris' response were correct. Boris got up silently from the table, head down, leather windbreaker open over St. Louis Cardinals T-shirt. When he returned a minute later, his face was red.

"How are you?" Jeff asked though he knew.

"Very bad," Boris said, flailing his arms. "Needs work. Too hard sit in house. Bad. Need . . . money. Welfare no good."

Welfare was $650 a month like the rent plus $250 more in food stamps. But welfare would take back half of whatever they earned so, what with losing 'medical,' he figured he had to make at least $300 a week to work at all. Jeff reassured him they were making progress and promised to help them make more. Boris looked skeptical.

"I know it's hard," Jeff said. "I've never been that good at it myself." He thought for their struggle they deserved somebody on top of his own life, someone with enough to give away.

Gradually Jeff came less often. He called off lessons and overlooked them, cutting the Russians back over time from twice a week to once and less. He called in to their newly taped phone message, more than once hanging up when they answered live.

"Weinberg family can come to phone right now. Please leave name after beep, we call you back. Thank you. Bye-bye."

It was getting to be more of the same. He told himself their English was not so much getting better as his own getting worse. He needed more time at home, hard as it was. He imagined new Russians, fresh Russians, true Russians, unspoiled, out of a fading old picture or a line from Shalom Aleichem or even Dostoyevsky. He could call a Jewish agency any time, Palo Alto, East Bay, San Francisco; Russians were a dime a dozen.

One night Boris shook Jeff's hand happily at the sliding door. He wore a smeared green T-shirt that read "Electricians Shock" in front and "Electricians Do It With Appliances" in back. He'd started helping two Russian electricians in San Francisco. These guys didn't bother with taxes or even checks but paid in cash "behind bench." He had to get out, he was going crazy in the house. He wouldn't make much, it was only a few hours a week.

Inside the apartment, though the TV screamed Ina and Yevgeny ignored it, sitting instead now around the phone, smiling and nodding, passing the receiver only reluctantly to each other. Boris soon joined them and two compared understandings while the other held the handset tightly to ear, shouting, "Stop! Stop! Quiet!" Jeff guessed it was his fault; he'd given them the numbers of the weather, time and free news lines.

Saturday two weeks later, sightseeing at the shopping mall, the Russians saw an ad in Domino's window. Soon Boris was delivering pizzas three nights a week with his big car. It was fine but for addresses. Streets here stopped suddenly and started again somewhere else entirely. Many houses didn't have numbers or lights. In Russia, everything was "number one, then number two." Streets didn't disappear or turn into something completely different. People knew their neighbor's addresses. Here nobody knew anything.

Ina finally got a letter from the steamship company that their container had arrived. It was giant, wooden, much taller than herself, weighing more than 300 kilograms, carrying furniture, clothes, cartons of books, musical instruments, records, papers and everything they could never replace: pictures, letters, bits and pieces they had written and received and kept all their lives. From growing up in Kiev, college, wedding, grandparents and great-grandparents and before, family killed by Nazis, Stalin, the Civil War,

Cossacks, children who had grown up and who hadn't.

Standing on a tall ladder, she unlatched the top of the box and saw straight to the bottom. She shrieked on the pier and everyone looked up at her. Blackness spread before her eyes. Maybe it was the wrong one? The few things left were tossed all about. She kept looking, looking, trying to make her eyes wider, trying to somehow let in more light. They were bad people at the border, she knew it even then in her heart. After ransacking the box, they sent it on almost empty, many months later, as if there were still something inside. Her eyes filled with tears telling the story. "Can't talk about," she kept saying. "Can't think. Broke country. Bad people." With nothing more to wait for, they were suddenly much poorer than they thought.

𝓧 𝓧 𝓧

At the party celebrating their first year in America, everyone but Jeff spoke Russian. It took three minutes to angle through the crowd from door to kitchen table where Boris and Ina sat between friends and family. Boris wore an uncharacteristic white shirt, buttoned at the collar. He smiled a cautious little smile and extended his right hand. Ina came up behind Jeff.

"Boris go for job," she said.

"He has jobs, I know."

"New job," she said. "Interview."

"Full time," Boris said, looking directly into Jeff's eyes, shaking his fist in the air in triumph. "Trainee engineer. Technik." The Russians around the table lifted smiling faces to Jeff in unison.

"Like start," Ina said. "Trainee engineer, trainee English."

"You had interview? This happened?"

"Today. This day," he said, pointing to the table with his right index finger. "Go good. Many Russian."

"That's wonderful," Jeff said.

"Forty-two thousand first year, with bonus," said Boris, eyes wide, features on his face stretched, then making motions like writing with his finger on a napkin in front of him. He shrugged and compressed his lips. "If get."

Ina smiled broadly and nodded. "Good start," she said.

"Great," said Jeff. His mind was blank. It was more than he'd made yet.

"English now better mine," Boris said, tapping his chest. "I can't job if you didn't."

"Thanks," said Jeff. "You've worked hard. You've done good work."

"English no good," insisted Ina, smiling. "Bad English. I want English. Need also job."

Jeff thought of his boys tumbling backwards and forwards across the living room floor, rolling over bars like acrobats, swimming like little water animals, things he'd never learned. He wondered again why he was there with the Russians while thinking he should really come more often. He didn't want to lose sight of them. Maybe they'd remember him like he would them. No one would know or care soon whether any of them were Russians or Americans anyway, soon when they sat side-by-side on the shelf or more likely in the box of some in-some-way-Jewish person, with whom he'd notice no particular resemblance if he could see them, pictures about which the names and places and so-called facts would be uncertain, the only hints dark letters scrawled in margins in some dead or dying language.

"I know you want to learn faster. I'm sorry I've missed so many times. I'm not a good teacher."

"No, no," said Ina. "We thank you coming us every time. You help too much." She somehow looked sad while smiling broadly. Boris's lips were flat.

"No one helps too much," he corrected her. "Can't help much."

The social worker warned any number of times that once you started talking like them, you were useless in the great work of Americanization.

"You help me too," Jeff added. "Make world bigger."

"Da," she said. She looked at him, nodding quickly, not speaking now, her green eyes as if on fire from the inside, wanting so much to understand, more, to have something, something he might not. She smiled extra-broadly. "Nice," she said. "Thanks. Da. Good. Good man."

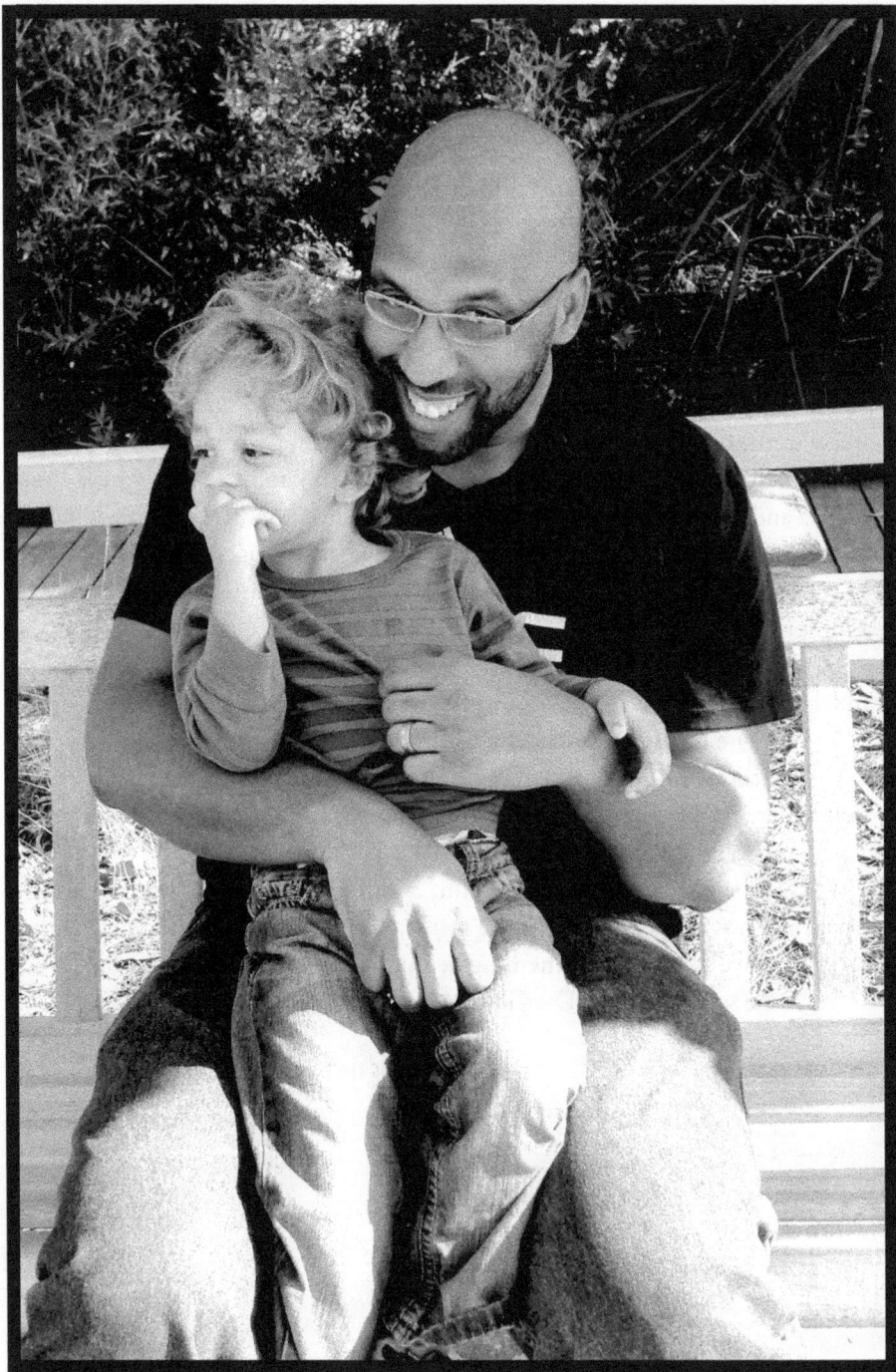

PAULINE KALDAS

AMONG NEIGHBORS

Our neighbor grills most summer evenings, even when rain threatens to cool the fire and pour on the picnic table set up in the middle of the driveway that he shares with his neighbors on the other side. The first summer we moved in, I'd watch out the kitchen window as he stood in front of his large gas grill, the cover propped open so he could turn whatever he was cooking with the long fork. David was tall with black hair and strongly accented cheekbones. In the summer, he wore jeans—often we'd see a row of them hanging on the clothesline—and no shirt, his slender body at ease with the sun and breeze of summer days. He moved with an air of calmness as if he were simply part of the changing seasons. Often, he'd stroll away from the grill to smoke a cigarette. It was a ritual that seemed integral to his life. "They're barbecuing again," I'd say to my husband, who preferred to keep the shades pulled down so no one could see us at our kitchen table as we ate.

When a young couple moved into the house next door on the other side of our neighbor, it wasn't long before they were barbecuing together, and that is when the picnic table was set up in their mutual driveway. "Well, no one ever invites us," I pouted to my husband, who responded with a flat hum. But maybe it's the nature of sharing a fence—soon my husband and David began to talk, and it was they, rather than David's wife and I, who began the relationship. We'd been there over a year, and perhaps that made us less threatening to them and the other neighbors since they realized we weren't the usual transient students. After my husband and I got married, we had moved to Egypt to teach at the American University in Cairo. I had immigrated at the age of eight, and this return was a reconnection to culture and family and an opportunity to introduce my husband to my homeland. The original plan was to stay one year but it had stretched to three. Now, we had moved to Binghamton to attend graduate school. Maybe knowing we were going to stay for a few years made us feel courageous enough to speak to those with whom we shared the street. From the kitchen, I'd hear David and my husband talking. Fortunately, they were both tall and had to crane their necks only slightly to see over the gray wood fence.

"What were you talking about?" I'd ask. Usually, the response was "nothing," but occasionally I'd get a tidbit of information: his wife's name is Emma and she's getting a degree in social work; he watches the weather channel; his father left the family when he was young.

Emma seemed more aloof, her lips thin and set firmly in place. I suspected she was the one who did most of the worrying in the family. As we tried to see each other over the bushes, it was difficult to find a topic for conversation, or maybe women just have a harder time chatting in that casual manner that men adopt so easily. Then Emma got pregnant and their first daughter was born. We went over with our two-year-old to offer congratulations and found common ground as we talked about children.

When the next summer arrived, David started gardening, and soon we found large zucchinis balanced on the fence for us. One day, I returned home to find that we had our own makeshift garden created by my husband and daughter. David had offered snippets of his own plants to get us started. The herbs survived, but the strawberries eventually became food for the squirrels.

After a few initial skirmishes, our cats learned to get along. Once, I saw David's black and white cat, Casey, and our gray tiger cat, Shango, sitting on opposite ends of our front porch, eyeing each other. Perhaps that was the moment of their truce. After that, I would often glimpse Casey strolling through our yard or even coming up to the back porch as if he were waiting for Shango to come out and play.

We slowly learned about our other neighbors. Mrs. Smith, who lived across the street, was in her eighties; she was a thin woman who still dressed carefully and went to the beauty parlor. Two things preoccupied her attention: the snow and parking. We quickly figured out that to qualify as good neighbors, we had only to respect what she considered to be her parking spot, which was directly in front of her house. As long as her spot remained reserved, we were praised as ideal neighbors and also subjected to stories about others who had lived in our apartment and violated the sacred laws, either by using her spot or neglecting the alternate street parking in the winter months. I watched in amazement as she shoveled out her own car during the winter and swept her stairs in the summer. On Christmas and Easter, she came by to offer candy to our children. She also made sure to let us know when garbage pick-up day was changed due to a holiday. We dubbed her the watchperson of the neighborhood.

Mrs. Sweeney, next door to us, also came over with small presents for the kids on holidays. I was amazed she could think of anyone else when she had nine grown children and numerous grandchildren of her own. She was a short woman with white hair that rested slightly on her shoulders. Something about her seemed rounded out, as if all the hard edges had lost their sharpness through the years. She spoke with a slight accent that sounded partly British, partly Australian—I think once she said she was from New Zealand. Our relationship began when her husband came over one day to introduce himself to my husband, who is African American, making a point of informing him that he had a son-in-law who was black. Mr. Sweeney was an older man, tall and well-built, usually wearing a baseball cap. He had spent many years in the Marines, but it wasn't until after he died that we found out he had been a school principal after he retired from the military.

Soon after Emma gave birth to Caroline, I became pregnant with our second daughter. Then David and Emma's neighbor on the other side, Lori, got pregnant. So the jokes began about something in the water and how many times it would go around.

Two summers later, Caroline turned two and Emma had another baby, a little boy they named Ben; our oldest daughter, Yasmine, was approaching five and the younger, Celine, was a year and a half; and Lori's daughter, Genevieve, turned one. It was that summer that our children found each other.

Caroline and Yasmine began to play, and, as soon as the weather warmed, their playing took them to the backyard. They would crawl through the overgrown wild berry bush next to the fence into each other's yard. I would watch them, or David, who stayed home during the day, would keep an eye on them. But the barriers became annoying when Yasmine needed to use the bathroom or if Celine joined them because she had to be watched more carefully or if David had to go in and feed Ben. One afternoon, the sun finally relenting its summer heat, the kids were running back and forth, and we all became a bit tired of stretching our necks over the fence. David began investigating the long poles on his side to see how the fence was put together. I nodded at his suggestion, and a few minutes later, a large section of the fence came down, carried away by David and my husband. Soon, our children were marking a path back and forth, claiming new territory.

David suggested a barbecue, and we compromised our varying dinner times to create a meal together. Between us, we had hamburgers, hot dogs, ribs, and chicken on the grill. Caroline ran back and forth to the picnic table and managed to consume almost the entire jar of pickles before we noticed. Celine sat herself in the center of the yard, the potato chip bowl firmly planted in her lap. If anyone dared to suggest she might want to share, they were given one of her lowered eyebrow squints and a sneer. The adults enjoyed the rest of the meal.

A few days later, standing in the kitchen wondering what nutritious, tasty dinner I could produce with turkey burgers, I looked out to see David standing by the grill. "Hey, David," I said without wondering if I was imposing, "Are you grilling tonight?" He nodded, so I asked if he had room for some burgers, and another communal dinner was on. When my husband returned, I announced we were eating with the neighbors again. His puzzled look subsided once he was outside, enjoying some male company with David and Lori's husband, Rick, instead of his all-female household.

Combined with David's spicy sausage and Rick and Lori's artichoke salad and barbecue beans, our burgers became part of a gourmet feast. And, with Rick's mother and his older daughters there, the child to adult ratio was in our favor as our children crawled and ran around the two yards. When the drizzle began, we ignored it and continued to eat. But when the raindrops grew louder and heavier, we covered the food, and our quick consultation over whose porch we should run to settled on Rick and Lori's, which was the closest. Everyone grabbed a plate, summoned a child, and we were off. Somehow, it was only the women and children who ended up on the porch while the men remained behind, presumably guarding the grill, although later I found them huddled on David's back porch. Soon Yasmine and one of Rick's older daughters were skipping up and down the steps, teasing the rain.

I wonder about this moment that rain, food, and children created. Had we met elsewhere, we probably would have never come to know each other. But sharing space can force an intimacy, stretching us beyond our seclusion. For me, that rainy evening was one of the rare moments when I felt located in one place, when cultural identity seemed superseded by being neighbors. At the end of that summer, we would move to Virginia. That evening, David, half-jokingly, said, "You'll find better neighbors and not even care about us anymore." Somehow I didn't think so. A friend who had grown up in Virginia had tried to reassure me recently about racial relations by telling me we probably wouldn't experience much direct discrimination, except maybe in housing.

The next day, David and Emma were not around. We used our own grill for a change and ate dinner alone. At the end of the evening, my husband tossed a few knots of sugarcane onto the still smoldering grill, and a sweet roasted smell spread over our neighborhood.

PATRICK CABELLO HANSEL

WASHING AWAY

He was washing his hands
at our kitchen sink, washing
and washing, the water running,
demanding more soap, this man
from Ukraine—writer, teacher,
speaker of many languages, now
reduced to one tongue even he
could not stand. A stranger in
his own mind. His wife of fifty
years leaned on the railing
of our back steps, pleading.
Each time she had passed us
on the street, she gave us a dollar
or two for our six-year-old's college.
Now she leaned, apologizing
for the man who barely knew her,
yelling at him that this wasn't his house.
I told him to take his time, offered
him a towel. My wife took his arm
and led him out the door and
into the late afternoon, patting
him on the shoulder and saying
"It's OK, it's OK, it's OK."

LOWELL JAEGER

AFTER SECOND SHIFT

She's stopped to shop for groceries.
Her snow boots sloshing
up and down the aisles, the store
deserted: couple stock boys
droning through cases of canned goods,
one sleepy checker at the till.

In the parking lot, an elderly man
stands mumbling outside his sedan,
all four doors wide to gusting sleet
and ice. She asks him, *Are you okay?*
He's wearing pajama pants, torn slippers,
rumpled sport coat, knit wool hat.

Says he's waiting for his wife.
I just talked to her on the payphone
over there. He's pointing at
the Coke machine. *What payphone?*
she says. *That one*, he says.
It's cold, she says, and escorts him inside.

Don't come with lights
and sirens, she tells the 911
dispatcher. *You'll scare him.*

They stand together. The checker
brings him a cup of coffee.
They talk about the snow.
So much snow.

They watch for the cop.
This night, black as any night,
or a bit less so.

NATURAL HISTORY

Young scholar leaving the Natural History Museum
steps into a sudden bluster of dust, a swirl
of dried leaves and curbside trash. Drops

her armload of file folders when she reaches
to save her hat, and a flurry of loose pages
scatter like a flock of white wings.

Boys across the street, passersby, rally and sprint
to help the girl chase after and gather
what can be caught, returning the salvage

soiled and creased. That's it; end of story—naturally
no single understanding is complete. These boys continue now
toward their college. The scholar un-rumples her work

and smooths it back into place. The impersonal
and insatiable wind goes howling. A few irretrievable
graphs and explanations have escaped.

NEIGHBORS

more than once i winched her car
back on the pavement
where she'd slid in the ditch

twice or three times
answered her call
to thaw frozen pipes

helped a delivery boy
heave a new fridge
up her back stairs

waved maybe in passing
but that's all there was
between us i think

and now that she's gone
unaccountably i miss
smoke rising from her chimney

and the one high window lit
i could view through the trees
in the darkened hillside yonder

WHAT SORT OF MAN

zips into a soiled red jumpsuit and pushes a broom?
Clears the plazuela, walkways, and greens.
Keeps the fountain clean. Sweeps cigarette butts,
gum wrappers, sticky discarded popsicle sticks,
plastic cup-lids. And dog shit.

The red jumpsuit says, Departmento de Parques.
He's working for us, and though it should single him out
—a cardinal in a field of sparrows—
this man melds into the jumpsuit like camouflage.

He's invisible to los estudiantes de la universidad
who spit their smokes and crush them. Faceless
to dog-walkers and aristocratic poodles, unleashed.
No obstacle to lovers who loiter nearby.
Just an empty pair of scuffed shoes to dark suits
hurrying past, tossing trash and missing the can.

I noticed him . . . because a devilish wind
stole pages from my notebook, and he ran
to help me gather my scribbles
scattered in the gutter across the street.
Gracias, I said and clasped in mis manos, clean and soft,
his gnarled knuckles and ragged nails.
De nada, he said. *De nada*. Kept his eyes downcast.

Noticed him at noon retrieve a brown sack
from a forked branch in a tree. And his hat
hung on another branch, same tree. His office,
I guessed. And noticed his granddaughter in navy blue
school uniform come to visit and share his tortillas,
help him hoist his waste buckets into dumpsters.

Noticed she hugged him. Noticed him waving, adios.
Heard him holler, *Gracias*, Maria. *Gracias por todo!*

THE LIBRARIANS

Why, as a teenage boy, would I savor the hushed solitude
and yellowed lamplight of a library reading-room
where bespectacled greybeards folded newspapers closed
on their laps, drowsed and mumbled?

What inner compass lured me
to the resplendent pillars, up the concrete steps,
and through the heavy glass doors? Can't explain
why those cracked leather chairs and dusty stacks
of all the stories in the world I hadn't read yet

comforted me weekends, while schoolmates
practiced their cool on the gymnasium dancefloor,
apprenticing themselves to the arts of coupling
and polite chitchat.

Or why the librarians . . .
my mother called them "spinsters." Why my dad raised an eyebrow
and made jokes about them I didn't laugh at.
Why I want to claim those ladies offered me kindnesses
of the sort I've rarely known through the husk of my loneliness
anywhere, elsewhere. When really all they did

was nod as I stomped my snowboots on the mat,
raise a finger to their lips to shush my bluster,
and dutifully wheel carts of titles back onto the proper shelves
where I might discover them. One of the ladies once
draped my wet coat over the steam heat, so that

at closing time I walked home, warm and dry.

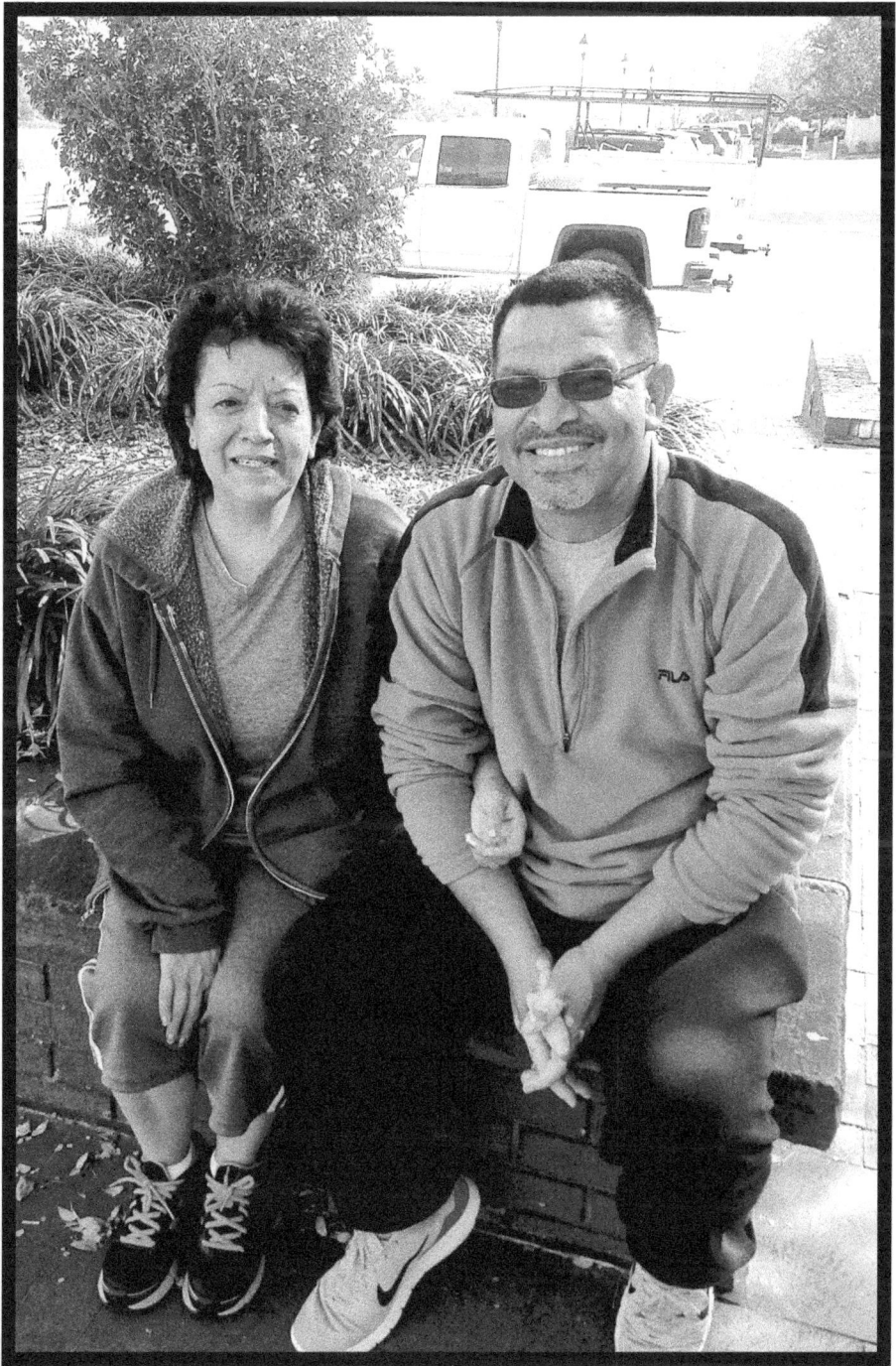

JOHN KING

COMMENCING AGAIN

I hold the graduation program above my face, and use it to shade my eyes from the sun as it comes slowly out from behind the clouds. For just a moment, I regret my impulsive agreement to "walk" with my classmates, but then I tune in again to the start of Commencement.

This is my third time to graduate from Rice University. The first had been as an undergraduate back in 1967, the second was when I received my MBA in 2006, and now I am receiving a Master of Liberal Studies degree. I would have skipped this graduation ceremony, except for one detail: the MLS Program is trying to grow, and wants to show its presence as the newest degree on campus. Even though I presented my Capstone and completed my graduation requirements back in November, when the emails started coming in from my classmates, pointing out to me that there were only eleven of us graduating and two would be out of the country, I quickly made my decision to send in my money, buy the cap and gown, and fly up from South Texas for graduation.

The one thing you can count on for a graduation ceremony on a Saturday in May in Houston is it will be hot. After a hundred and two of these ceremonies, the school has finally figured it out, and graduation started at 8:30 in the morning. This is fine by me, because it means I can sit here, listen to the speaker, have my degree conferred, and still get back to the apartment and change clothes in time for Liz and me to make the brunch service over at Local Foods.

Another thing different about this graduation is only Liz and I have come up to Houston. No kids, no parents, no friends, just a "being here, doing that" kind of a day.

The president of the university, Dr. LeBron, completes his introductory remarks, and then says:

"Ladies and Gentlemen, help me welcome, in Rice fashion, one
of the extraordinary leaders of our time, General Colin Powell. "

Powell steps up to the podium and appears to look over the sea of gowned graduates filling the quadrangle. The undergraduates have marched in by college, and each section has its flags and standards waving in the mild breeze. The rear of the courtyard is filled with family and friends.

After the introduction, most of the audience fish out their commencement bulletins to use as shade between them and the early morning sun. Powell is an entertaining speaker, but his commencement speech is probably not too different from those of the one hundred and one speakers who have preceded him. I certainly agree with his exhortations to serve humanity, but then my thoughts begin to drift:

My thoughts seize upon an event of more than fifty years before, when I was driving down Fannin Street toward Rice for an early morning class. The traffic lights were synchronized, and as I came to each intersection they turned green for me. In my rearview mirror I saw an old car, a "clunker," speeding up the street behind me. Because the street was three lanes wide, I pulled as far to the right as I could, and my first thought as the old car raced by me was, "Why is there never a policeman around when you need one?"

The car reached the next intersection before the light changed to green, and ran the red light. Luckily, there was no traffic coming through the cross street. I was struck by the realization that just beyond the University was the Texas Medical Center. Almost as soon as I realized that, I pulled to the right again and slowed down, since I heard a siren blaring as a blue and white Houston police car came rushing past me. As I drove up to the next block, I saw the policeman had pulled the old car over to the side of the road, and he had gotten out of his car and was walking toward the offending speeder. You could see aggression in his stance, his feet spread shoulder width, his right hand resting on the butt of his service revolver. He was a large man, powerfully built, and had a scowl on his face.

Then the officer stiffened as though struck with a jolt of electricity. The aggression was gone, and he began frantically fumbling with the back door of the old green Plymouth. He wrenched the door open, and grabbed a small, limp form from the back seat—a child, I saw—and with a tiny blanket trailing he ran to the door of his cruiser. The driver of the old car—a black woman—came scrambling out of her door, and around to the far side of the police cruiser, opening the back door and diving into the seat. By that time the policeman had shut his side door, run to the driver's side, and slid behind the wheel. The patrol car screeched off, taking a civilian and her child with him and headed for the medical center.

I braked to a stop while watching this, and then pulled up even with the abandoned car. The road was still deserted, and I stopped again for a moment when I heard the car's engine still running, got out of my car, turned the engine off, and left the keys in the ignition.

I drove on to school, and before my first class started I stood in the back of the almost empty room and related what I had seen to one of my friends. I still had a bit of a catch in my throat. Charles looked at me closely, took a breath, and then told me, "Johnny, maybe what you can't get over is seeing humanity in action."

That fifty-year-old memory of seeing the florid white cop sprinting to his car with the small child in his arms stays with me while I think of things like what happened in Ferguson, Missouri, and Baltimore, Maryland. I believe policemen are blue, not white, not brown, not black, and can see how difficult it must be for them to realize that every time they walk up to a car, they run the risk of being gunned down.

I stop wool gathering, and focus on Powell. He has just mentioned what it was like to go to college in New York, and points out one of the reasons he is proud to be the commencement speaker at Rice; he could not have been admitted here as a student when he started college—because of his color. For a moment I remember that while I was an undergraduate, the Board of Trustees of Rice University went to state court and argued before the judges that they had an issue with the school's charter, saying the charge to be a first class institution of higher education outweighed the restriction that it be just for white residents of Texas and surrounding areas. The judges agreed, and Rice voluntarily integrated.

Now he's talking about how it felt to be Secretary of State one day and then the next, when Condoleezza Rice was sworn in to take his place, to have all the members of the Secret Service detail take their equipment and abandon him, not even leaving a telephone behind that he could use to order Domino's Pizza.

The audience reacts with appreciative laughter.

✕ ✕ ✕

While flying up from the Rio Grande Valley to Houston the day before for the ceremony, I had been reading a collection of essays by a creative nonfiction writer named Karen Babine. Babine's book *Water and What We Know* talks of many different aspects of water and how it affects the land in which we live. In her essay "The River—1997," she writes of a flood on the Red River, the boundary between Minnesota and North Dakota. In it she quotes a flood story told by a classmate of hers, a young man named Jon Schauer. A portion of his story stuck in my mind. As Jon tells it: "So many people came in to help, busloads of people we'd never met before. They worked so hard, doing something that we can't ever pay them back for. . . . They came and did all that to help us, and we still couldn't beat the river."

Those simple lines remind me so much of what it means to be a person. Of what it means to be a human being. Of what it means sometimes to do all we can do for others, even when it doesn't succeed. It reminds me of doctors, firefighters, our service personnel, and so many others who give their all for strangers. Perhaps maybe, just maybe, their deeds offset the beheadings by ISIS, our napalming of civilians, the rapes and murders of innocents; maybe this allows this old world to continue to exist.

Now Powell is telling us an anecdote about his service with President Reagan. I lose track of his story because I'm thinking about James Taylor's song "Fire and Rain." Karen Babine had seen rain, and I'm sure when she hears the lyrics "I've seen fire and I've seen rain, I've seen sunny days that I thought would never end" she doesn't think there's anything funny or mundane about having seen the rain.

Thinking about the lyrics causes me to think about an essay by Kim Barnes. In her essay "The Ashes of August," she talks about the fires of August and the dryness of Idaho, and recounts just one night. Barnes and her family realized a lightning strike had occurred up around a farm she calls the Bringman place. Barnes writes: "I hung up, then began a series of calls, knowing that for each call I made, two more would go out, word of a lightning strike spreading faster than the fire itself, fanning out across the ridges and high prairie for miles, until every family would be alerted."

My thoughts range from Barnes's husband and the other men fighting fire to save the Bringman's farm, to the first responders who went up in the World Trade Center, and who sacrificed their lives trying to save so many people. Again, I think surely God balances these heroes, these humans who gave their lives trying to save others, against the horror and misguided fanaticism of the murderous men who crashed those jet airplanes into the twin towers in the first place.

Now, General Powell is completing another anecdote, this one about the White House parking garage. I glance behind the section where we MLS grads are seated and see the largest group of graduate students, the MBAs from Jones Business School, wearing their beige hoods. I remember ten years before when I started my second year of MBA school, when my best MBA friend, Mike Speck, missed almost ten days because he served in the Coast Guard Auxiliary. He'd been off making flights in and around New Orleans, the surrounding parishes, and Mississippi, trying to help FEMA and its workers coordinate their rescue efforts after Hurricane Katrina.

Everyone who was an adult in 2005 remembers Katrina, remembers the story of the Louisiana governor, Kathleen Blanco, who refused to ask for federal help, and President George Bush, who refused to ignore the laws of *Posse Comitatus*, not sending federal troops into a southern state without the required request from the governor.

But while they know about New Orleans, they probably don't know about Houston. Another governor picked up the phone at 2 a.m. on August 31st of 2005 and called Robert Echols, the county executive of Harris County, which is primarily Houston. What the Texas governor told the county judge was, "We're all in this together; they are our neighbors." Beginning with that 2 a.m. phone call, Echols got hold of the director of the Harris County Medical District, the emergency preparedness people, the Director of the Houston Astrodome. Within hours all events in the Astrodome for the next three months had been cancelled. The Aramark concession people who served food in Reliant Football Stadium as well as the Astrodome began contacting all of their vendors and persuading them to deliver water, ice, and food in massive quantities to the arena, and by noon of August 31, the first of 25,000 cots were being assembled. A field hospital equal in size to many of the Houston Medical Center hospitals was completed and certified and a full complement of doctors, including specialists, physician's assistants, nurses, and other healthcare providers, were signing up for rotations. A full scale nursery was begun, and representatives of the Houston Independent School District were downloading curriculum from Louisiana's public schools so they could match up children with the school rooms with space for them to continue their education. As the New Orleans refugees began arriving that afternoon, each of them was given toiletries, food, water, fresh clothes, blankets, towels, pillows, and access to not only public restrooms but also the restrooms and showers in the football team locker and training rooms. Although the convoys of buses delivered 25,000 people from the New Orleans Superdome to the Houston Astrodome, the total influx into the City of Houston was over 250,000 refugees, of whom it is estimated that a 150,000 now remain Houstonians.

There was no question of federal grants or FEMA money, the only question was how these folks could be helped. Texans have a reputation for being boisterous braggarts who are sometimes clueless about others' sensitivities. They are also among the most hospitable and generous people in the world, and this was just what we could do; just what neighbors do for each other.

As my musings and memories of Katrina ten years before come to an end, so does General Powell's speech. He has just talked to the graduates about the meaning of their lives, and concludes their lives have no meaning unless they help others. The general finishes up by saying, "If you help one child, your life is a success." Powell's speech and my thoughts have reached a confluence.

The degrees are conferred and the orchestra strikes up the Rice *alma mater*. The sun continues to shine down on the groups of graduates in their dark blue gowns who begin to surge together, ignoring the small hedges between the rows of now abandoned chairs. The traditional mortarboard toss occurs, then all of us walk out the Sallyport, and at least this one retread graduate is looking forward to the old cliché of this being the first day of the rest of his life, and in finding some new way to share this sense of humanity.

I start looking past the crowds of families and graduates posing for photographs, hoping to find Liz. We still have time to make our brunch.

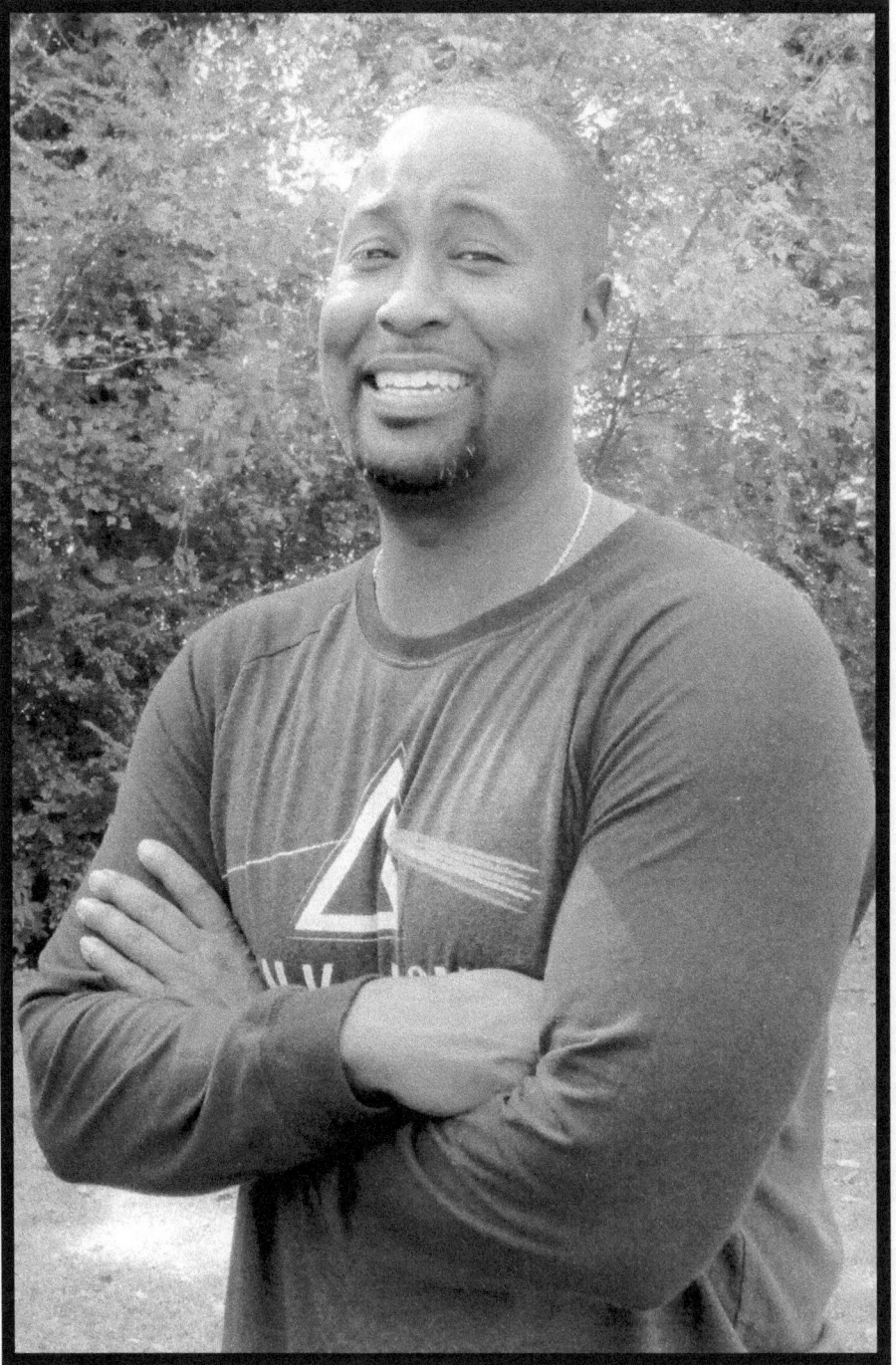

V. HOW MUCH IS ENOUGH?

ANUSHA VR

CORN ON THE COB

I was making my way towards the bus stop from the Central Excise Department when a light drizzle began. To call it an infuriating day would be an understatement. It was my first day at work and I was already on the verge of quitting. I tried to recall every motivational quote I had ever come across to prevent myself from having a full fledged meltdown.

I needed approvals on some forms from authorities who were the big wigs of the department. It didn't help my case that I was a mousy twenty-year-old girl. Right from condescending and patronizing looks to pure disdain, I had been served the complete spectrum of dislike by the authorities. It didn't matter than I knew the law as well as they did. Or perhaps that was the problem.

I was beat. All I wanted was to go home and curse myself for glamorizing the idea of being a chartered accountant.

"Chauvinistic imbeciles," I muttered under my breath.

The drizzle had turned into a vicious downpour in seconds in typical Bangalore fashion. I had always found the weather in my city to be quite bi-polar. Sunny one minute. Raining cats and dogs the next. I fumbled for my umbrella in my bag and tried to wrestle it open but to no avail. I raced towards one of the closed shops along the road to take shelter under a leaky awning.

It was one of those days when you think you've hit rock bottom but the universe likes to surprise you and bury you further down.

In my hurry I had forgotten to shut my handbag after fetching the umbrella that had ultimately served no purpose. I dug into my bag, praying that I hadn't dropped anything of significance in my hurry to get away from the rain.

A missing lipgloss, some old receipts and my wallet.

I could feel the hot tears blurring my vision. There was a knot in my throat and I wanted to be anywhere but stuck in the rain sans wallet, thinking of quitting the job I had dreamed of landing.

"Here," said a hoarse voice.

I opened my eyes and wiped the tears away. My hands streaked with mascara. I saw an old lady who looked like a shriveled up peach holding out a roasted corn on the cob. Bangalore had scores of these hawkers selling corn on the cob on pavements.

"No, no. Thank you," I said waving her away. In my haste, I hadn't noticed earlier that this woman and her cart stuffed with corn and a tiny charcoal stove had taken shelter under the same awning as I had. Just my luck to get stranded with a bothersome hawker, I thought to myself.

Helplessness is a funny thing. It either manifests itself as grief or to overcompensate for our insecurities we project it as anger at anyone who is inopportune enough to cross our path.

"Take it," she said again.

"I do not have any money," I said through gritted teeth.

"Doesn't matter, child. Take it. It looks like you need something to warm you up on this cold day."

I reached out and took that piping hot corn on the cob and devoured it. I didn't utter a word till I had tossed the remnants into a nearby bin.

"Thank you," I said.

"Whatever it is that you were moping about a while ago, it will get better. Things always get better. Till it does always eat something rather than throwing tantrums. Everything always seems worse if you have an empty belly."

I couldn't help but smile at the tough love she was handing out despite the fact that I was a stranger.

"Thank you so much," I repeated. I didn't know what else to say. I was on the verge of apologizing about my behavior earlier when she began:

"I put my sons through college. All on my own." A proud look spread across her face and her grey eyes twinkled.

"I worked odd jobs every day of every week. Now one is in Chennai and the other in Nellore. They are happy. They have families of their own. It wasn't easy. I fought hard to provide for them. And today I fight hard for myself. I didn't depend on anyone when my husband died. And I am not going to depend on my sons to provide for me now. If someone does something nice and expects something in return, they aren't nice people. I travel twenty-five kilometers every day selling corn. And these cops are always asking a commission else they shoo me away. Won't let me sell on the streets. If I had stood under a shop crying like it is the end of the world, then it would have been the end of the world. You have to fight for yourself," she said.

"I will," I said with a smile and tears of a different kind welled up in my eyes.

The very next day I went back to the same spot hoping I could find her. But she was nowhere to be seen. I hope that someday I can run into this old woman and tell her that I am fighting just like she asked me to on that rainy day.

This story is dedicated to Nithya and CV Reddy.

JENNIFER SCHOMBURG KANKE

CRANK CALLS FROM GOD

I
Dr. Moody wants to be homeless, just for a little while.
It's part of his plan to live a million lifetimes in one,
which sounds ridiculous. I seem to change lives

once every four years, no planning necessary,
and Now Me hardly speaks to Old Me. Sometimes
I can't help it though, like when she calls worried about insurance

a child is ill, someone is out of work.
I can't convince her I'm a wrong number.
I listen until I ascertain the issue. It's her dicey problem

solving skills, when you don't have a hammer,
everything looks like a nail. We get her a real
good action plan and the right number for Blue Cross,

and I get on getting on. I'm better when Old Mes call,
not so much if they stop by. When Walt Whitman
said, "Stranger, if you passing meet me and desire

to speak to me, why should you not speak to me,"
he couldn't have meant the homeless man on Monroe

dressed inappropriately for the weather
and smelling like fox urine. He reminds me
of my cousin Al who came to stay,
He'd been camping out
in a city park.

II
Behind every homeless man is an uncle tired of him
smoking near the house and drinking all the milk.
And I see in him a fine line clichéd rhetoric

trumped up by churches and hippies, a reminder
in my dickish moods, that if I hit hard times I'll trade
my Aveda Invigorate for Eau d' Renard and my six hundred foot

apartment for the wide open spaces of Lafayette Park.
So, I guess it's not Past Me walking by but Possible
Future Me and wouldn't PFM want someone to flip us

a quarter or at least not walk to the other side of the street?
But I've seen *Hobo with a Shotgun*, so I know
what I'm capable of and keep my distance

from all PFMs, including the woman in the parking lot
asking for a dollar to get a hot dog
because her sugar's real bad, repeating, "I don't mean

you no harm," which makes me think
she probably does. What if I went for my wallet
and she saw a five, then just like *If You Give*

a Mouse a Cookie, "no" was not an option?
Then again, maybe all those stories about homeless people
are made up, including the ones about Al and Dad screaming

every night while I tried to sleep? Maybe they're like sharks,
only bite when confused or taunted? My friend Brandi
thumb-wrestled a shark for five bucks once, or maybe

it was just a homeless guy, so he could feel like he earned it.
I think she's pretty noble, but it doesn't make me any less afraid.
It doesn't get me any closer to being Kiley Jon Clark,

a former homeless man, who runs a meditation group
for transients. Instead, I pass out cards to those in need
saying, "Sorry, I gave in my childhood," because I am no

infinite dharma font. I am a squirrel on a tree limb, balanced
on one foot scratching my fleas,
holding tight to my own little acorn.

FORGIVE ME KENJANEA

We are not used to knocks on our doors
in this neighborhood, we keep to ourselves
but may chat over chain link fences once a month or so.
Your mother and I know a little about each other.

I know more, I'm nosey, always asking questions.
Your brothers are football stars, get good grades,
don't like to mow the lawn. You've locked yourself out,
want to borrow my phone to call your mother at work.

Though you take it out to the porch, I can still hear
the tone if not the exact words.
It's familiar to me, the tense strains of not getting
what you need, being made to feel asking is unreasonable.

It's 9:30 and already eighty-five degrees, you are in your pjs.
"Just come do it," I make out, "Mom . . . just . . . just . . . ."
I haven't seen you much before now.
Were you away at college, rehab, the military?

No, not the military, your manners with me are the politeness
of the good Southern child, not a soldier.
When you come back in, you say she'll be back shortly
and I ask if you're home for good or just a little bit.

I'm home now, you say and I laugh, telling you
your mother never mentioned she had a daughter before last week.
I'm sorry, you didn't need that reminder.

BRING YOUR OWN REDEMPTION

Look up from changing the station, notice
how it all happens so quickly somewhere
between Q-FM and The River. Young
men from the gas station running to see
if help is needed, the school bus driver
worrying over her safety record.
It becomes clear the girl in the Honda
will be lucky to be alive in all
that metal and glass.
It's 7:30.
You are not yet late.

MARIANNE PEEL

HAPPY HOUR AT PF CHANG'S

When he asks me why I piled the green peppers
into the side bowl
I want to tell him the truth:
That they repeat on me, make me belch.
That my middle age gut cannot handle them anymore.

Instead, I tell him I just don't like them,
that I forgot to order the cashew almond chicken
minus the peppers.
I don't tell the truth,
because he leaned in when he took my order.

Because he pointed out tasty items,
touched them on the menu, between my hands.
Because he sat down next to me.
Because he mixed just the right amount
of hot mustard in the special sauce to make it sizzle.

These college boys are well-trained
to romance the middle-aged clientele.
They never ask *Just one?* when they seat me here.
They don't make me feel alone and lonely on a Monday night.
Poor lady, eating all by herself. Not here.

I could sit here for hours,
sampling exotic teas
and maybe order a mai tai. Or two.
I could practice picking up cashew pieces
with my chopsticks.

I know he is schooled to look at me hungrily, to whet my appetite
with the five o'clock shadow beard
that other reputable restaurants do not allow,
to look at me with those *I want to dance eyes.*
Calls me "miss" not "ma'am."

He keeps coming back, refilling my Passion Fruit tea.
Leaning in.
He doesn't seem to mind
that the sauce from the lettuce wraps
oozes down my fingers, onto my wrists even.

My fortune cookie tells me
You will soon be surrounded by good friends and laughter.
Again, he returns to my table.
Lingering. Leaning in.
Asking me if I am satisfied.

Perhaps I will stay for dessert.

TEETLE CLAWSON

FOLLOW-UP APPOINTMENT

On the steel table, shivering
in a frayed cotton gown,
my naked feet are wedged into jaws
of metal stirrups set too far apart.
It doesn't matter. Sitting on a couch,
eating in an Oakland dive, splayed
on the exam table—it's all the same.
Just five weeks earlier Greg and I were living
in an old farmhouse in the Colorado Rockies.
When he walked into our kitchen,
put the rifle to his temple, he didn't know
I was pregnant. When I found him
in a spreading halo of bright blood,
I didn't know I was carrying the baby
we had been hoping for.
The door swings open,
"Hi, I'm Doctor Kline. How are you feeling?"
Grabbing the stool, he wheels it
between my legs while the nurse adjusts
a rectangle of quilted paper over my knees.
It's supposed to be that way—a nurse
there with the doctor, the paper between us
a flimsy curtain of privacy.
The doctor talks while he probes,
asks if I had any unusual pain
after the abortion, any unusual bleeding,
and what kind of birth control would I like?
"My husband is dead," I say, "I don't need birth control."
He asks again. But it's unthinkable.

Doctor Kline tells the nurse he needs something
from another room and when she leaves,
for a few brief moments he gently circles
his thumb on the soft folds above my clitoris.
I know he's doing this for me.
I know he's risking his career.
"Yes," I say, "maybe you should fit me for a diaphragm after all."

WILDERNESS SARCHILD

CHARITY

I navigated
the New York City subway system
like a native. Except I wasn't good
at ignoring the young man
who got on at Park Slope and rapped
a story about losing his mother
and his father
when he was eight. How
he entered the Life
and now his woman has
a new baby and he wants to be
clean and live God's blessing.

I gave him a dollar, tempted to give more
but still hadn't decided whether
to act like a seasoned New Yorker
or to open my heart and my wallet
like I did that time in Mexico
with two niños and within seconds
was bombarded by a child army
demanding "pesos, pesos, señorita, por favor."

Chuck would have given him
fifty, not because he believed the story
but because the guy might be
one of the chosen thirty-three
secretly protecting the world;
or paid him for his great voice,
the hard work it takes

to get on train after train
and sing it fresh.

The next day two men
with dreadlocks, jeans
and tie-dyed T-shirts
hopped on the train at Times Square,
each with a wagon filled with fast food.
They asked for money or blessings or a smile.
They told us to help ourselves
because "though not everyone
is homeless, everyone gets hungry."
I gave one some money. He told me
I had a nice smile.

One week later a middle-aged man
with an earring in his left ear,
the shadow of a beard, and a worn
green army issue pack on his back
got on the train at Columbus Circle,
told us his house burned down.
He lives in a shelter and has no food.

I ignored him.

That worries me.

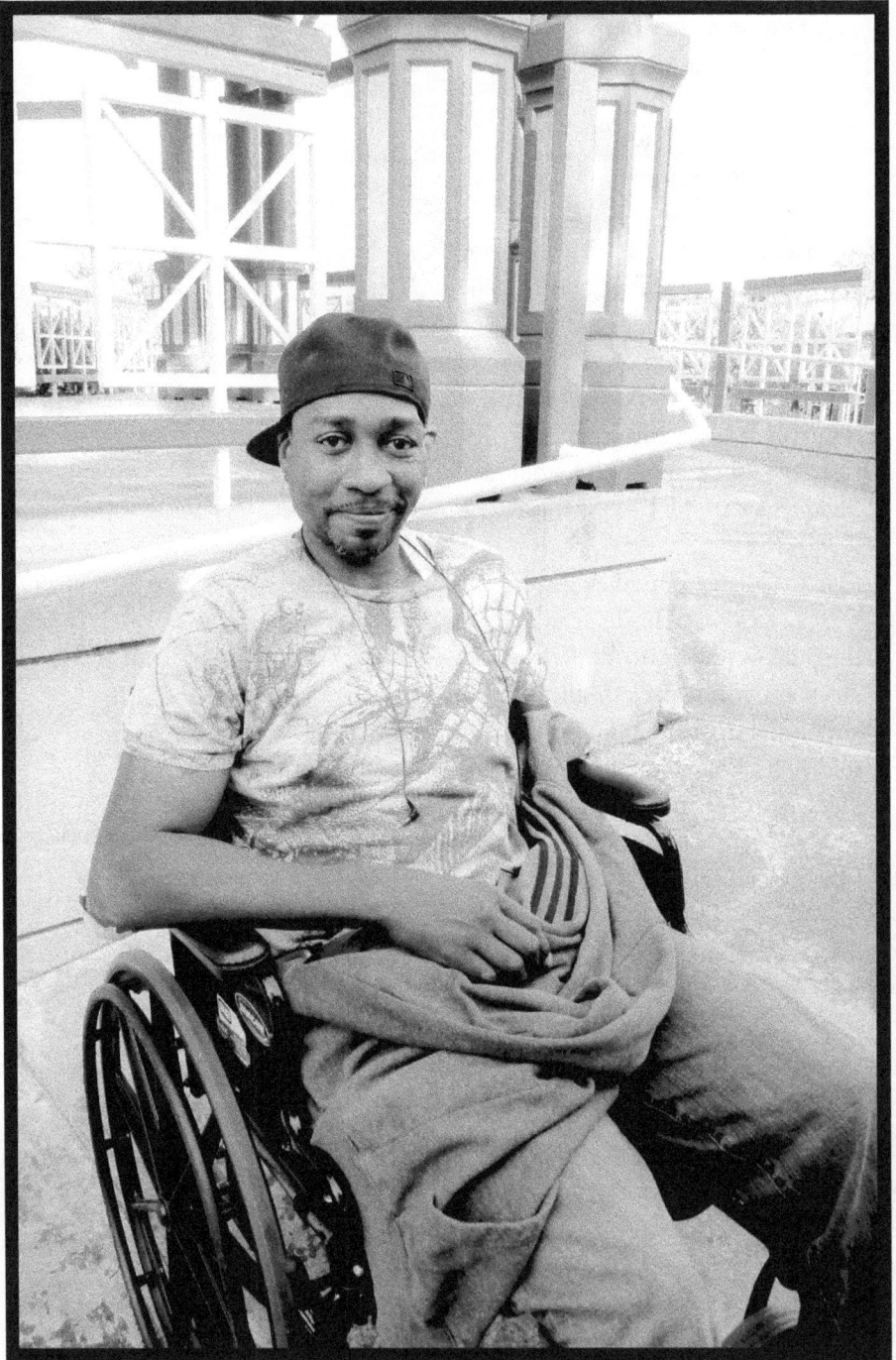

JOHNNY TOWNSEND

THE GIRL FROM TREPONEMA

The young woman at the window grimaced in my direction, giving her best approximation of a smile, her teeth showing a long history of meth. She didn't need to tell me her name. Some customers one remembered instantly. I pulled Cathy up on the computer and saw that she had three pieces of mail waiting, two regular and one DSHS. We had the mail separated for more than 3000 clients according to type: 1st class, DSHS checks, special, oversize, Affordable Care, EBT cards, and so forth. Most of the people who came to Mailing Address were homeless, or addicts, or mentally ill, sometimes all three.

I had Cathy sign for her check, handed her the mail, and wished her a good day. Since I knew she liked macaroni and cheese, I also handed her a coupon before she walked away. I tried to clip a few coupons every week for the items I knew various customers liked, though I only had time to hand them out if the line wasn't too long.

I quickly flipped through my small stack to make sure I still had the one for kitchenware. Sharonda was due to stop by sometime over the next few days. She had a phobia about washing dishes after cooking. Rather than rinse her pots and pans, she'd set them out in her back yard so the food wouldn't stink up her apartment as it rotted. When all the pots from her kitchen were eventually outside, she'd either break down and wash or, more often, go out and buy new ones. Last week, she'd come in crying, saying that when she went to go set out her latest pan, she discovered someone had stolen all the others sitting in the yard. I'd started looking for coupons as soon as I returned home. She could always go to Goodwill, of course, but she wouldn't be caught dead eating from pots someone else had cooked in.

A Hispanic man came up to the window next, so I used the Spanish I'd learned on my mission to Honduras decades ago and that I practiced with my husband now. The man withdrew $60 from his account and shoved it into his pocket. The morning dragged on, one client after another after another appearing at the window. I opened an account for a guy who wanted to deposit $20 "for emergencies," and I handed out a daily allowance for one of our payees who was not able to budget his own money.

"Time for your lunch break, Buddy," said Chryssie, another one of the tellers, coming to relieve me. This week, Chryssie had blond hair with magenta trim, making her look younger than her forty years. She and I took turns throughout the day, working the window, sorting and labeling mail, and then going back to the window. There were three tellers, three case managers, our actual manager, and a couple of volunteers on any given day.

"Thanks," I said. "I'll be back in half an hour." I grabbed my jacket and headed out the building. Most of the others ate in the mail room, and I usually did, too, but lately, I'd felt the need to get away for a few minutes each day. I'd been working here over ten years, ever since moving to Seattle after Hurricane Katrina destroyed my apartment and thousands of other homes in New Orleans.

One my coworkers there had been unable to face starting over at forty-six and killed herself. I had been only forty-five at the time and had used half of my savings to buy a ticket to Seattle, once the computers in Hammond were up and running again.

The sun was shining brightly in Seattle today, and the temperature had warmed to over fifty degrees. I looked out over the Sound, the snow-capped Olympics on the far side. Working in Pioneer Square, right on the water, was always a little nerve-wracking. These were the oldest buildings in town, all vulnerably brick, built above "underground Seattle." The early inhabitants had suffered so many problems with the water, spouting toilets for one, that they'd eventually built a street one floor up over the original city. People could still visit the former ground level buildings for a fee, interesting enough, but I was never able to get the idea out of my mind that in any sizeable earthquake, we'd all be the first to go. If we weren't killed by the quake itself, there was always the tsunami we were unlikely to escape.

Things like devastating hurricanes had a way of warping how one viewed the world.

I knew Antonio was going to die.

I turned the corner and walked up to 1st Avenue, passing a chunky black guy masturbating in an alleyway. A few feet farther on, a white guy in a wheelchair, with two prosthetic legs, was urinating against the side of a building. He seemed unperturbed that his stream was hitting his feet as well.

I ducked into a Thai restaurant and ordered. There was no lack of eateries in the neighborhood. One served passable New Orleans cuisine, but I could never eat there without thinking of Don, who'd died of pancreatic cancer just before the hurricane hit. Even after all the time we'd been together, he hadn't left a will, so his brother inherited the house and the car, and I moved into a tiny apartment in St. Roch. My friends had warned me against the neighborhood, about 97% black, but ethnicity had not turned out to be the problem. I'd just bought a stackable washer and dryer, the most expensive available because it was also the smallest, when I had to evacuate by bus, taking just one suitcase. I'd never seen my apartment again.

I sat near the plate glass window facing 1st Avenue, watching people walk by. At least half of them were tourists, oblivious to the other half who were destitute. This was the only neighborhood I could afford when I'd moved here in 2005. Then I met Antonio and we bought a house together in Hillman City, the first house for either of us in our own names. He was a laborer, mostly cement work, still hunky at fifty, but breathing had become more and more difficult over the last year, and finally I was able to convince him to see a doctor.

The career I'd wanted to have. Back in the mid-90's, I'd dated a guy with full-blown AIDS and become frustrated with both the care and the information available to patients. "Do you think both sides of your brain work?" Stevens asked while we were shopping one evening for a new pillbox. He still used make-up then to hide the black Kaposi's marks.

"What do you mean?" I'd asked in return. I tried to remember what the right side of the brain was responsible for.

"Why don't you go to medical school so you can be sure I get the treatment I need?"

I'd already earned three English degrees by this point and was an adjunct at two different schools, but I enrolled in remedial math and started over again.

Stevens was dead by my third semester. But I kept at it. Physics, anatomy, histology, statistics. I remembered struggling with chemistry, irritated when the solution in the back of the book was different from my answer on a homework assignment. I went over the problem again and again, and I kept coming up with the same wrong answer. So I stopped by the professor's office to ask about it, and he said dismissively, "You're right, obviously. The book's wrong," and ushered me out the door in a manner indicating he thought I was being a show-off. It had never occurred to me that I might actually be good at this stuff.

A couple of semesters later, it had been excruciating in Genetics class to have to tell the professor after every single exam that he'd graded my answers incorrectly. He always said, "Oh, I see. You're absolutely right. Sorry about that," and adjusted my grade. Was that really supposed to be my job?

Only a few minutes left for lunch. I pulled out my cell and called Antonio. "How's my honey feeling today?" I asked. He'd lost at least forty pounds in the past six months.

"Not so good, Buddy. I tried to pull some dandelions in the yard and got winded in five minutes."

"Don't worry about it," I said. "I'll take care of it."

"But you're doing everything," Antonio protested. "I'm not dead yet."

I stared out the window. A man with a huge herpes lesion on his face walked by. "I wish . . ." I said. "I wish . . ."

"There's no wishing," Antonio said sternly. "And there's no praying."

I'd hung onto a belief in God decades after being excommunicated from the Mormon Church, but these last few years, I'd joined Antonio in becoming an atheist. Still, enough residual Mormonism lingered to make me wish he'd never taken up smoking when he was a teen. "Want anything special for dinner tonight?" I asked.

"I'll fix burritos," he replied. "You like my burritos."

So did he. I'd suggested months ago that we eat his favorite foods every day. That meant tacos five to six days a week, and burritos when he was feeling depressed. "See you in a few hours."

"Love you, Buddy."

I walked back to Mailing Address, put in the code to the office door, and reopened my window. "Arthur was here," said Chryssie. "He was asking for you."

Arthur was one of our regulars who came almost every day. He only received at best three pieces of mail a month. He didn't come for that, of course. He came because we were his only social outlet.

I found some mail for the next customer, but one piece was missing. With over twenty boxes of mail spread out all over the office, there was no telling where it was, or if we'd already given it to the customer and simply forgotten to scan it. Two people withdrew money, one deposited money, three asked if they had any mail but didn't, and four more people picked up checks.

During a lull, I logged in the fifteen new EBT cards we received today.

"Need you back at the window," said Tyresia, just out of college and working here almost six weeks now. She still acted like a student, studying at work just for fun when things were slow. I couldn't remember what it was like to be that young.

I pulled up the metal grid over the adjoining station and asked an Asian man if I could help him. He thrust his ID at me without saying a word. Lots of the customers never talked to us. Which was often better than if they did.

The next person asked where he could take a dump, and I directed him to our Hygiene Center downstairs, where customers could use the bathroom or bring their laundry. The staff in that department handled all the laundry, at no charge, of course. They just had to wear thick gloves when emptying the customers' pockets, because of the needles.

Telling people where to go to the bathroom. It was a far cry from curing HIV infections. Or treating cancer.

Or prolonging life in any meaningful way at all.

I thought back to my Cell Physiology class, where the professor had been so consumed with a textbook he was writing that he completely abandoned students in the lab. We tried to figure everything out on our own, but every single one of us received low marks for that portion of the grade. I had the highest GPA in the class by the end of the semester, and even I ended up with a B.

I wondered if I should buy some ice cream for Antonio on the way home. I never had any myself, needing to keep in shape. But Grocery Outlet had a sale on Häagen-Dazs for 99 cents a pint. Tres Leches, Antonio's favorite.

Of course, his taste buds weren't working well these days because of the medication.

I had wanted to save the world.

I remembered my Biochemistry class, the single hardest class in over twelve years of college courses, far harder than Organic Chemistry, which had actually been kind of fun. But Biochem—sheesh. I'd made out over five hundred note cards while hunched in my library cubicle, drawing each of the molecules I needed to understand. I learned dozens of complicated pathways and knew every step, able to draw every molecule from start to finish.

I interviewed five years in a row for medical school. In the end, the dean told me I just didn't have the right personality to be a physician. It was a terrible blow, and the insecurity from all those years as a Mormon, constantly being told I never measured up, came flooding back. But then I met Don, an ex-JW, and I worked hard to leave the last vestiges of Mormonism behind me forever.

Mail was sorted for the day, so all three teller windows were open now. I asked Susie about her Chihuahua with cataracts while I withdrew some money for her, asked José about his aunt who'd been having seizures, and asked Phuc about his new job at a warehouse in Sodo. But mostly, I just smiled and handled the transactions as quickly as I could to keep the line down. With three of us at the window, things were moving along pretty smoothly.

"What did you think of that windstorm the other day?" asked Chryssie during a slow spell. A man had been killed in Seward Park when a tree landed on his car.

I thought of an old boyfriend in Lakeview who'd drowned in his attic.

"Freaky," said Tyresia. She began talking about how the storm had knocked over all her daffodils.

"You okay, Buddy?" asked Chryssie. Tyresia turned to stare at me.

"I think I might leave early, if that's okay with you guys."

"Sure, sure, we'll see you tomorrow. Feel better."

I clocked off the computer and picked up my jacket before heading back out the door. An obese man in a motorized wheelchair was staring at rust-colored water bubbling out of a manhole on the street. I turned the corner and saw three gobs of spit in a row on the sidewalk. I trudged up to the gem and fossil shop on 1ˢᵗ, looking through the window at a three-foot high geode, the purple amethyst crystals forming a breathtaking cave. A piece of natural artwork I could never afford as a nobody making minimum wage. I looked about me, at the intricate brick, stone, and cement work around the windows, doors, and along the roof lines of most of the buildings in the area. For a dilapidated neighborhood, it was still quite beautiful here. Things could be worse.

I thought about the blood Antonio sometimes coughed up.

A long-haired Native American man walked past with a short Latino man, sharing a cigarette. They were followed by a well-tailored white man who trotted up the steps to a law firm. A professional making a difference in the world. Then a middle-aged woman probably only a couple of years younger than I was tapped me on the shoulder. Pus was oozing from a sore on her face.

I thought of my Microbiology class, where we had to bring samples of our own E. coli to culture in Petri dishes. I'd sung "The Girl from Treponema" to my lab partner during one class. She'd laughed, wagging her finger and saying, "Better watch out for her!"

I'd also volunteered to correct the lab manual the professor had written. Lots of grammar errors on every page. But I realized now that my offer had probably been pretty obnoxious.

"Come on," I said to the woman, putting my hand on her arm. She was someone I had never seen before. "Let's get you signed up for some help." I walked back with her to Mailing Address and stood with her in line until Chryssie's window was free. She was still the best at registration. And she could set the woman up with a case manager after she finished.

I walked five blocks to the bus stop near the old train station and headed for Grocery Outlet, where I picked up that pint of ice cream I needed to make sure Antonio knew how much I loved him.

JOHN TIMM

A GOOD DAY AT THE OFFICE

I have a Bachelor of Arts degree (*cum laude*) in marketing, a minor in communications, seven years experience at a major consumer products company (a name you'd recognize immediately), Lindsay and I owe $21,348 in student loans, we have a mortgage payment of $1,247.06, a car payment of $350, two kids under the age of five, and today I began my second week as a cashier at Walmart.

Monday
"You want a bag for the milk? Yes? Thirty-eight-ninety-four. . . . Have a great day."

Nobody else in line. Slow. They told me Mondays can be slow. Just so I don't get sent home early.

The job hasn't become as routine as I thought it would. And it's harder than it looks when you're just a customer. Really. I'm still going back to the employee manual all the time. I want to get this right. I have to. For now, there's no other choice.

"Good morning. Did you find everything you were looking for? Great. Twenty-seven-thirty-three. Credit? Press cancel."

Six hours and forty-five minutes to go. . . . I've got to stop looking at the time.

On another Monday morning six weeks ago, they called us to a meeting right after nine. That's the way they do it now. Mondays, not Fridays. No long weekend for you to brood over it. Do it on a Monday. More humane that way. Or so the experts say.

When I saw the director of HR standing at the front of the conference room—the big one on Level 3—I'm sure I knew what was coming before the others. I wouldn't gasp or mumble like some of them. There'd been rumors, of course, but there are always office rumors. For me it was almost anticlimactic when she broke the news and started into the details: severance based on your longevity, outplacement assistance, personal counseling, the ins and outs of COBRA and a "helpful list of websites and phone numbers for additional information on your rights as a terminated employee."

It was a bad day at the office.

"The sign on the shelf says these are seven dollars."

"They ring up at nine. Let me have someone check."

Getting busier. That's good. Better than just standing around. Or having to go home early.

The next person in line is growing impatient, stacking everything from her basket in a big pile at the end of the belt. Glaring at me. *Come on, come on. What's the damn price?*

"Thanks, Nadya. Yes, sir, we'll ring them up for you at seven."

The Director of HR asked for questions. There were none. On behalf of the company she offered "heartfelt appreciation for your understanding" and then dismissed us. It was over just like that. As we headed to our work areas, no one spoke—not even in the elevator—each of us in our own compartmentalized world.

"Sorry about the wait, ma'am."

Lady, at least you could acknowledge my apology with something besides another dirty look. Things happen, okay? Get a life.

"Seventy-five-oh-two."

Security walked us to the front door and out to the parking lot. At the main gate they inspected our boxes of personal items and pulled our IDs and parking passes. I thought it demeaning at the time. Now, I guess I understand. Everyone reacts differently, and these days you never know.

I couldn't decide whether to call Lindsay from the car, or just show up at home in middle of the day and deal with it that way.

"They dropped a bottle of orange juice in the aisle in front of the coolers back there."

"Thanks. We'll get someone to clean it up right away."

I finally opted to break the news to Lindsay face-to-face. I mean, how do you start a phone conversation with something like, "Hi honey. We all just got fired"? I needed some extra time to think about how to soften the blow. I needed it both for her and for myself.

"At least they gave me a severance."

"How much?"

"A month's salary for every year of service. They gave me credit for eight years. I guess you could call it generous."

"That's supposed to be *generous*?"

"Nowadays, yes."

"So how do we get by on that?"

At that point, I ran out of answers.

The front end customer manager appears at my side. "Need change?"

"Yes. Lots of bigger bills today. Getting low on tens."

"They must still have something left over from payday. Wish I did."

"Me too." *If you only knew. If you only knew . . .*

The front end customer manager quickly reappears, money bag in hand, swaps out the larger bills, resets the register and walks off. *Routine. She could do it in her sleep. All in a day's work. 10 o'clock. Break time.*

In the break room there are half-a-dozen conversations going on in half-a-dozen languages. Over to one side of the room I recognize Ali and head his way. Ali is about my age, maybe a little younger. He's got his green card and his dreams. Freedom, a job, opportunities for him and his wife.

We're sitting two tables away from Jeffry. Jeffry's on his daily rant to no one in particular. Today it's about the front end customer manager. "She's the worst. She is the worst." The others in the room must be used to him—they don't even look over his way.

When Jeffry's done, he leaves the room and Ali turns to me. "He's like that. It's always something. He complains about store management and the company and the rest of us. And sometimes his parents and his girlfriend."

"How long has he worked here?"

"He's been here as long as I have. Two . . . two years. Somebody said it's the longest he's held a job. He's like twenty-one and worked six other places already. Lives at home."

What a jerk. Really got it tough kid, don't you? Try my life on for size.

They post the previous day's stock price outside the door of the break room. It's $75 a share. *Don't remind me, please don't remind me. I don't want to have to tap my IRA like I hear some of the others are already doing.*

Sometimes I pay close attention to what people buy. You're just supposed to make sure it gets through the scanner and into the bag. But certain things get your attention. I try to imagine what happens when they get the stuff home.

Lipstick . . . vitamins . . . WD-40 . . . dog food . . . athletic socks . . . a birthday card . . . candles. I get everything but the WD-40. How does that fit in?

It helps me pass the time.

Other than Ali, the only associate—*man, I'm really getting into the lingo here*—the only associate I've gotten to know is Harold, a refugee from decades of corporate warfare. He can relate to what I'm going through. He's seen it all. Kind of fatherly, too. He only works a couple days a week. Says it's to help pay his health insurance. I also think he just likes to work.

Tuesday

Somebody suggested I get a job driving long-distance semis. At least until something opened up in my field. Begging for drivers. Great pay. Steady. But me? It's not that I'm too good for that. I'm just not cut out for it. I'd last a month—at most. Not a good job for a young family man, either. Someone else suggested work in the oil fields. Same thing—a college educated fish out of water. Everybody means well, I'm sure.

They tell us to park away from the front of the store to make it more convenient for the customers. No need to say it twice. I keep the Mustang as far out of sight as I can. A bright yellow Mustang GT calls attention to itself—and the driver—and too many people in town know me and my car. Okay. So maybe it's false pride. What of it?

There's a McDonald's at the front of the store next to the south entrance. So far, I've been packing a lunch. Today, I need a change, if only for one day. I'm trying to stay under five dollars. Not always easy. I have a crumpled five I found in my jacket over the weekend. The credit cards are going to remain dormant for the foreseeable future. *Crap. I have to worry about how much I'm spending on lunch. At McDonalds, for crying out loud. McDonalds!*

First customers of the day. And lookee here . . . my old girlfriend. And this must be the dick she ended up marrying. Should I recognize her? . . . Just act casual about it? . . . or wait and see what she does first? Awk-ward. He looks like a loser. . . . Yeah, well, I should talk.

She sets the tone for the encounter with a mechanical smile, the kind you'd flash at the random person who holds the door for you at the mall. I reciprocate with my own version of the happy-to-see-you-and-thank-you-for-shopping-at-Walmart smile. The guy has no clue about what's going on. That's good for all of us.

"Fifty-four-fifty-six . . . Thank you. Have a nice day." *While you're at it, have a nice life.*

My mother used to say that in times of trouble, God is testing you, but he'll never give you more than you can handle. If that's true, today God is pushing the limits. Here comes Mr. Andersen, my high school English teacher.

"Good to see you."

"Good to see you, too, sir."

"Miss having you in class. How long has it been?"

"Ten . . . twelve years, maybe? At least that long."

Is he just being patronizing? This is tough for me. It's probably as tough for him. What will he say to Mrs. Andersen when he gets home? "I just saw Erv Brooks' boy at Walmart. He's working there now—at the checkout. Do you believe it? I didn't want to ask him about it. I thought I heard he had a good job in marketing somewhere. What a waste of talent"? Or, will he just say, "Guess he's finally found his niche"?

<u>Wednesday</u>

Today it's me who's the target of Jeffry's daily lunchroom rant. Lucky, lucky me. I suppose I couldn't expect to remain invisible forever.

"New guy, works here two weeks—not even two weeks—gets weekdays only. How does he rate when the rest of us get shit schedules and shit hours and have to work nights, weekends and holidays, whether we like it or not?"

Jeffry doesn't have the *cojones* to look at me; he just stares at his sandwich like he's addressing it, says his little piece and then takes a savage bite of whatever lies between the layers of bread. I'm not the only one who's uncomfortable at this point. Even those who usually ignore Jeffry are staring, first at him, then at me, then back at him. Waiting.

I won't rise to the bait. Tempting. No, can't do it. Funny thing, I really need the job, he doesn't. He's got mommy and daddy who probably feed him and do his freakin' laundry—and pay his damned bills.

Break time at Walmart 8068 ends without bloodshed, and we all return to our appointed tasks: Nasrin to Seasonal, Tina to Housewares, Hector to Produce, Riya to the Deli, Raj to Electronics and Joe to Automotive. Jeffry is probably hiding out somewhere in the storeroom today. Me, I'm at Checkout Six.

A guy comes up. He's on his cell and he's maybe three feet from me, but for him I don't exist. He gestures as he talks, not at me but at the person on the other end, more visible to him than I am. He breaks from the conversation to signal for me to put the ice cream in a separate bag, which I would have done anyway. Then he's back to that all-important conversation.

"Twenty-nine-fifty-one."

He struggles to find his wallet. He apologizes to the unknown party for the interruption and hands me three tens.

Three-thirty. School is out. Four teenage boys approach. *No cart.* One has something in his hand. *Shoelaces.* Overactive hormones raising havoc with his complexion. His companions are fooling around. They catch my eye and start passing candy bars back and forth. They put the candy bars back on the shelf. They look at me, look at each other. They laugh. Then they pick up more candy bars and start their little game over.

Was I that big an idiot at their age?

"Two dollars and eighteen cents."

My acne-challenged customer replies, "Here. I only have two dollars and seventeen cents."

"Two dollars and eighteen cents, please."

"I don't have it."

Come on Mr. Pimply, I'm not giving in. It's a standoff until another customer approaches, pushing a full cart, forcing the issue. Glances exchanged among the four. One of the other three flips a penny on the belt. They head towards the door as I greet the next customer, then stop and turn around. "Hey Jared, that's what you're going be doing if you don't stop screwing off in class. You'll end up working at a Walmart like that dude. A checker at Walmart." More laughter.

Some couples shouldn't be allowed to breed.

At the end of the day I tell Lindsay about all these kinds of people. She stops me after a while. Hearing it makes her sad for a whole bunch of reasons.

Thursday

The front end customer manager comes up to me. "Go ahead, take your break."

I'm getting to hate break time. Then I see Harold. *Great. He's working today.* I take a chair on the opposite side of the table. "So what did you do on your days off, Harold?"

"Every day is a day off for me. But to answer your question, yesterday I did all the honey-do things a man who's been married forty-eight years does . . . and then we went out for some barbecue. How about you? Are you getting the hang of it around here?"

"Little by little. I can deal with the customers and management. What gets me the most is sitting right over there. I can't wait until he cranks it up again."

"We all look at the world though our own lens."

"He decided to take me on the other day."

"Ignore him. You're a survivor, he's not."

As if on cue, Jeffry starts in. *Speak of the devil.* As usual, he talks to his sandwich. "So you're the dude with the hot Mustang out in the lot. Nice car. Bet all the ladies like it."

No, I can't resist any longer. I stand up. "See this thing? It's called a wedding ring. Yes, the ladies love it—both my wife and my three-year-old daughter. Any more questions?"

The two women over in the corner smile at me. Jeffry says nothing more. He makes much of crumpling up his sandwich wrapper and tossing it in into the garbage as he leaves. Harold gives me a wink.

Here's hoping you get the trots from that sandwich today, stupid bastard.

My last customer of the day is a real piece of work. She's another one of these cellphone addicts who has to be jawing away about nothing in particular while she shops. Meanwhile, her two kids are left to entertain themselves. One is grabbing a box of cookies out of the basket and starting to open it. The mother does a good job of ignoring him, while the other, a little girl, tugs on her mother's pants leg, whining for attention. I'd like to say: "Lady, you're showing some great parenting skills there." But I don't, of course.

The customer is always right.

Friday morning

For whatever reason, I was thinking about Mr. Andersen this morning while driving to the store. He'd talk in class about the coming-of-age novels we were reading and say things like, "We never stop coming of age." It sounded so profound when I was sixteen or seventeen, but I really didn't know what he meant. I think I'm finally beginning to understand.

A couple comes wheeling up to my check out with a full basket. *No wedding ring. A baby. Another on the way.*

The cart is filled to the top with life essentials. Cereal, corn meal, boxes of macaroni and cheese, eggs, milk, fruit juice, diapers.

Another child comes running up from back in the store. She's about the same age as my daughter and has something in her hand. A toy? Her mother bends down and whispers something to her. After several moments, the little girl heads towards the back of the store with the object.

"One-hundred-seven-oh-three." The couple exchanges a glance. She swipes the EBT card. Not enough. He gestures for her to swipe it again. She knows better and shakes her head, but swipes it anyway. Same result. Same silent exchange between the two of them.

She pulls a credit card out of her purse. It's mostly symbolic. Maxed out.

I suggest, "Maybe we can take a few things back. How short are we?"

"About twenty . . . dollars." She doesn't look up at me as she says it.

I pull a credit card out of my wallet. "Here, it's covered." The man motions for her not to accept it.

Her hand is small, but warm. Wet with perspiration.

I'm on camera. You're always on camera here. Most of the time I forget about it. Sometimes I resent it. Right now I don't give a damn. *If they want to give me crap because I helped out a customer, too bad. Mom would have said, "There, but for the grace of God, go I."*

I print out the receipt and hand it to her. She whispers something to me. I don't catch what she says, and I don't know if it's in English or Spanish. It doesn't matter.

When I got home, I hugged Lindsay. I hugged my daughter. I kissed our sleeping child in his crib. It was a good day at the office.

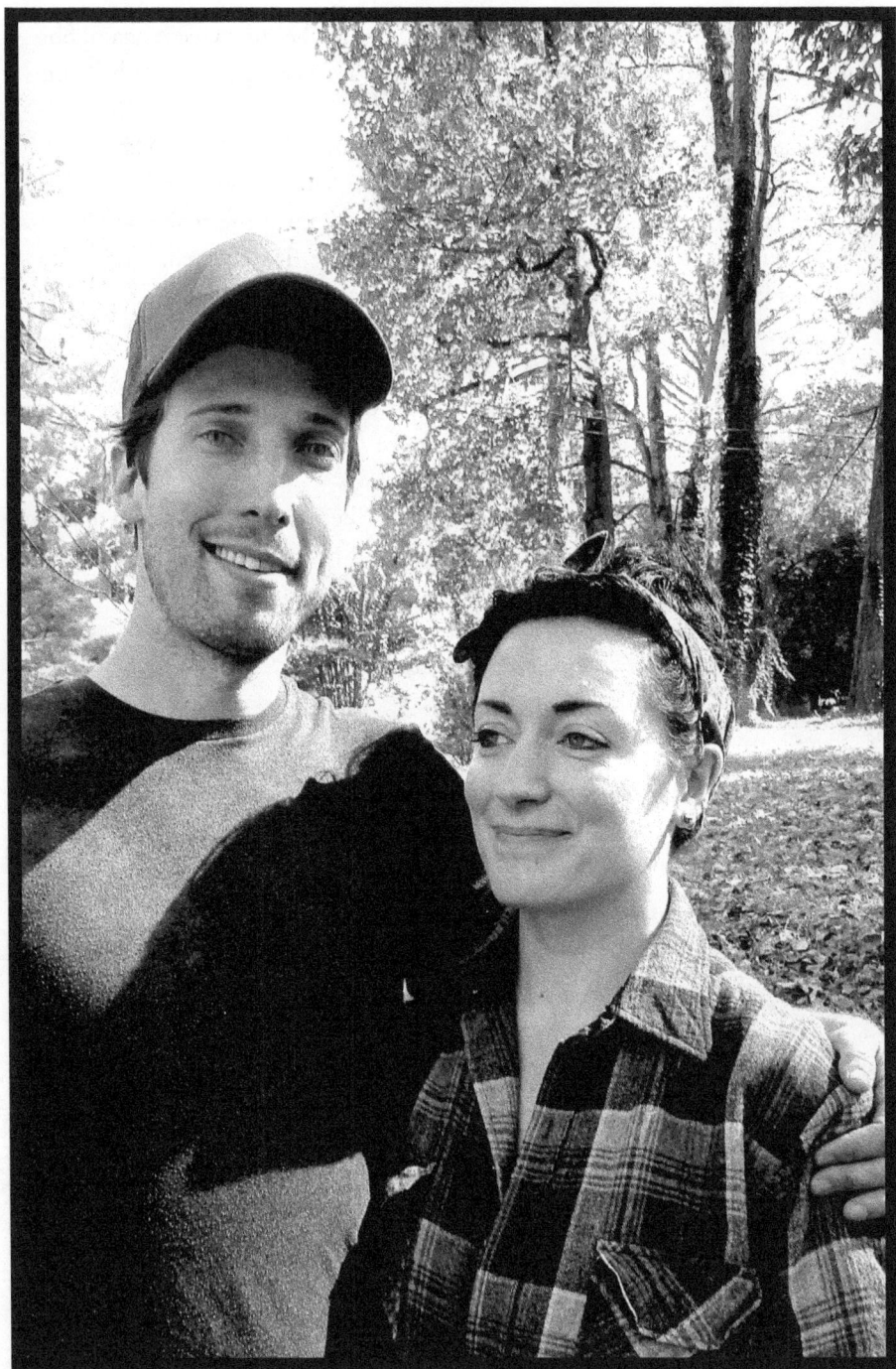

JASON A. NEY

UNTIL IT HURTS

The dinner was my wife's idea. She said it would give me an opportunity to meet Mackenzie, hear her story, and ask her any questions that would help me come to a decision. If we were going to do this, we needed to be on the same page.

So over a meal in our dining room—Erin and I on one side of the table, Mackenzie on the other—she told us how her relationship with Ryan had seemed like a dream at first. How he'd told her he'd never been married before, never had kids. How, when she'd unexpectedly got pregnant and told him that there was no way she'd be able to carry the baby to term, that she and her ex-husband had tried for years but her body couldn't support a viable pregnancy, he'd been so sweet and supportive. How he'd said he would marry her. How once the baby looked like it would make it, he'd turned into someone she no longer knew, a vicious, controlling abuser who constantly demeaned her and was now demanding an abortion.

How she'd found out he had a wife and two kids in Connecticut, his job here in Colorado allowing him to ferry surreptitiously between two lives. How he was threatening to throw her out of their shared rental, and how her ex-husband had destroyed her once-sterling credit by stealing their chiropractor business away from her and then somehow still forcing her to pay spousal support, leaving her in the kind of financial shape that made her unattractive to landlords. How (and at some point in here, the tears started falling), because of her Lupus and rotated hip, she wouldn't be able to continue to work alongside Erin in the hospital where the two of them had met. How she just needed to stay in Colorado long enough to have the baby on her employer-provided insurance and recover from the pregnancy so she could then safely move in with her mom in South Carolina. How it wasn't ideal, given how cruel and judgmental her mom had been toward her and her pregnancy, but it was her only option.

How she'd be so, so grateful for the chance to stay in our spare bedroom for a few months once her lease with Ryan expired on May 1. How it would cover the time from just before her delivery to when her maternity leave would end.

Later that night, after I'd walked her out to her car in the icy December cold and she'd given me a hug and told me how welcome we'd made her feel, Erin asked me what I thought. Should we do this?

"I'm leaning toward yes," I told her, "but I still need to think and pray about it some more."

I already knew.

Ⅹ Ⅹ Ⅹ

"What do you mean, she traded her car in?" I asked Erin over the phone on my drive home from work. "I offered to come by her house, take pictures of it, put them on Craigslist, field the offers, and meet with buyers. She wouldn't even have had to do anything."

"I know, babe. I don't have all the details. I just know she said the dealer said it would need several thousand dollars of repairs, so she freaked out and went to the nearest dealership and traded it in for a leased new car."

"I just talked to her about this last night at dinner. Why didn't she wait to talk to us before rushing this through?"

"I don't know."

"So how is she going to pay for it?"

"I don't know."

"So yesterday she owned a car, and today she doesn't."

"Yes."

Ⅹ Ⅹ Ⅹ

About a month later, Erin waved me over to where she sat at the kitchen table. She put her hand over the phone and whispered, "Mackenzie's freaking out."

Almost every night since our initial dinner, Mackenzie had called Erin, who would see the number, hesitate, pick it up, and then be unable to get a word in edgewise for the next three hours. Sometimes, when Ryan was back in Connecticut on the weekends, Mackenzie would ask Erin to come up to her house for vaguely defined "help." The consummate servant, Erin could never say no and would never get home before midnight, even when Mackenzie knew she had to work early the next morning.

"What else is new?"

"This sounds different."

She put it on speaker.

"Mackenzie, it's Jason. What's going on?"

"I just feel so stupid!"

"Why?"

She started sobbing. "I just found out that Ryan's wife is pregnant, too!"

X X X

In subsequent conversations, we tried to convince her to just move in with us immediately, that living with Ryan for the next four months was a bad idea. She hemmed and hawed, claimed they were trying to work it out, said that even though he'd lied about having a family, and even though his wife was pregnant (something he didn't know she knew), he still asserted they weren't together anymore and he wanted to be with Mackenzie—just not with both her and the baby. We spent hours trying to get her a lawyer, especially since he'd threatened that his "$1,000 an hour" team of sharks would make sure she got nothing in child support if she pushed him, a claim we assured her was ridiculous.

He did have money; that much was certain. His job paid quite well, footing the bill for him to fly back and forth between Connecticut and Colorado every week and paying his rent while he was here. And through Mackenzie's amateur detective work, the details of which remained murky, she'd figured out he'd married into a family whose name would be instantly recognizable to anyone who heard it—a family with the kind of money that begins with a "B."

"It's what attracted her to him, because he's not good looking," Erin told me. "You should see all of her stuff. She has more designer clothes than I've ever seen before."

"Where is it all going to go when she moves in?"

"I have no idea."

"If she's that hard up for money, why isn't she selling some of it?"

"She would never do that."

Without fully realizing how or when, this had become our evening routine. Come home from work and talk about Mackenzie's drama. Discuss how Erin needed to spend less time on the phone with her and at her house, how it was placing unneeded stress on both her and our marriage. Worry about the logistics of moving her in, how she and the baby would fare once here. Go back and forth about the concrete "move out" date we would set for her. And she wasn't even here yet.

)( )( )(

It was after 1:00 am, my car was stuffed, and I still wasn't even close to getting everything out of her house.

"What am I supposed to do with all of this?" I yelled to Erin over the phone as I surveyed the detritus piled throughout the living room. "I'm going to have to drive a half hour to our house, unload all of this shit, come back up here, and even *then*, I don't know if one more trip will be enough."

"I don't know, babe. Mackenzie and I are just trying to get through everything that's already here."

"I have classes to teach tomorrow. It's the end of the semester, and I'm buried under a mountain of grading. I wasn't supposed to be here this late. In fact, I wasn't supposed to be here at all."

"I know, and I'm sorry. This day didn't go as planned."

"Is her precious tarp okay?"

"Yes," she sighed. "Thank you for getting it."

"I still think it's ridiculous that we couldn't just put her boxes on our garage floor."

"She doesn't want the bottoms of the boxes to get dirty."

"They're boxes!"

"Listen, I know she's being ridiculous, but you've been so helpful so far. Can you just give me a little bit more?"

My turn to sigh. "Sure."

Mackenzie had packed nothing in advance, so Erin had just spent all day diverting her from her panicked micromanaging of thousands of small items while the movers loaded up a twenty-four-foot truck, dropped it all off at a storage unit, came back, loaded the truck up again, and then dropped all of that stuff at our house, where our garage was now overflowing with large boxes labeled with phrases like "Holiday Shoes." Ideally, this would have been wrapped up by dinnertime, but we'd hit an afternoon-long snag when Mackenzie had claimed some expensive diamond earrings had gone missing and demanded to know which one of the movers had stolen them.

Her friend Dexter had only complicated matters. A slow, methodical engineer who hadn't packed competently or quickly enough for her, he'd endured a full day's worth of abuse as she berated him for not doing things exactly how she'd wanted.

By evening, even though the job was far from finished, everyone else had thrown in the towel, leaving me to pack up the rest of the house and clean it—and the garage—so Mackenzie could get back her deposit.

)( )( )(

So, Dexter. Her only friend. A tall, spindly nerd who'd gone on a date with her several months ago, only to have her meet Ryan at the bar while he was busy parking the car. The guy who was still hanging around, for reasons that remained unclear. Why was he always doing her grocery shopping and personally delivering her handpicked, overpriced Whole Foods delicacies? Why was he suddenly at our house every evening once Mackenzie moved in, ferrying an ever-shifting list of items back and forth from the garage and the upstairs bedroom next to ours, where Mackenzie perched on Erin's childhood bed, barking orders? And when she yelled at him for not following her exact instructions, why did he never push back?

"Does he still want to date her?" I asked Erin after he'd helped her move yet another box of stuff into her bedroom. "Does he know what's going on with Ryan?"

"I don't know. But I do know that she's not interested in him—at least not in that way."

)( )( )(

Jesus talked regularly about helping the poor. He said that when you give a feast, you should invite the castoffs, the lowly. He also said if you have two coats, you should share with the guy who doesn't have one. He fed the hungry, healed the man with the withered hand, and had compassion on those whose infirmities kept them from earning a decent living and functioning as a regular part of society. These were the teachings on which both Erin and I were raised, on which both of us still believed we were supposed to act.

But by the time we moved Mackenzie, her mom, and her two yappy dogs into our house, I began to wrestle with how applicable his example was to our specific situation. Should we help this woman, even when her depressed economic condition had resulted not from outside misfortune, but from a lifetime of irresponsible decisions? When she refused to buy groceries at the Kroger down the street but would send Dexter to Whole Foods three times a week, always making sure he picked up the tab? When she was stuffing boxes of designer handbags into our garage instead of selling them for much-needed cash? When she had so much clothing, she required two large closets to the one Erin and I shared?

What does helping a poor person like this even mean? Was she even poor?

✕ ✕ ✕

The first major sign she was maybe, possibly not being completely honest with us came when we started to get to know her mom, a flighty but kindhearted woman who waited on Mackenzie hand and foot from sunrise to sunset—making her meals, doing her laundry, helping her schedule doctors' appointments in the run-up to her scheduled C-section—and did it all with constant cheer. A woman of humble standing who was herself divorced and working part-time at Cracker Barrel, she'd not only put her job at risk by taking a leave of absence and traveling across the country to help her daughter through her transition into motherhood, she'd also emptied her meager life savings to make sure Mackenzie's financial "needs" were met.

"Where's the woman Mackenzie described?" I whispered across the dinner table to Erin one evening. "She made it sound like her mother was the Wicked Witch of the West."

"I know," Erin whispered back.

"Didn't you tell me she got emancipated when she was a teenager?"

"At sixteen. That's what she told me."

"From that sweet woman? Why?"

"The details were sketchy. But she said it had something to do with her stepdad making a pass at her."

✕ ✕ ✕

It didn't take long for us to realize that while we had the physical space to house another family, Mackenzie's daily demands on Erin's time and energy over the last four months had stretched our psychological space to the breaking point. A few days after she'd settled in, at my behest, Erin and I sat with her in our living room to explain a few house rules.

1. Dexter was welcome to come by and help her out, but he had to leave by 9:30 pm.

2. Ryan was not allowed to visit her at our house.

3. She would need to be completely moved out by July 16.

That last rule had been suggested to us by more than one person who had also housed folks in transition. They'd said if you don't set a concrete move-out date, the people you're helping are liable to push past their welcome and end the situation on a sour note when you finally put your foot down.

We didn't have to wait that long.

"I just don't know about this move-out date," Mackenzie sputtered. "Having no flexibility will be really difficult for me, especially if Zachary has doctor's appointments he still needs to go to."

"I understand," I said, trying to keep my voice from matching her elevated volume and speed. "But we want to make sure you have adequate time to prepare for when you will be moving out. This way, we're all on the same page."

The exact date had been the source of a good deal of back and forth between Erin and me as we tried to nail down a day that would give her time to adjust to motherhood but have her gone before I had to start prepping in earnest for my fall classes. In advance of this meeting, we'd game planned how we would stay strong together, not budging for anything she'd throw at us.

"It's just, no flexibility—"

"Well, look at this way—there's actually quite a bit of flexibility. The day you choose to move out is completely up to you. You can move out any day between now and July 16."

She actually laughed at this. *Maybe this is working*, I thought.

"I just want to make sure that Zachary can stay through his ten-week appointments and any follow-ups he'll need."

Mackenzie looked at Erin with wide, woe-is-me eyes. Erin looked at me. I could see her silent pleading, could feel her resolve crumbling. No, my eyes shot back. We'd already factored all of this into the date we'd chosen. Why move it back even further?

But after some haggling, move it we did, back to July 23. "But this is it," I told her. "This is the date."

"That's fine," she beamed.

)( )( )(

As I sat in my doctor's office in mid-May, explaining how my depressive anxiety had returned and that I needed to go back on my meds, I knew what he was eventually going to say, and I didn't want to hear it.

Three months earlier, under his supervision, I'd decided to try weaning myself off the Zoloft I'd been taking for nearly a decade. For years, I'd wanted to know if I had a truly chronic mental illness that would always require medication, or if my symptoms were only the result of a particular set of circumstances long since passed. For years, I'd waited for the "right" time to try, and eventually, after realizing there would never be a "right" time, I'd decided to quit waiting.

And for a while, during March and the first half of April, I'd felt great, my energy levels rising, my emotional spectrum expanding into feelings I hadn't experienced since college. *So this is what it's like to feel normal,* I'd thought, ecstatic at the prospect of never again picking up a prescription while wondering if the pharmacist was silently judging me. But as I explained to my doctor, the day-to-day chaos Mackenzie had thrown into our lives had dovetailed with my eventual mental deterioration. I could no longer think straight, could no longer remember to do basic tasks like show up at the classes I was supposed to teach. I was falling out of sync with the world around me and back into frighteningly unhealthy thought patterns. I was worried about losing my job and being unable to function at the most basic of levels.

"Do you think the Mackenzie situation caused this?" I asked. "Would I have been okay staying off my meds if we hadn't taken this on?"

"50/50. This might have happened anyway, but we won't know for sure unless you try to go off them again after all of this is over."

As he wrote down my prescription instructions on his pad, he asked me how long they were staying.

"About three months."

"Well, you're doing a good thing. You and your wife are good Christian people."

There it was. It wasn't the first time I'd heard it, our friends and family constantly mentioning what a "good thing" we were doing. *Then why doesn't it feel like it?* I would think. *Why has doing this "good thing" made us so miserable?*

)( )( )(

By mid-June, we'd started discovering additional details about Mackenzie that cast doubt upon her version of her relationship with Ryan. When Erin and Mackenzie's co-workers—all of whom hated Mackenzie and couldn't wait for her to leave—would talk to Erin about her, they would relay what Mackenzie had told them, and a lot of details, both big and small, didn't jive with claims she'd made to us. Her story about how she'd needed to get the leased Jeep had also omitted a few important details—mainly, that she had cajoled Dexter into co-signing on it, leaving him with a $600/month payment if she couldn't make ends meet.

Now that we knew where some of her money was going, we knew more about why it wasn't going to other expenditures—and one kind of expense in particular. Since the day she'd moved in, her mail had been piling up on the desk we'd moved out of her bedroom and somehow crammed into our living room. When the stack grew to nearly a foot high and I—not for the first time—pointed it out to her, she told me, "Just keep throwing all of it on the desk. It's only medical bills. They call me every day, too. I just ignore them."

Erin had work as an escape. I was home for the summer, but "home" had become something alien, a set of constantly constricting walls, a pressure cooker of agitation and stress. I found myself leaving for hours at a time, spending entire afternoons in a cubicle at the public library, the temporary silence my only salve.

Mackenzie had delivered Zachary on her scheduled C-section day, which had gone about as well as we'd expected. And then, as soon as she had pumped and stored enough breast milk, she started leaving her baby, at that point only a few weeks old, for more than 24 hours at a time, foisting him onto her mom so she could spend the night with Ryan at his new executive suite in the downtown Marriott. She was always able to drive to these rendezvous, but any time she needed to run errands, her hip started "acting up," pulling Erin into service as her personal chauffeur, regardless of Erin's pre-existing responsibilities. When these situations arose, I gently reminded Erin that she needed to stand up to Mackenzie, that if she kept giving in, Mackenzie would completely burn her out.

And sure enough, one night, the dam broke. As Erin and I sat parked in our driveway, the darkness almost completely obscuring us from one another, she began to cry.

"It's just been so hard to see the way she treats Zachary." Her voice was quiet and even, at odds with her steady stream of tears.

"I know."

"I just look at that sweet baby boy and wonder how she could spend all day, every day tanning in our backyard, leaving him upstairs by himself. She hasn't even changed a single diaper."

"Her poor mom."

"He's going to be raised by his grandmother, that's for sure. It's just—I wonder when it's going to be my turn."

For a long time, we'd been trying but failing to get pregnant, and none of the fertility doctors who had examined Erin could tell us why. "Everything looks good," they'd told us again and again, leaving us only more desperate for answers. Erin had been taking her temperature every day, charting her ovulation cycle, timing our sexual activity, all to no avail. I'd put myself through embarrassing medical procedures to try to get any kind of answer for our inability to conceive. All the tests had come back clean. We'd prostrated ourselves before God, begging, pleading for an affirmative answer.

"If she would put Zachary up for adoption, I would take him," she said, staring straight ahead. "I wouldn't even hesitate."

"I know."

"I just wonder why God gives children to people like her who clearly don't want them, and then for someone like me, who wants a child more than anything, He says 'no.'"

X X X

With about two weeks to go, I had lunch with Mike, a long-time friend, at a local restaurant. It wasn't long before the conversation turned to Mackenzie.

"You wouldn't believe how incapable this thirty-seven year-old woman is of taking care of herself, let alone Zachary," I told him, giving way to the bitterness more easily than I liked. "The other day, her wine refrigerator stopped working, and she couldn't get it to turn on, so she asked me to fix it."

"Did you?"

"I turned the power switch off and then back on. That was all it took. When I told her it was working again, she acted like I'd just discovered how to cure cancer."

"Jeez."

"That kind of thing has happened so many times since she moved in. But we've also noticed something she's doing to other people that she'll probably do to us. She'll use a person for as long as she can, and once she's used them up, she'll invent something wrong that the person has done and then use that imaginary slight as a reason for cutting them off. She's done it with people at her work, in her family, and she's done it with Dexter—at least until she needs him for something again."

"How's Erin dealing with all of this?"

"About as well as she can. She finally started standing up to Mackenzie, which has made her pull back from some of her more ridiculous demands."

"Well, that's something, at least."

"It's just amazing to me that someone can be so consistently demanding of others while at the same time doing absolutely nothing for anyone other than herself. But when you're always painting yourself as the victim, I suppose it makes a twisted sort of sense." He took a sip of beer. "What's the latest with her and Ryan?"

"It depends on the day. He still hasn't met Zachary. He's not sure he wants to, and she's not sure if she wants him to or not. Some days she says she does, but then he'll do something—or, she'll *claim* he does something—that makes her never want to see him again. But that hasn't stopped her from sleeping with him regularly."

"What does her mom think of all of this?"

"She's been telling her that she's going up there to 'work things out' with Ryan and make sure they're both on the same page before she moves to South Carolina."

"And her mom believes her?"

"Her mom believes everything Mackenzie tells her."

"So how are you doing?"

"I just honestly don't know if we're doing the right thing or not. Are we helping her or just enabling her bad behavior? Would she have been better off if we had said no to letting her move in with us? Or maybe if we'd charged her rent instead of letting her live for free, would that have helped?"

"So she's staying with you guys completely for free?"

"Yeah. She offered to pay about $40 a month to help with our increased electricity bills, but I said no. I can just see her using that as leverage to bilk us even more, or at least to use it as a defense whenever we'd need her to do something she didn't want to do."

We both paused, settling into the uncertainty of what to say next.

"In these situations," he ventured, "it can be really tough to figure out what you're supposed to do."

"Yeah, no kidding. After she'd been really disrespectful to Erin about a month ago, I wanted to throw her out, but Erin reminded me that there's a child involved, and that if we can give him a stable home for the first few months of his life, it's still worth it."

"Do you believe that?"

)( )( )(

Moving day.

From behind the closed door of our upstairs bedroom, I could hear Mackenzie screaming at the top of her lungs and stomping around the kitchen below, tearing into Dexter for not packing her/his car exactly how she wanted it.

It wasn't her first ear-piercing, heart-stopping outburst. The previous evening, as we were getting ready for bed, our suddenly wide eyes had locked in response to what we'd just heard, our minds racing to the same conclusion. I'd ripped open our door and we'd both torn across the hallway and into her room, fully expecting to find Zachary lying in a pool of his own blood.

Instead, Mackenzie was just sitting there next to her mom, in the same propped-up position she'd taken for most of the past three months, looking not even a little sheepish. Zachary was asleep in his top-of-the-line, multi-directional swing.

"Oh, hi guys. I just got stressed out about the move," she'd stated matter-of-factly.

After listening to her tantrum make its way outside to the car, I went into her bedroom to find Zachary by himself, wrapped up in his swing. I lifted him out and held him close.

"You know, of everyone who lived here this summer, you were my favorite," I said softly, rocking him back and forth.

Whenever I'd become especially frustrated over the past month, Erin's comment about providing a home for Zachary had circled back into my mind, mingling with my own thoughts about the nature of sacrifice. I'd thought about how true sacrifice means helping someone even and especially when that person's only reciprocation is spitting in your face. I'd thought about how hard it is to turn the other cheek, how Jesus must have spent so much of his time in a state of utter emotional exhaustion, and how truly miraculous it was that he successfully fought off the temptation to just scorch the earth and be done with all of us.

And I'd thought about how little of my life has been defined by his kind of sacrifice.

Once everything was loaded into the moving truck and the car, I ventured outside. (Erin was at work, mercifully exempt from our final day's responsibilities.) Mackenzie's mom hugged me tightly, crying and thanking me profusely for what we'd done for them. Then she asked me to pray for them.

I didn't want to, but if it got them going, fine. As we all stood holding hands in a circle next to Mackenzie's car, I briefly asked God for the standard "safety while traveling" as well as for a blessing upon Zachary. *Sorry, God,* I thought as I prayed aloud. *This is as good as it's going to get today.* Mackenzie and her mom loaded Zachary into the car, while Dexter, ever the browbeaten lackey, climbed into the driver's seat of the moving truck and started the engine.

Not long after she moved out, Mackenzie would do exactly as we'd predicted. She would text Erin and tell her she had a fun update on Zachary, and could she talk? Erin, who had checked Mackenzie's Facebook profile several times since her move and had showed me the pictures Mackenzie had proudly posted of herself out partying, would text her back and let her know she was in the middle of her workday but would definitely call her later. Mackenzie would text back a snippy response, saying she just thought Erin would have cared enough to talk about the baby she'd said she'd cared about, but she guessed not. And that was that.

But that day, as I watched them drive away, I breathed deeply, slowly, releasing the months of tension. As I went back inside to call Erin and let her know they were gone, I was reminded of what a friend of ours had told us a few months earlier: "In eighteen years, you'll get a knock on the door, and a young man will be standing there, waiting to thank you."

I wasn't so sure. But I also wasn't sure it mattered.

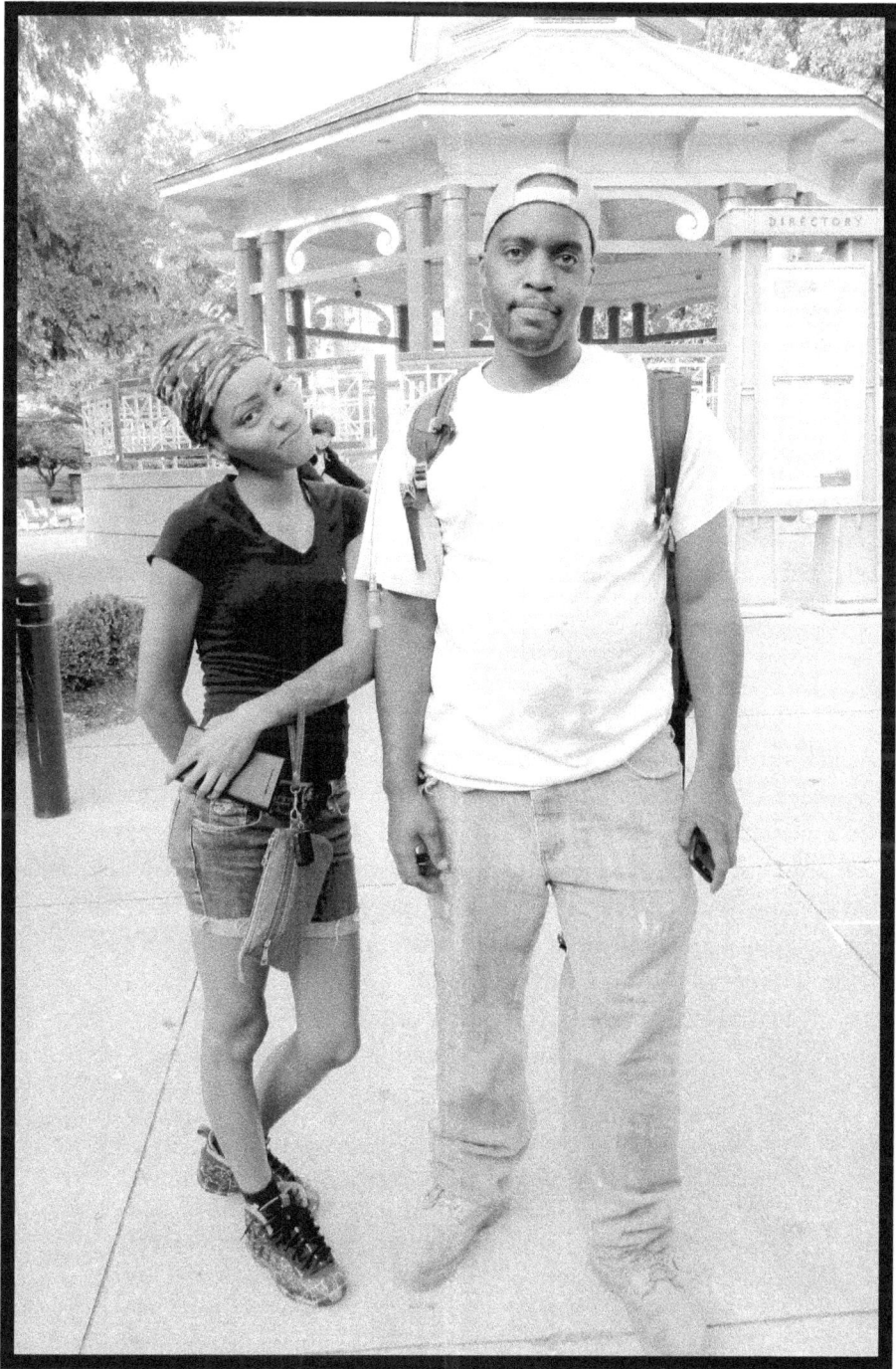

JANA ZVIBLEMAN

BUCKET OF WATER

There's a place you pass on the highway, between those two funky little hill towns of Paradise and Egypt, where a bucket pours water down—do you know where I mean? A huge bucket up in the air, tipped; a stream of water is falling out of it, into what looks like a well. The bucket is just hanging from the sky, and you can't see where the water comes from—at all. I've passed it time and again over the years, and I've yet to figure it out—real water keeps pouring and pouring.

)X( )X( )X(

On Wednesday, I received the special Bridal section of the local paper, which carried my ad about being a wedding officiant. It gives a link to my website, which has photos of me with brides and grooms, in gardens, at inns, in a manicured park by a river, in a gazebo. . . . I'm wearing a long velvet dress draped with a purple scarf in one, an off-white tuxedo suit in another, and in the most recent wedding, my new silver silky duster. It says that "I'll help create your perfect ceremony," that I am "ordained" by Universal Life, and that "I'd love to help you with your special event."

On Thursday morning, I opened an email.

> *Hi,*
> *Can you give me an estimate for tomorrow-or Sat? We got our licens tues and I excited to get married sooner, the better. There will only be like 8-10 people and we will probably all be in jeans and tshirts, including me, the bride. (: No kidding, we love each other dearly but can't aford a real wedding so we just want to get the basics and some down the line when we can afford a real wedding, we will do it again right now we just need someone spirtual and kind to read the words and marry us. It will take like 20 minutes top you know more than I, I guess how long it takes. Everyone keeps wanting to send*

> *me wedding stuff and charge arms and a leg. One said it was 250 for*
> *10 minute servuce and that's just out landish to me. So if you can help*
> *me at all, hopefully for around $50.*
>
> *Thank you,*
> *Loreen* ☺

Fifty dollars for my vast experience, my unique style, my customized care?
Fifty dollars when I am worth real money? I dragged the message to the trash
folder.

Yet, something about that message . . . I opened the trash, and read it
again.

I did some deep breathing, and invented an exercise for "letting go": *I*
can just say no. I need to do only elite affairs, classy weddings. I am establishing a
profit-making endeavor.

I read the message again, lingering on her word: *spiritual.* And: *kind.*

I hit reply.

Then I again saw that tacky smiley face, and I closed the program.

What would the Dalai Lama do?

I opened my email again, and I found myself smiling back to the smiley
face. I replied to Loreen, asking where she lives and that I *may* be able to help
her. I told her to send her phone number and we'd talk.

Within an hour, I received a reply:

> *Thank you so much! We really can't afford a hole lot. My fiance*
> *lays pipe but work has been so slow. He didn't work all of May and*
> *only part of June towards the end. So we have enough $$$$ to live*
> *but not a hole lot. I only wish I could afford a big, beautiful elaborate*
> *wedding. I doubt if we will even have a cake, but it will still be the*
> *most beautiful day for me. A couple months ago it would have been*
> *easy paying 200 or so, but it's just hard right now. You are helping me*
> *so much by doing this and i will never forget you.*
>
> *Also, we live in between Egypt and Paradise. I hope that is ok*
> *and not too far.*
>
> *Are you free tomorrow or Saturday?*
> *Thank you*

Oh sure, I thought. *She really means she wants her wedding to be tomorrow?*
Did Miss Loreen think I had nothing else to do? Did she have nothing else to do?
Why wasn't she out working so she could pay a decent price for a specialized

service by a professional? I closed her email.

I thought about Loreen never forgetting me. I wondered what had happened two months ago and where their $200 went so quickly.

Then: *I could do it. I should do it. The poor girl lives between Paradise and Egypt. She can barely write. She deserves a special wedding! I could do it the way other officiants I've heard of do weddings: in-and-out, practically a drive-by. I could dig up a short, sweet, standard quickie ceremony, deliver it and get out of there, just keep it at that.*

I wrote back:

> Loreen, I would like you to have a lovely ceremony and will be able to help make it special. I am available this Saturday. You can pay me $50, plus $10 for the gas.

Then I changed it to $40, and $7 for the gas. *Maybe I could write it off as a charity donation.*

But I would not create a personalized poem for this couple—about living just south of paradise. Or compose flowing comments, say, about his laying a pipeline to her heart. Nor describe how their dream will someday manifest, a spectacular affair complete with a huge, cream-laden, flower-encrusted cake. I would not embellish a fable of how their paths crossed in a mysterious world where there really are no coincidences. I would not take the time to interview them and elicit a heartwarming story, perhaps about the one set of great or great-great grandparents who had gifted the family with a model of a long, devoted marriage. This would be my first instant-wedding. Really.

)(( )(( )((

Early that evening, Loreen and I met on the phone.

She sounded the same as she wrote: you could hear the misspellings in her high-pitched little-girl voice. I meant to set my terms and get off the phone quickly.

I heard myself asking how she and her fiancée met.

"Well, kindof in bad circumstances," she said. "Billy and I both were in alcohol, it wasn't too good. But once I got pregnant we made huge changes, we really did, and we cleaned up. We moved here into a little trailer, well it's a big trailer actually, on my stepmom's goat farm."

I found out that both she and Billy were twenty-eight years old, and that they had a two-year-old son, Perry.

Fine, that was enough for me to get going on.

But I went on. "Loreen, to help me customize your ceremony, tell me about what you treasure about Billy."

She said, "He's ADHD, and he's like a kid, that makes him very challenging. But," she added, "it's kindof cute."

"I meant your fiancée, not your son," I said.

"Yes," she said. "My fiancée, Billy."

"Tell me what you two take pleasure in together."

"Oh, we go up the hill. There's a creek. We like that. He calls it 'our crick.'"

I found myself asking to talk with Billy. I heard some calling and muffled discourse, and there Billy and I were.

"I dunno, we watch a lots of movies," Billy said. "We go to our crick, since we got to get the kid out of the house sometime."

With that, Loreen was back on the phone.

I asked her, "Are you exchanging rings or other mementos?"

She said, "I've been wearing one for a couple weeks. It's real nice one, I kindof found it in the park, so it's special. But someone had the engagement and wedding ring welded to each other, but its okay. I like wearing it."

I reminded myself: *don't get involved.*

I immediately started coaching Loreen on various options to make the ceremony special. I said we must consider the venue.

Silence.

"*Venue*," I repeated. *Where* will we be?"

"Oh," she said. She guessed everyone could stand out in the pasture.

I said she might want to set up chairs. I suggested that she consider a circular configuration.

"Would you like to kindle a columnar candle together? Some couples drink from the same wine glass, or . . ."

Loreen said, no, she guessed they didn't want candles—her Perry, and something about fire. "And we'll have soda pop. *Only* pop."

I continued with my usual ceremony prompts. "Are there any traditions, such as rituals that your parents or grandparents or someone in your lineage hold dear, that you would like to honor? Anything from your heritage, or his, that the families would appreciate? Elements that make the wedding authentic for them?

"For example," I said, "And this is just an example, in a Jewish wedding the groom smashes a glass."

"Oh, my mother, she's Jewish," Loreen said.

"Oh really?" I said.

I thought, *Knock me over with a chuppah by a trailer.*

"Yeah, Mom is—she was—she is. But she's not around."

So, I launched into educating Loreen about the Jewish wedding *chuppah.* "I'm sure your mother and your grandmothers had it at their weddings. Perhaps. There's something called a, um, a canopy. During the nuptials, the betrothed stand under a special cloth— it means protection, and home, metaphorically"

She said, "We don't have special cloth like that."

"If you have a decorative tablecloth people could hold up, maybe an embroidered one, or even just white on white. . ."

Silence.

"Or how about, let's see . . . a tree as a natural canopy? If there's a tree in the pasture, you could stand under the tree."

She said, "The only trees here are inside the goat corrals, I think."

"Never mind," I said. "You don't need a canopy."

"How about the sky?" Loreen said. "Would it be okay to use the sky?"

"Nice," I said. "Perfect."

I was becoming fond of Loreen.

I asked if she'd thought about a bouquet. How about flowers growing around the farm, that she'd want to hold?

"Nope. There's no flowers here," she said.

My heart tugged.

She said, "But we could go buy two roses from the ShopRight to give each other."

Supermarket flowers—ugh. I started mentally surveying my own gardens. *What colors would Loreen like? NO, stop.*

"Two roses, for each other; that will be nice," I said.

I asked if she wanted any music. Silence. I told her to consider it.

)( )( )(

Early Friday morning, Loreen called again. When she was excited, her voice became even higher and little-girly-er.

"I spent three or two hours last night in Walmart! I found some white Capri pants—you know, to be special. But they'll be okay if they get dirty in the field."

Then she said, "Please don't be offended. But my stepmom is kindof worried about me, because she knew some people who went to get Social Security and found out their marriage was never legal."

I assured Loreen that her marriage would be legal. I could bring documents that showed I was certified, and that providing she had obtained the license, it would be fine.

"You have obtained the license?"

"Yes, my stepmom has it under lock and key," she said. "Oh, by the way, my Pop plays banjo and sings and maybe he'd sing if we twist his arm up."

Sweet, I thought. "Sweet," I said.

)( )( )(

Another email from Loreen:

> "By the way I didn't tell you my sisters are lots of us, but most of them won't be there, only 1. I'm Loreen and every one of us is EEN: Maureen and Koleen and Maxine and the youngest is Laleen. Billy always says if there was more 1 is Magaz-een and Pop always says there was a Canteen but he thinks she got empty. You know all the jokes. Anyway its nice to let you know because I'm not the only girl in the family but now I kindof am except for the 1. who might be here."

I opened up Word and became immersed in creating a unique ceremony, one worthy of a lifelong memory for Loreen and Billy.

I had her father singing three songs of his choosing: before, during, after.

I decided Loreen was the "something old, new, borrowed and blue" type, and that the tradition would be therapeutic for her.

I wrote "Your son is old—he's been here two years, and he has already changed your lives so much."

(I wrote, in parentheses, a message to Loreen: "Please think of something new you can wear that day, in addition to your Capri pants. Maybe a pretty ribbon?")

I wrote, "The sky sheltering you right now is blue, and it is a symbol of your fresh start on life today."

(In parenthesis I asked, "Does Perry have blue eyes? Or do either of you? If so, I could add that.")

(And I asked: Did your sisters ever let you *borrow* something nice? Or your stepmom?)

I incorporated a light mention of God. I usually would be extra careful to ask couples about that: people who seek out independent officiants tend to belong to the "I don't believe anything" or "We like *spiritual*, but can you *not* mention *God*, please?" camps. But I decided to just insert the Divine in this one and see whether it would fly with Loreen.

I played around with how to mention the EEN sisters. *Eenie meenie . . . very eenteresting family . . . eench by eench . . . .* I abandoned that track.

Where were those women, anyway? Their own sister's *wedding*. They don't deserve to be mentioned if they're going to be so *meen* and not be *seen*. I liked my stupid joke, and wanted to remember it to tell my husband. With some effort, I managed to get my mind off the *eens*.

After two hours of refining the ceremony, I clicked the opus off to Loreen, telling her to decide on any changes, and asking her to send directions to her place.

As soon as I hit "send," this message arrived:

> *Hi,*
> *I am so sorry. My mom (step) just told me she thinks she found a pastor to Marry us in a Church. Thank you for help all your help. If for some reason he says no, I still like you to Marry us.*
> *Loreen ps. I guess Pop could still sing in church or maybe not thatd be something for him allright. ;)i*

I found myself feeling sad. And it wasn't for the $40.

A short time later, another message came in:

> *Hi its me again,*
> *I just read all this that you sent me and I really like what you said and how you planned it, so I am going to go with you on marrying us and tell my step-mom and everyone that it is our day we have it all set up all ready. Billy and I both like the vows, it says what we truly feel.*
> *My sister might not show because she is busy a lot working, but that's okay. My stepmom is calling everyone right now.*
> *Pop is kind of very excited He has other daughters but never got to go to the weddings. So maybe if you can put something about*

my pop giving me away or something, that would make his day. And mine to. (:

She gave me directions, adding,

> *"You can't miss it. Oh, we are on the left side of the road. If you get to the pouring bucket you are one drive way too far.*
> *Oh and we all have blue eyes, so we have the blue covered. :-) I borrowed my sister's cowgirl hat when I was little and that was not so good she got mad, so I'll have to think. I guess our marriages good for new, right?*
> *Pop is also happy he gets to sing. You will like my family, we are all kind of goofy.*
>
> *Thank you,*
> *Loreen*

Goofy. I need more goofy in my life.
We exchanged subsequent emails. In one, she said:

> *Thank you again. I was beginning to think every one was just marrying people for the money and not in it for ... I don't know how to say it.but I thank you from the Bottom of my heart because I know you could be making a lot more $$ doing this and you R doing us a HUGE kindness. Your bride well you know what I mean. Loreen*

My bride. Sweet.
That night, I set about convincing my husband, Thomas, to accompany me to this event.

"Just this once . . . I might get lost . . . Who knows what these people will be like? I may need you to drive the getaway car, it might be the McCoy feud and a shotgun wedding . . .."

No sympathy.

Then I hit upon, "You can take wedding photographs. I'm sure it will be quite an interesting visual, a sociological study. Come on, dear, you *love* photographing picturesque characters."

Got him.

)( )( )(

Saturday morning. I nervously rummaged through my closet. *Not the velvet dress. Not the silky duster. For sure not the tuxedo suit . . .*

I pulled out a blue denim dress I hadn't worn in years, and never to a wedding.

I usually wore Mother's diamond ring and tennis bracelet when I conducted weddings, to supplement my own jewelry. I put them on, took them off.

)( )( )(

Thomas drove us past the pouring bucket, because I wanted to look at it; then he turned our automobile back, found the driveway, and found the trailers. Next to them, two trucks, a car, and the insides of a car—all covered in mud, dents, and rust. Scattered around were components of a red swing set, a half-smashed horse saddle, a baby bottle filled with neon-green matter. And more. We parked.

Blazing heat. Flies smacked into our windshield and bombadiered through our open side windows.

"Roll up the windows!" Thomas said.

Up bounded a glowing young woman. *Oh, she's attractive.* Buxom, with a dragonfly tattoo emerging from her abundant cleavage, her bosom bursting from a clinging white cotton blouse. Very shiny-lips, pretty smile. Dark auburn, flowing, curly hair. Freckles.

In her high little-girl voice, Loreen exclaimed, "Carla, look!"

She held out her left hand, wiggling her ring finger. At the same time she pulled over a pale, skinny young man. Close-clipped crew cut. Faded plaid brownish shirt, faded blue jeans.

"Billy, show yours," she said. She pulled his hand toward me. "Look, we got a ring for Billy!"

I didn't ask where.

Billy was eying Thomas's camera, and Thomas started telling him about the lenses he brought and all the paraphernalia he didn't bring.

I noticed Loreen was wearing a skirt: gathered, three-tiered, pale pink, skimming the knees of her bare Rubenesque legs.

"Come look, we made a *ven—ven-you.* Under this *tree!*" she said. "Billy made it like an ark, like you said!"

The tree trunk was on the other side of a wooden fence; a spindly branch hung over and offered no more than one foot of shade. A few pale flowers were strung around the trunk.

Loreen said, "Look, he put them—we found wild-carrot it's called, in the field. I couldn't sleep!"

Long black and red feathers and gold beads hung on fishing wires from the branch, with plastic medallions dangling at the bottoms.

"My stepmom makes these—they're dream-catchers. She said one is to keep for our wedding present, so we'll have dreams about it!"

Facing the tree were several dingy white plastic lawn chairs, and two bent aluminum-frame chairs with seats and backs made of woven yarn, black and orange. Plus a few wobbly green wooden kitchen chairs.

A large, silver house trailer leaned behind us, with cinder block steps, and just beyond it crouched a small, dented turquoise trailer. The fence consisted of several sections of chain link, several of weathered wood. It bordered a small square of clumpy dirt and scattered piles of dark brown pellets. One section was separated with chicken wire, and through its squares poked and bobbled a gaggle of dingy gray-yellow chicken heads, making a cacophony of hoarse clucking.

"I'll go tell everybody you're here!" Loreen said, "And get you the papers and try calling up my sister again."

Thomas and I stood watching a goat approach the fence, then two, then more goats than I had ever seen. Their *bahs* competed with the *clucks* and the noise of trucks rushing by on the highway.

I noticed that Thomas was swatting his neck, his arms, waving his hands back and forth in front of his face. He said *sotto voce*, "When and if we tell this story to our friends, let's not mention the flies."

But I do have to mention the flies. Swarms. Flocks. *Bevies* of flies. *Mobs* of flies. *Truckloads*. Mysteriously, they kept their distance from me.

And now, human members of what I assumed was the wedding party, and guests, straggled over. Almost one for every chicken. Thomas was absorbed in fiddling with his camera lens. I introduced myself to people, one by one.

Grandpa looked smooth, pale, and drippy, like a melting candle in overalls. He and his aluminum walker wobbled over, barely making it to one of the yarn chairs, and almost tipped it over when he plunked into the seat. I shook his oily hand.

Boney, short, Pop dangled from his thin-lipped mouth the longest cigarette I'd ever seen. When I greeted him, he took the cigarette out of his mouth and held it down at his side, cradling the burning end towards his cupped palm. I told him we were looking forward to his singing and playing, and I wondered what compositions he had chosen, and that I'd signal to him at the times I designated in the ceremony for the music.

"Naw," he said, in a cement-mixer voice. "Can't play. My thumb hurts an' I been sleepin' on the floor."

He put the cigarette back in his mouth.

Far behind me, I knew Thomas felt in visual haven. I saw Billy at his side.

A woman whose arm muscles bulged in her sleeveless red shirt appeared and poked her elbow into Pop's side. She said, "He might come through, you never know, ya know? Hello, I'm the stepmom. Did you meet my goats? I can show you the goat grave later."

She added, "I hope it's all legal. You know, these two had enough trouble with the law. Don't say that in the wedding. Ha ha."

I guessed her age as mid-forties, despite the scarcity of teeth in her mouth, and a face that matched the wooden fence.

Loreen bounced up to Pop, plucked the cigarette from him, took a drag, turned her head to aim the smoke behind her, and put the cigarette back in his mouth. Then she disappeared, appeared, disappeared.

Billy approached, carrying a metal highchair in which was strapped Perry. I've witnessed many a toddler, and I have no fantasies about picture-perfect children, but this was the stickiest, grimiest-faced young one I'd ever seen. His stubby legs, equally grimy, dangled and kicked. His chunkiness was crammed into a too-small, faded black cowboy shirt; a neon green price tag was stapled to the outside of the collar. Billy plunked the chair-with-child down in the center of the *ven-you*.

Then Billy set a lopsided card table next to the chair, and items were distributed on it: cigarette pack, lighter, plastic bathroom cups. A silver whistle. A cardboard box marked in red: *DoNuts*.

One man had a red Amish-style beard—the under-the-chin kind—a black porkpie hat, and dark brown suspenders. Sticking out of his side pants pocket was a dull gray metal flask. He caught me eyeing the flask and said, "Gatorade. This is Billy's first weddin', I wouldn't do that to him."

There were other people. I knew Thomas was in ecstasy with character-studies, framing brilliant compositions. I noticed him handing his camera to Billy—I was sure he was coaching Billy on the rule of thirds and such.

A middle-aged bald man wore the local college team T-shirt, tucked into brand new blue jeans; he was barefoot.

A 20s-something guy with a beer belly and shaved head said to me, "I'm just the camera man."

They all wandered away.

Thomas, the chickens, and I stood there next to Perry in his high chair. He was reaching and straining toward the table, turning red. I was amazed that he managed to reach and grab both the cigarette pack and the lighter.

Thomas said sweetly, "Oh Perry, look what you have. I'll take your picture with them. Now, will you hand those things to me please?"

Before Perry could refuse, a 70s-looking woman with coke-bottle red hair, quite overweight, appeared and swapped the things in Perry's hands for half of a Baby Ruth bar. She was holding an infant. Clinging very close to the woman's side was a 20-something, dark-haired woman, extremely emaciated looking. "We'll behave ourselves," the older woman said. "Don't you worry."

A teen girl came up to me, "I'm getting married next month. I don't have a preacher yet neither. Maybe you'll hear from me."

Everyone else shuffled back to the *ven-you*, as did three or four newcomers. Some settled into the chairs; others stood near the fence; and one spread a raggedy red quilt on the ground and spread herself down on her back. The young skinny woman was tearing up tufts of grass and pushing them through the fence to the goats. The flies were congregating and getting their hankies ready.

I heard a TV somewhere in the background, with a laugh-track: "No! No! NO!" "Oh, *please*, Rickie? *Pretty please*, Rickie?" An old "I Love Lucy."

Loreen and Billy stood at attention before me. She winked at me.

"Welcome!," I said loudly, to signal the start of the ceremony.

Pop lit another cigarette.

There was some shuffling around, and grumbles from The Camera Man. Loreen said "Back in a 'sec," running toward the trailers; she returned and handed him a tape. We began again.

All went like clockwork, for several minutes: Welcome, Introduction . . . I asked Pop to come up and stand by Loreen.

"Do you bring your daughter Loreen, with your whole heart, to this new phase of her life? Are you open to the extending of family, and will you support this union fully?"

He moved his cigarette down to his side and held it slightly behind him, saying, with smoke coming out of his mouth, "Yes, ma'am, I do."

Then he muttered, "That support better don't mean money 'til death do 'em part."

Some who heard it chuckled; someone laughed outright. Billy turned red, and I saw Loreen shooting Pop a look.

"Loreen and Billy, a marriage is sacred, a blessing from God, and a promise." Are you ready?"

Loreen said "Oh, yes!"

Billy said "Sure am."

"Let's all take a moment in silence, while each in our own way gives blessings, or good wishes, to this marriage."

. . .

The chickens prayed up a storm.

"Loreen, repeat after me please . . .

> *"I give you my promise*
> *that from this day on*
> *you shall not walk alone,*
> *May my heart be your shelter*
> *and my arms be your home . . . "*

They each in turn repeated after me, phrase by phrase, perfectly. We proceeded swimmingly.

Then I said softly to Pop, "If you *would* like to, um, lead us *all* in a song, now is a perfect opportunity."

He gave me a tobacco-stained *thumbs-down*.

"And now," I said, "I am happy to pronounce you, Loreen and Billy, spiritually joined, legally bound, and lovingly wife and husband!"

The bride's cheeks were wet with tears. And *ah*, her smile—it made me think of how I love the sun shining forth during a light rainshower.

Silence.

No one moved. People and chickens and goats stood looking at me. The flies held their collective breath.

I surmised that the entire clan was waiting for that "you may now kiss" proclamation—which I always avoid. It's not up to me, I figure, to give a couple permission to kiss. I'm sure I've yet to marry a couple who hasn't been doing quite a bit more together for quite a while.

At least they didn't insist upon the "Speak now or forever hold your peace" clause.

As I stood my ground, I thought, *How ripe Loreen looks.* I imagined kissing her myself.

She and Billy still looked at me. *Too many old Western movies,* I thought.

Loreen whispered "Can we?" and Billy said "Is this the *you get to kiss* part?"

Perry threw down someone's key ring loaded with bottle openers, Swiss Army knife, whistle, and flashlight; it landed on my foot.

Thomas' camera was aimed at the audience, not at the couple.

They all seemed to be staging a sit-in. They won.

"You may now share your first *wedded* embrace," I said. "You may now and forever do whatever you'd both like together—you are truly married!"

So they embraced dramatically, as the masses gave out a few *whoops,* which made some of the goats startle and jump onto each other, while a shout rang out, "Do we get to eat yet?" and someone else whistled and yelled "OH BILLY BOY!"

When bride and groom pried apart, The Camera Man growled "Hold it, I didn't get that this *friggin'* thing, smooch her once more okay?"

They laughed and kissed again, and the baby shrieked, and the chickens garbled.

Bride and Groom, Grandpa and Pop and Stepmom and everyone resumed looking at me.

And stayed looking at me.

Someone said "What now?"

"Well," I said. "Does anyone have a story they'd like to tell about our newly married couple? Maybe their courtship?"

Grandpa and Pop and Stepmom and everyone looked as if no one were home. Silence.

Loreen said, "You're not going to hear *them* tell any stories."

Even the chickens had nothing.

"How about something you *wish* for Billy and Loreen?" I said. "Or, marital *advice?*"

Stepmom came up to Loreen and Billy, pointed her small camera inches from their faces, and snapped a photo, saying, "Well, *it's about time!*"

The Camera Man said, "I was gonna say that, but I figured I shouldn't."

Loreen laughed, saying, "There's a lot of stuff *you should not say.*"

Everyone was standing, and shuffled closer together into a cluster under the tree. The chickens were paying more attention. The flies all landed on Perry.

Stepmom said, "I wish you a good one. At least one. I've had six good years married to your father, I think like a thousand sometimes, and it's rough times and good times like she said, and I hope you have a good one."

I applauded, and by making eye contact encouraged a few claps.

Stepmom elbowed Pop. He said, "Time's fun when you're having flies."

Loreen said to me, "Thank you thank you thank you."

Billy muttered, "Yeah."

The bride leaned closer to the groom and said, not very softly, "Itch me on my back, I just got a fly bite real bad," and he did so.

Then she strutted away and cuddled the baby. The groom cleared the things off the card table and moved it to under the tree. He left and came back carrying a supersized cooler, opening it to reveal soda cans—seemed like one hundred of them: Western Family brand cream and Western Family brand lemon lime. Perry whined and struggled to get down from the high chair. Ignoring him, Billy got down on his stomach on the ground and aimed Thomas's camera at the goats.

The flies were dancing the first waltz.

People called to each other "Who's got the church-key?" and "Don't forget those cookies" and "Give me a hand let's move those crates over here for a table" and "I'm so hungry I could eat a goat" and "You don't say *that* around Lucy here."

Most of the women left. Two returned carrying huge red-and-white cardboard buckets of a knock-off brand of to-go fried chicken.

The live chickens were straining their necks through the fence, stomping each other and squawking to join us.

"Hey, stay 'n eat. It's that time anyway," the Amish-ish man said to me, taking a pull from his flask, and Camera Man handed Thomas a can of Western Family, and the flies were bringing in their cousins.

Thomas and I looked at each other.

"Oh, we ate prior to our arrival," I was saying.

At the same time, he was saying, "Thank you, no I, we need to get to a, a dinner, thanks, we have a dinner waiting. What a nice wedding. I'll send you photos."

The bride and the groom hugged me at the same time, while Perry in his high chair under the tree raised his arms to me, shaking something gooey. I bent down and pecked his cheek.

I said to Loreen, "Keep in touch," feeling teary.

As I backed our car out of the driveway, Thomas said to open all of the windows *quickly* so the flies would get out and stay home, they were driving him crazy.

)( )( )(

An email the next day:

> *Thank you again that was the best. I am a bit worried because I just realized my parents signed in handwriting instead of print when they signed as witnesses and it says they were supposed to print. Is it still going to be legal? I'm going to give Billy a real good camera for our aniversary someday.*
> *Thank you,*
> *Loreen*

> *To the beautiful new wife,*
> *You were a lovely, glowing, gracious bride! Your family is so full of energy! Thank you for the honor of being part of your special occasion. Don't worry about the paperwork. Ask your Pop and Stepmom to print their names next to or above where they wrote. You can call the office where you are required to turn it in, and tell them—it will probably not make any difference. If they say it has to be reissued, post a new form to me with your sections filled in, and I can sign and mail it in. Enjoy! Carla*

> *Hi*
> *thank you for saying such nice things! You were wonderfull, too, and I thank you for coming and helping us! You made it a wonderfull day for me (: us!*
> *I guess I am just worried because it was such a beautiful that they would make me start all over again and do it again! I think I am just being silly, there is noway such a small thing would be such a big deal. I will do what you said and have them print above there names.*
> *Thank you,*
> *Loreen*

A few days later:

Dear Loreen, How are you all faring? Did you get the paperwork mailed in? How is Perry? I wonder if the video came out, and the photos by the people there.
Fondly, Carla

From her:

If there's ever thing we can do for you . . .

The next week, I wrote:

Maybe if you are ever over in the city . . . Does Billy still need work? Do you think he could climb a ladder to our roof to clean out the gutters? And maybe he can figure out what's wrong with our skylight closure. Is he willing to saw tree branches? We would love to hire him for various chores.

)X( )X( )X(

It seems ages ago that Loreen proposed the idea to design a concise poster for my wedding business, and she did it—complete with a smiling-sun-and-sky-and-tree drawing. She went around her town push-pinning the posters onto supermarket bulletin boards and masking-taping them to laundromat windows and thrift-store doors. Her marketing strategy brought in several calls.

She and I would talk about the business and take Perry for walks and cook together each time Billy did some handyman jobs for us, and then while he assisted Thomas in constructing a darkroom in half of our tool shed.

So we were in touch, when one day I received an email:

Carla you won't hear from me any more, maybe but I don't know where were going, Step-mom I mean Pop's wife or x I guess what ever is kicking all us out its not being fun around here. Good luck.

My friends still don't understand, but I couldn't allow Loreen to reside in a tent, or worse.

She and Billy and Perry don't take up much space in our house—they truly don't.

Most evenings, Loreen and Billy are in their room watching movies anyway, and they keep the volume fairly low. Their bedroom is the one that used to be our Master. They needed the space, and the attached bathroom, much more than did we. She made the walk-in closet the sweetest little bedroom for Perry.

When her Pop is around, he's fine sleeping on the den's leather couch.

When the remainder of their family visits, they bring their own chicken or burgers, and they usually remember to smoke outside. (I decided if you can't beat 'em . . . so I keep a pack or two for when they come.) Loreen actually did stop smoking—she seems to be able to do anything to which she sets her mind.

Thomas and Billy spend hours out in the darkroom. They're currently creating a calendar: twelve portraits of chickens being cradled by men wearing fancy hats.

Perry is quite a child. He is maturing so rapidly. He's extremely sweet, eager to participate in household activities. When the family all comes over, he so enjoys emptying the ashtrays, concentrating so hard on carrying, and he tips the ashtrays so carefully into the bin, without spilling much at all, and brings his miniature dustpan for the butts that do end up on the floor. That's thanks to the skills from the Montessori school in which we enrolled him. Thomas and I have met many sweet young parents there, and a few other "grandparents" too, when we take him and pick him up. Thomas even says Perry looks—just a *tiny* bit, around the eyes—like me.

Loreen is an amazing asset to my wedding enterprise. She began by walking around behind me right before I left for an event: *Did you print the ceremony? Should I check to make sure it's the final version? Do you need to bring the music stand for this one, or do they have a podium? Um, your shawl may clash with that bride's colors. Make sure you know how to pronounce his last name— seems like a tricky one.* She printed a checklist.

In addition, she designed a logo—eye-catching yet tasteful—and expanded the poster-hanging strategy to bookstores and coffee shops in our area. Then she produced full-color brochures and business cards, and she sets them in unique holders shaped like three-tiered cakes, which she had Billy make of copper wire. She brings them to fine women's dress shops, jewelers, and nice restaurants, as well as to temples and churches. She inserted us on Craig's List, plus she keeps finding new social-media ways to advertise. I was amazed when so many calls began coming in, now in the high-price bracket.

And Loreen used to love listening in on my pre-wedding telephone interviews. I found that the ideas and insights she jotted down were quite beneficial. For instance, once she noted, "Groom wants you to talk about his grandad but I got it that grandad's wife is *not* his Gramma, and Groom isn't down with that. You could say, 'Grandad's got love big enough for all of us here at this wedding even those who are not here anymore.' *Don't* say his Gramma, but don't put in that new wife."

So Loreen began accompanying me to my in-person consultations, and then to the rehearsals; it was natural that she became my assistant at the weddings. She oversaw the choreography of who stands where, and walks in when, with whom—all of those wedding *planner* details that people attempt to persuade me to manage. In addition she designed—and had Billy construct—the most lovely portable archway, and coordinated altar and podium, which they customize for any bride's style and colors.

One thing led to still another, and it turns out Loreen's quite the talented officiant. She has a knack for speaking to people's hearts, and for bringing forth the joyous tears. I'm losing my *oomph* for such—during the "til death do us part" phrase, my mind keeps wanting to forewarn "til divorce-proceedings do rip us to shreds." Loreen is abundantly starry-eyed and maintains enough romantic bounce to marry the whole county. Her couples seem to be vowing *to her* to stay committed.

Billy is perpetually occupied, of course. His chickens out back, for one thing, and his puttering to maintain our household gadgets. Also, perusing salvage yards and hardware stores. Our neighbors used to complain about the clucking and the digging and the pipes and the tools, as well as the toys and little forts around the yard, *and* the bluegrass music. But Billy got on their case, and now they pretty much *mind their own beezwax*, as he says. Thomas and I had never established "community" with this neighborhood anyway.

Billy has become determined to create a mystery-water-pouring sculpture for our front lawn.

His aesthetic design began as a jug and mug, but it seems to have evolved into a rainbow with a waterfall streaming down into a large round vessel. He says little girls like rainbows.

The sticking point is his trying to figure out exactly "how in the heck those dang contraptions work." He's photographed the bucket of water from a variety of perspectives.

Loreen encourages him, professing her faith that he'll get it "up and running," and he'll be able to use the one here as a "demo" and build up quite a business. She's already strategizing her marketing.

I've been envisioning myself relaxing near it on a quilt with their new baby, Carleen, after she arrives—which will be soon. I love that Carleen will assume it's *très naturel* for water to be pouring from nowhere, perpetually. It will be years before she even begins to wonder from whence cometh such abundance.

ACKNOWLEDGEMENTS

Susan Austin's "The Sweet and Dark" previously appeared in *Clerestory: Poems of the Mountain West* (2015).

Rachel Squires Bloom's "Who Is This Girl" was previously published in *Clackamas Literary Review* (2001).

"New Year's Eve" by William Cass was first published in *Zest.*

Norita Dittberner-Jax's "Jazz Trumpeter" and "Universal Donor" were earlier published in *Stopping For Breath* (Nodin Press, 2014).

Rupert Fike previously published "Tutoring Mohammad Mohammad" in *Duende* and "Our Street Preacher, Miss Edna" in *Lotus Buffet* (Brick Road Poetry Press, 2011).

Frank Haberle's "Road to Haines" appeared previously in the *Adirondack Review* (Summer 2006).

"And All Points West" by Margaret Hasse was previously published in *Poet's Lore* while "Blood Oranges" was previously published in *Flurries* and *The Saint Paul Almanac*. Both also appeared in *Earth's Appetite* (Nodine Press).

Lowell Jaeger previously published "After Second Shift" in *Soundings Review*; "Neighbors" in *MIRAMAR*; "The Librarians" and "What Sort of Man" in *Or Maybe I Drift Off Alone* (Shabda Press, 2016).

Murali Kamma's "Brahms in the Land of Brahma" first appeared in *Lakeview International journal of Literature and Arts.*

Marianne Peel's "Happy Hour at PF Changs" was previously published in *Muddy River Review* (Fall 2016).

"Take Care of Each Other" is excerpted from MK Punky's *Report from the Street: Voices of the Homeless.*

Versions of Patti See's "To Give Away: One Used Kidney" previously appeared in newsletters of her high school and college as well as the newsletter from the transplant center where she made her donation, *Inside View: University of Minnesota Medical Center-Fairview* (2005).

Karen Skolfield's "Wait Five Minutes" was previously published in *Zone 3*.

Ken Staley's "Missing" first appeared in *From the Porch Swing: Memories of Our Grandparents I* (Silver Boomer Books, 2010).

A somewhat different version of Rebecca Taksel's "Omega" was published in *Redwood Coast Review* (Summer 2004).

Johnny Townsend previously published "The Girl from Treponema" in *The Washing of Brains* (BookLocker, 2016).

Photographs in this book are part of the *Remembering Kindness* project, to which numerous people have participated, many anonymously. We would like to thank Kerry Langan, Robert Geitz, Madeline Geitz, Katie Glauber Bush, Jessica Naab, Meia Geddes, Tyree Wilson, Charles M. Beattie II, Ashley Smith, William Reilly, and Marcus Stallworth for contributing photographs. Heather Tosteson thanks Geanie, Stephen, Alex and Cameron Brown, Robert and Gladys Reynolds, Shahidah Muhammad, Daniel Nesatu, Karen Davis, Linda Duque, Shelia Harkleroad, Scott and Maggie Nesbit, Tyrone, Maurice, Mr. Smith, Stanley, Mimi, Cynthia, Albert, Bryson, Paula, Manuelo, and many others for so generously agreeing to be photographed and sharing a moment of remembrance with us.

We again give special thanks to Kerry Langan, Michele Markarian and Kathleen Housley, members of the Wising Up Press Writers Collective, for so generously sharing their skills as editors and engaged and thoughtful readers. We couldn't do what we do without them.

CONTRIBUTORS

Susan Austin lives in the foothills of the Teton Mountains. She loves maps, all kinds of maps, the topographic maps stacked in the mudroom closet. She was the recipient of a James Michener Fellowship. Her work has appeared or is forthcoming in *BOAAT, High Desert Journal, Clerestory, Borderlands, Hanging Loose, Best New American Writers 2003*, and elsewhere.

Rachel Squires Bloom has published poetry in *The Hawaii Review, Poet Lore, Fugue, Main Street Rag, Kimera, Poetry East, Nomad's Choir, Mad Poet's Review, Bluster, 96 Inc., Bellowing Ark, Slugfest, Taproot Literary Review, True Romance, Lucid Stone, Green Hills Literary Lantern* and *California Quarterly.* She has also had poems in several anthologies. She teaches in Quincy, MA.

Katie Glauber Bush is a memoir and humor writer in Louisville, KY. Her story "Queen of the May" appears in the Wising Up anthology *Siblings: Our First Macrocosm.* Katie's story "Woman's Work" appears in the award-winning anthology *Times They Were A-Changing.* Her work was honored by the San Francisco chapter of the National League of American Pen Women in 2012 and 2013.

William Cass has had a little over a hundred short stories accepted for publication in a variety of literary magazines and anthologies. Recently, he was a finalist in short fiction and novella competitions at *Glimmer Train* and Black Hill Press, received a Pushcart nomination, and won writing contests at *Terrain.org* and *The Examined Life Journal.* He lives in San Diego, CA.

Laura Chaignon is a twenty-one year-old Paris-based author and a graduate student at the University of the Sorbonne where she studies the effect of artificial intelligence creativity on the world of literature. She is primarily a French writer and has never been published before.

Teetle Clawson had a long career as a visual artist and art educator with at-risk youth before co-founding a medical product design company in Santa Cruz, CA. Her work has appeared in the *Midwest Quarterly, San Pedro River*

Review, Syracuse Cultural Workers and *The Sun Magazine*. One of her poems published in *The Sun* was nominated for a 2014 Pushcart Prize.

Susan Clayton-Goldner's poetry has appeared in literary journals and anthologies including *Animals as Teachers and Healers* (Ballantine Books), *Our Mothers/Ourselves, The Hawaii Pacific Review-Best of a Decade*, and *New Millennium Writings*. She is the author of a collection of poetry entitled, *A Question of Mortality*. Her novel, *A Bend In The Willow*, will be released in January 2017.

Shireen Day grew up in New Jersey, the U.S. Virgin Islands, Iran and Iowa. She earned her BA in Sociology from Colorado College, and an MS in Social Work from University of Denver. Her essay, "Unexpectedly White and Privileged," was published in the 2016 anthology, *What Does It Mean To Be White In America? Breaking The White Code of Silence.*

Norita Dittberner-Jax has published four collections of poetry, most recently, *Stopping For Breath* (Nodin Press). She has won numerous awards and fellowships, among them several nominations for the Pushcart. One of the poetry editors for Red Bird Chapbooks, Norita lives with her husband on the banks of the mighty Mississippi River.

Alethea Eason is a writer, artist, and educator, living in rural Northern California. Recent stories have appeared in *Lamplight Magazine* and *The Del Sol Review*. She has published three young-adult novels: *Hungry, Starved,* and *Heron's Path*. "Holiday Cove" was written as part of her work as writer-in-residence for the Putah-Cache Creek Watershed Project sponsored by U.C. Davis.

Rupert Fike was named the Finalist (2nd place) as Georgia Author of the Year 2011 after his collection, *Lotus Buffet* was published by Brick Road Poetry Press. He has been nominated for a Pushcart Prize in fiction and poetry, with work appearing in *Rosebud, The Georgetown Review, A&U America's AIDS Magazine, Natural Bridge, The Southern Review of Poetry, Alligator Juniper* and others.

Meia Geddes is the author of *Love Letters to the World* and *The Little Queen*. She graduated from Brown University and has been the recipient of a Fulbright grant.

Frank Haberle's stories have won the 2011 Pen Parentis Award and the 2013 Sustainable Arts Foundation Award. They have appeared in journals including the *Stockholm Review of Literature, Necessary Fiction, Adirondack Review, Smokelong Quarterly, Melic Review, Wilderness House Literary Review, Cantaraville,* and *Hot Metal Press*. Frank works as a nonprofit development professional and volunteers with the NY Writers Coalition.

Patrick Cabello Hansel has had poems published in over thirty anthologies and journals, including *Painted Bride Quarterly, Hawai'i Pacific Review, Switchback, The Meadow, subprimal, Ash & Bones* and *Lunch Ticket*. He has received awards from the Loft Literary Center and the MN State Arts Board. His novella *Searching* was serialized in thirty-three issues of *The Alley News*.

Stephanie Hart is the author of the book *Mirror Mirror: A Collection of Memoirs and Stories* (And Then Press). Her work has appeared in anthologies including *Connected: What Remains As We All Change* (Wising Up Press) as well as literary magazines: *The Sun, Jewish Currents, And Then,* and *ducts.org*. She is currently at work on a novel entitled *Two Brothers*.

Margaret Hasse is author of five poetry collections, including *Between Us*, published in 2016. Her poems have been featured on *The Writer's Almanac* (American Public Media) and her poem, "Truant," was part of the *American Life in Poetry* newspaper project (Poetry Foundation of America). Margaret is a recipient of a National Endowment for the Arts poetry fellowship, among other grants and prizes.

Paul Hostovsky is the author of eight books of poetry, most recently *The Bad Guys,* which won the FutureCycle Poetry Book Prize for 2015. His poems have won a Pushcart Prize, two Best of the Net Awards, and have been featured on Poetry Daily, Verse Daily, and The Writer's Almanac. His new book of poems, *Is That What That Is,* is forthcoming from FutureCycle Press in 2017. Paul makes his living in Boston as a sign language interpreter and Braille instructor.

Lowell Jaeger is author of six collections of poems, including *How Quickly What's Passing Goes Past* (Grayson Books 2013) and *Driving the Back Road Home* (Shabda Press 2015). As editor of Many Voices Press, he compiled *New Poets of the American West*, an anthology of poets from Western states. Most recently Jaeger received the Montana Governor's Humanities Award for promoting thoughtful civic discourse.

Pauline Kaldas is the author of *Egyptian Compass*, a collection of poetry; *Letters from Cairo*, a travel memoir; and *The Time Between Places*, a collection of short stories. Kaldas was born in Egypt and immigrated with her parents to the United States in 1969. She is Associate Professor of English and Creative Writing at Hollins University.

Murali Kamma is the managing editor of *Khabar* magazine. His fiction has appeared in *Rosebud, South Asian Review, Asian Pacific American Journal, AIM, The Missing Slate* and elsewhere. He has interviewed, among others, Salman Rushdie, Anita Desai and William Dalrymple. His columns have been published in *The Atlanta Journal-Constitution*, and his essay on immigration appeared in the Wising Up anthology *Complex Allegiances.*

Jennifer Schomburg Kanke's work has recently appeared in *Prairie Schooner, Nimrod*, and *Fugue*. Originally from Columbus, OH, she lives in Tallahassee, FL where she teaches creative writing and critical theory at Florida State University. Previously Poetry Editor at *The Southeast Review*, she is currently Reviews Editor for *Pleiades* and reads poetry submissions for *Emrys.*

John King's essays have appeared in *The MacGuffin, The Examined Life, Open Minds Quarterly*, and *Foliate Oak*. He is a graduate of the Master of Liberal Studies program at Rice University and the MFA program in Creative Non-fiction at Vermont College of Fine Arts. He lives in McAllen, Texas with his wife Elizabeth, where he enjoys the practice of law.

Laurie Klein has published award-winning prose in numerous journals and anthologies. Her poetry collection is titled *Where the Sky Opens*, and she has a chapbook, *Bodies of Water, Bodies of Flesh.*

Norman Klein has published poems in *Ploughshares*, *EPOCH*, and *The Beloit Poetry Journal*, and twelve short stories so far this year. He has taught at Simmons College and UMASS Boston, then ten years plus in Chicago. He now lives and writes in the woods of New Hampshire.

Steve Koppman has contributed fiction to anthologies and literary, regional and Jewish magazines including *ZYZZYVA*, *The Berkeley (CA) Monthly* and *Jewish Currents*. His short plays have been produced across the U.S. and Australia and anthologized. He co-authored *Treasury of American-Jewish Folklore*. He has contributed to many publications including the *San Francisco Chronicle*, *Nation*, *Village Voice*, *Huffington Post* and *Chicago Tribune*.

Rick Krizman took a sabbatical from his decades-long career as a composer and songwriter to earn an MFA in Writing at Pacific University. He is the father of two grown daughters and lives with his wife and animals in Santa Monica, CA. His short fiction has appeared in *Star 82 Review* and *Flash Fiction Magazine*.

Fr. Robert J. Kus, RN, PhD is Pastor of the Basilica Shrine of St. Mary in Wilmington, NC. Fr. Bob is also a sociologist, psychiatric-mental health nurse, and writer. He has taught at the University of Iowa, the University of Montana, the University of Texas at Austin, North Carolina State University, and was a research scholar in Hungary and Czechoslovakia.

Linda Maxwell has published her poetry in *Chaffin Journal*, *Wordriver*, *The Litchfield Review*, *Southern Women's Review*, *Word Hotel* and *Poetry as Prayer: Appalachian Women Speak*. Her essays have found homes in *Catholic Digest*, *I to I Life Writing by Kentucky Feminists* and *Dazzle*. While teaching in coastal South Carolina, she is currently completing a young adult novel.

Jessica Naab first fell in love with the world of books in grade school. From then on, all she ever wanted to be was a writer and author. Today, she participates in several critique groups and judges various writing contests. In 2013, she won the Rocky Mountain Fiction Writer's Colorado Gold contest and continues to participate as a judge.

Jason A. Ney holds a PhD in English from the University of Denver. He works as an Assistant Professor of English and the Director of the Writing Center at Colorado Christian University. His creative nonfiction has also appeared in publications from *Fiction Attic Press* and *Little Did She Know*, and he is a regular contributor to *Noir City* magazine.

Marianne Peel taught English at middle and high school for thirty-two years. She has been published in *Encodings: A Feminist Literary Journal*; *Write to Heal*; *Writing for Our Lives: Our Bodies—Hurts, Hungers, Healing*; *Mother Voices*; *Metropolitan Woman Magazine*; *Ophelia's Mom*; *Jellyfish Whispers*; *Remembered Arts Journal*; and *Muddy River Review*. Marianne also received Fulbright-Hays Awards to Nepal and Turkey.

Dorothy Oliver Pirovano has been writing professionally since high school when she reported for a local weekly. She went on to a decade-long career as an award-winning journalist, and, for the next thirty-three years, worked her way up through the ranks to become CEO of a national public relations firm. Now retired, she has returned to her love of writing.

MK Punky was a member of the 80's hardcore band The Clitboys. The author of ten books, most recently *The Termite Squad*, and a winner of the 2016 Stratford-upon-Avon Literary Festival's creative writing prize, MK serves as poet laureate of Vista Street Community Library in Los Angeles.

Wilderness Sarchild is a psychotherapist, poet, and playwright. Her play, *Wrinkles, the Musical*, will be produced in 2017. Her poems are published in several anthologies/journals. She won awards for poetry/play writing from Veterans for Peace, Women's International League for Peace and Freedom, Chicago's Side Project Theatre, and in 2015, was a winner of the WOMR National Poetry Competition.

George J. Searles teaches English and Latin at Mohawk Valley Community College and has also taught creative writing for Pratt Institute and graduate courses for New School University. Along with many poems, articles, and reviews, he's published three volumes of criticism and two textbooks. Honored with several awards, he was a Carnegie Foundation New York State "Professor of the Year."

Patti See's work has appeared in *Salon Magazine*, *Women's Studies Quarterly*, *HipMama*, *Inside HigherEd*, and many other magazines and anthologies. She is the author of *Higher Learning: Reading and Writing About College*, 3rd edition (2011) and a poetry collection, *Love's Bluff* (2006). Her blog "Our Long Goodbye: One Family's Experiences with Alzheimer's" has been read in over ninety countries.

Pegi Deitz Shea, two-time winner of the Connecticut Book Award for Children's Literature, has published more than 400 articles, essays, and poems for adults. Her poetry has appeared in *The Christian Science Monitor*, *Slag Review*, *Connecticut River Review* and other journals and anthologies. She teaches Creative Writing at UCONN, the Mark Twain House, and the Institute of Children's Literature.

Karen Skolfield's book *Frost in the Low Areas* (Zone 3 Press) won the 2014 PEN New England Award in poetry. She's received fellowships and awards from the Poetry Society of America, New England Public Radio, Massachusetts Cultural Council, Ucross Foundation, Split This Rock, Hedgebrook, and Vermont Studio Center. Skolfield teaches writing to engineers at the University of Massachusetts Amherst.

Darcy Smith works as a professional sign language interpreter. Her poems have been published in the US and abroad. Publications include: *Boyne Berries*, *Up The River*, *Chronogram*, *Mom Egg Review*, *Sadie Girl Press*, and *GTK Creative*.

Ken Staley lives and writes in Eastern Washington. His published works appear in several anthologies. When not writing, he can be found working with stained glass or visiting one of the wineries in the area.

Rebecca Taksel is a writer, teacher, and activist who lives in Pittsburgh, PA. She wrote on animal rights for *Animals' Agenda* and on sustainable design for *Natural Home*. Her essays appeared between 2003 and 2014 in *The Redwood Coast Review*, where she was contributing editor. Her novel, *Come Away*, is slated for publication by Little Feather Books in late 2016.

Jennifer Thornburg grew up in the desolate beauty of northeastern Montana. She holds an MA in English at Montana State University, and an MFA in Creative Nonfiction at Vermont College. She teaches writing at MSU, spends summers tending a greenhouse full of heirloom tomatoes, and has five grown children. She lives with her husband and super-model cat in Bozeman, MT.

John Timm writes at his home in the Sonoran Desert that he shares with artist wife Susan. He has published numerous short stories in a broad range of genres, appearing in *Bartleby Snopes, Blue Bonnet Review, Fiction Attic, The Story Shack*, and elsewhere. When not writing, he teaches communication and foreign language at a university in the Phoenix area.

Johnny Townsend earned an MFA in fiction writing from Louisiana State University. He has published in *The Washington Post, The Los Angeles Times, The Humanist, The Progressive, Glimmer Train*, and in many other publications. His books have been named to Kirkus Reviews' Best of 2011, 2012, 2013, 2014, and 2015. He is an associate producer for the documentary *Upstairs Inferno*.

Gina Valdés's poetry has been published in journals and anthologies in the U.S., Mexico, and Europe. Recent work appears in *Calyx, Spillway, The Pedestal, Off the Coast*, and *Mizna*. She's the author of two bilingual poetry collections, *Eating Fire* and *Bridges and Borders* (Bilingual Press).

Anusha VR is a chartered accountant residing in India. Her short stories have been published in various anthologies such as *III Goan Anthology, Death and Decorations, In a Flash and It's an Urban Style of Love*.

Joel Wachman is a writer and computer technologist. He has written for *Harvard Review* and the Boston *Globe*, and has won awards for his works of creative nonfiction. His self-published zine, *Par Avion*, was widely read by the Anglophone ex-patriot community in Paris in the 1990s. Joel lives with and derives inspiration from his wife and son in Cambridge, MA.

Jana Zvibleman, an Oregonian, collaborates poetically with sculptors, painters, costumers, scriptwriters, and a flugelhornist. Her poems are in journals and anthologies including *Calyx, To Topos, Faultlines*, and *The*

Knotted Bond, and have been featured in The Magic Barrel, The Silverton Poetry Festival, and Northwest Poets Concord. A painter and photographer, she's illustrated her chapbooks. She has taught poetry and humor writing, and critique response.

EDITORS/PUBLISHERS

HEATHER TOSTESON is the author of *Breathing in Portuguese, Living in English; Germs of Truth; The Sanctity of the Moment: Poems from Four Decades; Visible Signs;* and *God Speaks My Language, Can You?* She has worked as executive editor of two public health journals and in health communications with a focus on communication across disciplines, racism, social trust, and how belief systems develop and change. She holds an MFA in Creative Writing (UNC-Greensboro) and PhD in English and Creative Writing (Ohio University).

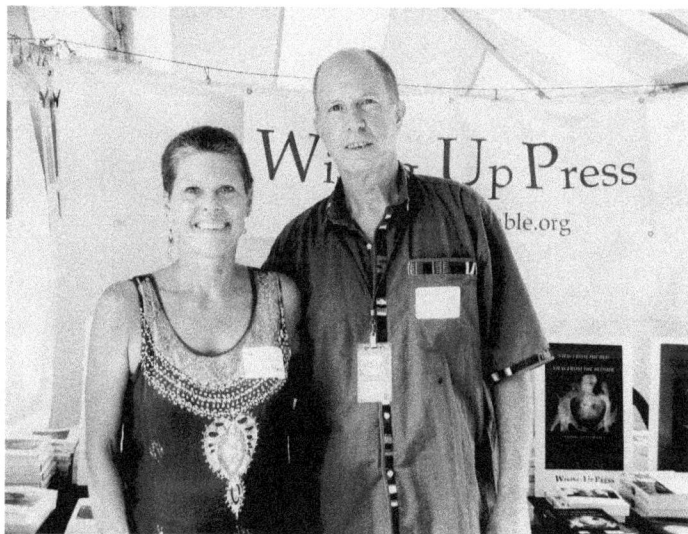

CHARLES BROCKETT has a PhD from UNC-Chapel Hill and is a recipient of several Fulbright and National Endowment for the Humanities awards. A retired political science professor, he has written two well-received books on Central America, *Land, Power, and Poverty* and *Political Movements and Violence*, and numerous social science journal articles and book chapters. With Heather Tosteson, he is co-founder of Universal Table and Wising Up Press and co-editor of the Wising Up Anthologies.

Visit our website and learn about our other publications,
our readers guides, and calls for submissions.

www.universaltable.org
wisingup@universaltable.org

P.O. Box 2122
Decatur, GA 30031-2122

www.ingramcontent.com/pod-product-compliance
Lightning Source LLC
Chambersburg PA
CBHW020604270326
41927CB00005B/162